Makerspaces for Adults

Makerspaces for Adults

Best Practices and Great Projects

Edited by
Jennifer Hicks
Jessica Long

ROWMAN & LITTLEFIELD
Lanham • Boulder • New York • London

Published by Rowman & Littlefield
An imprint of The Rowman & Littlefield Publishing Group, Inc.
4501 Forbes Boulevard, Suite 200, Lanham, Maryland 20706
www.rowman.com

6 Tinworth Street, London, SE11 5AL, United Kingdom

British Library Cataloguing in Publication Information Available

Library of Congress Cataloging-in-Publication Data

Names: Hicks, Jennifer, 1987– editor. | Long, Jessica, 1981– editor.
Title: Makerspaces for adults : best practices and great projects / Jennifer Hicks, Jessica Long.
Description: Lanham : Rowman & Littlefield, [2020] | Includes bibliographical references and index. | Summary: "This book highlights how to integrate your makerspace within university and public libraries and the wider community. Discover how you can connect your makerspace with service learning to support different groups, take your makerspace tools to various points of need through community partnerships, and build relationships with faculty, students, and patrons through makerspace projects."—Provided by publisher.
Identifiers: LCCN 2020001522 (print) | LCCN 2020001523 (ebook) | ISBN 9781538133316 (cloth) | ISBN 9781538133323 (paperback) | ISBN 9781538133330 (epub)
Subjects: LCSH: Makerspaces in libraries. | Libraries—Activity programs. | Maker movement.
Classification: LCC Z716.37 .M355 2020 (print) | LCC Z716.37 (ebook) | DDC 025.5—dc23
LC record available at https://lccn.loc.gov/2020001522
LC ebook record available at https://lccn.loc.gov/2020001523

Contents

Preface

The rise of makerspaces within public and academic libraries has led to a wide variety of sources that cover how to set up your space, what technology works best, and, in smaller numbers, how to get your administration or the community to support the addition of a new space within your library. For publications that branch out from the initial setup of the makerspace, their focus turns to projects that are generally aimed at the K–12 younger audience set. *Makerspaces for Adults: Best Practices and Great Projects* aims to shift the makerspace discussion to show how we can support and encourage making for adults, from college students to octogenarians, educating readers on ways the makerspace can connect outside of the library and make a bigger impact on the community through making.

We begin our discussion by highlighting how to integrate your makerspace within university and public libraries, as well as the wider community. You will discover how to build a makerspace that is welcoming and supportive of people from different backgrounds and abilities. You will see how you can connect your makerspace with different course assignments and service learning projects, how to take your makerspace tools to various points of need through community partnerships, and ultimately how to build relationships with faculty, students, and patrons through a variety of makerspace projects. Intended for academic and public librarians, faculty, and staff who would like to implement more making into their classes and build productive collaborations, this book includes sections that cover theory, best practices, and project ideas that provide a clear guide on how to develop and implement your makerspace within the curriculum and make connections with outside partners.

To help discover how to best utilize your makerspace, this book is broken down into four main parts: Academic Libraries, Connecting to the Curriculum, Public Libraries and Community Outreach, and Projects in Action.

Part I features six chapters that cover best practices for running a successful makerspace within academic libraries including programming, marketing, and collaboration. These practices and tips can also apply to public and community makerspaces that have just begun or have been in existence for a while and are looking for new ways to grow their space and maker projects.

Chapter 1, "Made for Each Other," aims to justify the addition of makerspaces within the academic library by making the connection between libraries as knowledge centers and makerspaces as creators of knowledge.

Chapter 2, "Building an Accessible and Inclusive Makerspace," examines what is required to build an accessible and inclusive makerspace that is welcoming to patrons of all ages, backgrounds, needs, and abilities. These best practices for inclusivity can be applied to new or existing makerspaces to ensure they reach their goals in connecting and supporting makers within their community.

Chapter 3, "Making an Academic Makerspace and Making Assignments by the Moment: Successes and Challenges during the First Year of Operation," highlights best practices on how to build your makerspace, connect with faculty and students, and integrate makerspace programming that helps users develop and exchange creative ideas. This chapter also addresses the challenges that many of us face when trying to build up our space and extend maker programming throughout the university.

Chapter 4, "Intergenerational Learning and Crafting through Stitch 'n Bitch," offers an example of how the library can develop a makerspace that offers supplies and programming to support the reemergence of different making trends within our culture, in particular needlecrafts. By creating a place for needle crafters to convene, libraries are aiding in the expansion of making skills, as well as the building of community, which ultimately helps encourage positive change through craft.

Chapter 5, "Constructing and Critiquing Learning Pyramids in a University Makerspace," aims to go beyond acknowledging the innovation potential of makerspaces to focus on how they enable students to forge diverse learning pathways.

Chapter 6, "Collaborating Across the Institution to Deliver Makerspace Services to Students," explores the various models of collaboration found in academic library makerspaces, along with recommendations for how to work with partners more effectively.

Part II focuses on how the makerspace can be used by faculty within their courses or by students on class projects. Despite makerspaces existing in many academic libraries, little has been published that focuses on the groups that would use these resources. The six chapters within this section cover a variety of subjects, utilizing a mixture of makerspace tools, technology, and equipment.

Chapter 7, "Applying Design Thinking, Collaboration, and Makerspaces to Encourage Innovation in the Classroom," covers how to utilize the tools within a makerspace to provide a hands-on learning experience that connects innovation, design thinking, and cross-functional teamwork.

Chapter 8, "3D Printing in a Senior Seminar Fashion Course," covers how 3D printing and fashion work together, showing the links that can be made between technology and design, while encouraging students to think beyond the boundaries of fabric.

Chapter 9, "Sculpting Synesthesia: Using the Makerspace to Develop Creative Writing and Creative Minds," seeks to explain how makerspaces can be used to engage students' creative process in innovative, rich, and complex ways.

Chapter 10, "The Makerspace as a Place for Social Justice Learning," outlines the framework for incorporating experiential learning within makerspaces into social justice courses.

Chapter 11, "City of Galadriel: How It Is Used to Explore Understanding Surface and Groundwaters," highlights how students can use makerspace tools and equipment to make functional models of different aspects of the hydrologic cycle.

Chapter 12, "Little Shop of Horror," connects digital making within a philosophy class through the creation of short horror films, showing how the library can support making in course assignments.

Part III offers programs and best practices for work aimed at adult makers in the public library and greater community.

Chapter 13, "Growing a Maker Community: Planning and Implementing a Local Community Maker Fest," covers the generation, planning, organization, implementation, and assessment of a maker fest to promote and share the creativity of makers within the community.

Chapter 14, "I Saw It on Pinterest: A Choose Your Craft Adventure," provides details on how to build makerspace programming utilizing public opinion, voting, and examples from Pinterest.

Chapter 15, "Moving beyond Craft Programs: Encouraging Creative Confidence in Adult Learners," provides guidance, as well as specific examples, for incorporating making and tinkering into craft programs, showing how to ease adult learners into the world of making.

Chapter 16, "Design Thinking in a Goal-Oriented Makerspace," identifies how to use design thinking when setting up and choosing the technology that will be most utilized in a library makerspace.

Chapter 17, "Busting the Doors Open: Makerspace Programs and Services That Engage with the Community," discusses new takes on makerspace programs as well as ways to take the makerspace to the community.

Chapter 18, "Maker Programming for Adults with Disabilities: 'Library for All' Best Programs and Best Practices," covers how a library program helps to remove barriers for adults with developmental and/or physical disabilities so that they may participate more fully in STEAM activities within the library makerspace. Their list of programming and best practices can easily be duplicated within other libraries to support an often underserved population.

Part IV includes all of our great projects. These chapters cover a wide variety of makerspace projects from academic libraries to public libraries with a focus on making by students and other adult groups.

Chapter 19, "Multimedia Dickens: Teaching Language and Illustration through the Makerspace," connects literature assignments with the makerspace, having students create a visual representation of classic stories.

Chapter 20, "Sharing a Common Thread: Quilting Projects in the Makerspace," discusses how to create quilts through community collaboration.

Chapter 21, "Building a Simple Oscillator and Engaging Makers through the Building of Lunetta Electronic Music Instruments," shows makers how to create simple electronic "musical instruments."

Chapter 22, "Design, Cut, Etch: Using Vinyl Cutters to Create Custom Etched Glass," explains how to use vinyl cutters and etching cream to create one-of-a-kind pieces for participants.

Chapter 23, "Laser-Cut Snowflake Workshop: Introducing Design and Fabrication to Makerspace Beginners," gives participants an introductory project with 3D design and fabrication that provides them with a take-home item.

Chapter 24, "Why Don't You Make Me? Laser Cutting a Statue/Bust," discusses 3D scanning and laser cutting material to build a custom bust.

Chapter 25, "A Tale of Two Tortoises: How the Cline Library MakerLab Is Building Curriculum, Community, and Cohesive Service Design," explains how the MakerLab worked with a local vet to help repair turtle shells with 3D printing.

Chapter 26, "Bringing the Field to the Classroom using 3D-Printed Fossils," covers the creation and implementation of 3D-printed fossils in the classroom and community.

Chapter 27, "3D-Printed Selfie," guides participants in 3D scanning and 3D printing themselves.

Chapter 28, "Chemical Education in the Digital Makerspace," discusses how a chemistry department works with the library makerspace using VR and 3D printing for hands-on learning.

Chapter 29, "Taking a Virtual Archaeological Site Tour: A Class Visit to the Baths of Caracalla," helps guide readers on how to create site tours with VR technology.

Chapter 30, "Using Virtual Reality in Teaching Education Students," covers how students can take virtual "field trips" with the assistance of VR.

As you read through these chapters, we encourage you to try some of the technology and programming suggestions within your own makerspace. Remember: don't just build a makerspace; make the most of your makerspace.

Acknowledgments

First and foremost, I would like to thank Jessie Long for her persistence, organization, and help with this book. I couldn't have done this alone. I would also like to thank our director, John Burke, for always being encouraging and supportive. I have never had, and probably never will again have, a boss as awesome as John. Thank you to my parents, Brenda and David, for always being there for me and supporting my goals. Thank you to my fiancé, Andrew, for being you because life is better with you in it. Finally, even if he doesn't realize it, I want to thank my son, Landon, for being the motivation behind every accomplishment and the reason to keep pushing toward the next goal. I am definitely surrounded by amazing people.

—Jennifer Hicks

This book could not have been completed without the creativity and determination of Jennifer Hicks. I too would like to thank our director and fearless leader, John Burke, for all of his support and feedback. I feel privileged to work with people who constantly push me to try new things. And lastly, I want to thank my family for all of their support through my different career paths, those that worked and those that became hobbies instead, for helping me stay focused and persistent to get where I am today.

—Jessie Long

Part I

ACADEMIC LIBRARIES

Chapter One

Made for Each Other

James Mitchell

For the past two decades, public discourse among librarians, learning theorists, makerspace advocates, and politicians has juxtaposed the maker ethic with the consumerist mentality inculcated in American society today and encouraged their communities to be producers instead of consumers.[1] Framing makerspaces as spaces of production rather than consumption, especially as more libraries continue to incorporate these spaces, elicits important questions for librarians: where do libraries fit within this picture? Have libraries traditionally only been spaces for information consumption? Do makerspaces offer something essential to the libraries that add them?

The aim of this chapter is to initiate a discussion by attempting an answer to these questions with special focus afforded to academic libraries. Academic librarians have seen early success establishing makerspaces, even though some justifications provided for them aren't fundamentally tied to a traditional view of what libraries are. Justifications such as supporting curriculum among STEM disciplines,[2] promoting hands-on learning, providing access to cost-prohibitive equipment,[3] and functioning as a neutral learning space for multiple disciplines[4] are provided within the literature. Yet, it is difficult to see how these justifications ensure a long-standing relationship between libraries and makerspaces in the far future, especially as academic libraries face challenges to maintain and expand resource offerings with shrinking—or, at best, stagnant—budgets. If makerspaces truly are integral to the identity of libraries in the twenty-first century, then the justifications put forth ought to be able to bear the weight of scrutiny not only when makerspaces are growing and easily justified[5] but also when fiscal accountability is stricter about demanding demonstrated value. To achieve this goal, this chapter will attempt to expound upon some of the aforementioned justifications. This chapter will argue that makerspaces are more than appendages to libraries. Both makerspaces and libraries foster communities of practice, promote learning as a process in constructing meaning, and share core values. Consequently, libraries benefit from makerspaces because they allow libraries to more fully reach their potential as centers of learning and knowledge creation.

COMMUNITIES OF PRACTICE

Libraries and makerspaces consist of more than the spaces they occupy. They both, in fact, support communities of practice. Wenger et al. defines communities of practice as "groups of people who share a concern, a set of problems, or a passion about a topic, and who deepen their knowledge and expertise in this area by interacting on an ongoing basis."[6] Libraries have long been more than book repositories, and their history as institutions that support communities of practice stretches back to the library of Alexandria. The Egyptian rulers, the Ptolemies, who established this library recruited geographers, philosophers, anatomists, and other academics to make use of the library. Lionel Casson has likened this community to a modern-day think tank instead of a simple book repository.[7]

Similarly, Benjamin Franklin established the first subscription library in Philadelphia in 1731, a precursor to the United States' first public libraries. By pooling their resources, members of the Library Company were able to buy books for enhancing learning and curiosity, tools that no one individual within this group could have afforded.[8]

Makerspaces, likewise, have a history of fostering communities of practice. The maker movement grew out of a desire by Dale Dougherty and others to revive learning through tinkering and curiosity. Dougherty established *Make* magazine in 2005 and started the world's first Maker Faire in 2006.[9] In 2006, TechShop, one of the movement's most well-known makerspaces, opened its doors in October 2006.[10] Since then, makerspaces have become a global phenomenon, with the number of makerspaces growing yearly.[11] Like the Library Company established by Benjamin Franklin, makerspaces have arisen to provide cost-effective access to tools for individuals who share interest in making. As a result, makerspaces foster their own community of practice geared toward the practice of making.[12] Makerspaces as communities of practice with a focus on learning through hands-on experience are an important complement to libraries that identify as centers of learning and knowledge. As the next section demonstrates, makerspaces enhance the concept of learning and knowledge already implied in the academic library community.

CENTERS OF KNOWLEDGE CONSTRUCTION

In addition to complementing libraries as communities of practice, makerspaces augment theories of learning already taking place in libraries. Learning theories are conceptual models that attempt to describe the learning process.

Constructivist learning theory, for example, is "the belief that learners, having some prior knowledge and experience as a basis from which to test out their hypotheses, build their own set of problems posed by the instructor." Unlike earlier traditional theories of learning, constructivism situates the instructor as an aide to the learner rather than as an intermediary of knowledge. Learner-centric theories that stem from constructivism are already present models within the practice of librarianship.[13]

Constructionism, additionally, is a sort of constructivist learning theory. Seymour Papert, educational theorist and coiner of the term "constructionism," linked these two theories together by arguing that they both fundamentally share the belief that learning is the process of building knowledge. Papert additionally believed that learning is best achieved when a person is actively engaged in the process of physically "constructing a public entity."[14] This key feature is what distinguishes constructionism from its parent theory.

At first glance, the connection between these two theories, makerspaces, and libraries may not seem evident. However, Papert's statement is an important key. It is significant that Papert does not say that learning happens when a learner constructs a physical, tangible object. Papert does not preclude the possibility that a "public entity" could be a computer program or even a poem. The importance of constructionism is that learning be expressed outside of the mind in a variety of forms.

As a result, constructionism is an important theory, not only to makerspaces but to academic libraries as well. Academic libraries, in addition to offering instruction on the use of resources, also seek to facilitate learning by creating contexts for learners to participate and express knowledge beyond their minds. Librarians must see themselves as doing more than teaching learners how to use information resources. This common thread constructionism provides between makerspaces and libraries when it comes to learning is essential, especially if librarians view themselves as facilitators of all, and not some, knowledge creation.[15]

EMBODIMENT OF CORE VALUES

Another significant reason makerspaces are complementary to academic libraries is that they share fundamental, enduring values. Makerspaces, like libraries, are often superficially identified with the physical resources they make available to their users. The library has historically been exemplified by the book; the makerspace, it may be argued, is exemplified by the 3D printer. Anyone who has made use of either of these spaces soon realizes, though, that both the library and makerspace are more than the sum of the tools they provide to their communities, important as they may be. The tools are a means to an end.

Both libraries and makerspaces value openness and sharing.[16] With these common values, these two spaces have the potential to make a significant impact in the lives of an academic community that frequently delineates learning along disciplinary lines.

Openness

While makerspaces and libraries both share the concept of openness, the history of how the communities around these spaces came to adopt this value differs. Makerspaces, for example, were influenced by the hacker ethic and history of the open-source movement. As Steven Levy points out, adherents to the hacker ethic value the free access to information because it's what allows them to improve the tasks to which they put themselves.[17] It does not matter if this ethic is applied to computer programs, electronics, sewing, or creating art. A quality hack is clever, playful, and curious.[18] Yet, how can adherents hack their environment if they do not have physical and intellectual access to the world around them? It's this desire for openness so that the curious mind might interact with and improve the physical world that has imbued the maker movement and makerspaces with the value of openness.

The concept of openness permeates both the profession of librarianship and the idea of library as space. The concept of intellectual freedom as articulated in the bill of rights[19] is little if it isn't a codification of the value that free and open access to information is integral to and for the benefit of society. Within an academic setting, libraries are important because they provide access to resources for the benefit of all constituents of an academic community, regardless of what course of study a particular student has chosen, for example. It is irrelevant to an academic library whether an engineering student wishes to read a book on philosophy, a faculty member within the English department wishes to create e-textiles, or an administrator wishes to create a podcast. Even if there are other similar services outside of an academic library, what distinguishes the library makerspace from other types of makerspaces within an academic institution are the complementary values that both of these spaces bring together to enhance the learning experience of their communities. You only need the desire to learn something to use these resources. No other strings are attached.

Sharing

Another core value of the maker movement is the concept of sharing. In the words of Mark Hatch, "Sharing what you have made and what you know about making with others is the method by which a maker's feeling of wholeness is achieved. You cannot make and not share."[20] Librarians have also long understood, as detailed earlier in this chapter, the importance of sharing information and constructing knowledge both inside and outside the library space. Academic libraries already often provide both communal and social spaces for students to learn and share knowledge.[21] Makerspaces are an extension of these spaces and emphasize hands-on experience and learning. If academic libraries already value the idea of providing a space where their communities are encouraged to share and learn together, then how can librarians fail to see the significance of adding makerspaces?

In the beginning of this chapter, the question was posed whether makerspaces added something essential to academic libraries. This chapter has attempted to show that libraries have a long history of being more than book repositories. Instead, exemplary libraries throughout human history have supported communities of practice, both in the sciences and the humanities. Furthermore, libraries and makerspaces are both spaces for the construction of public knowledge and are more than storehouses of tools. Finally, makerspaces share important values with libraries, making them important partners as both communities serve the greater good of society. If academic library leaders understand the significance of these connections, library makerspaces should have a comfortable place in the future of academic libraries for the long term. Makerspaces have the potential to become more than a novelty. Instead, makerspaces ought to become permanent fixtures of academic libraries that foster learning through hands-on experience, establish communities of practice centered around making, and enhance the values of sharing and transparency that the library profession has cherished for centuries.

NOTES

1. John J. Burke, *Makerspaces: A Practical Guide for Librarians* (Lanham, MD: Rowman & Littlefield, 2014), 2; Deborah Fallows, "The Library Card," *The Atlantic*, March 2016, under "Technology," www.theatlantic.com/magazine/archive/2016/03/the-library-card/426888; American Library Association, "American Library Association Supports Makerspaces in Libraries," News release (June 13, 2014); Erin Fisher, "Makerspaces Move into Academic Libraries," *TechConnect* (blog), ACRL, November 28, 2012, acrl.ala.org/techconnect/post/makerspaces-move-into-academic-libraries.

2. John J. Burke, "Making Sense: Can Makerspaces Work in Academic Libraries?" (paper presented at the annual meeting of the Association of College & Research Libraries, Portland, OR, March 25–28, 2015), 500.

3. Ann Marie L. Davis, "Current Trends and Goals in the Development of Makerspaces at New England College and Research Libraries," *Information Technologies and Libraries*, 37, no. 2 (June 2018): 99, ejournals.bc.edu/index.php/ital/article/view/9825/pdf.

4. Jennifer Harris and Chris Cooper, "Make Room for a Makerspace," *Computers in Libraries* 35, no. 2 (March 2015): 7.

5. According to a U.S. Department of Education press release, this department committed $279 million in Fiscal Year 2018 alone to STEM grant funding. Makerspaces are an important part of STEM/STEAM initiatives.

6. Etienne Wenger, Richard A. McDermott, and William Snyder, *Cultivating Communities of Practice: A Guide to Managing Knowledge* (Boston: Harvard Business Review Press, 2002), 4.

7. Lionel Casson, *Libraries in the Ancient World* (New Haven, CT: Yale University Press, 2001), 33–34.

8. Library Company of Philadelphia, *"At the Instance of Benjamin Franklin": A Brief History of the Library Company of Philadelphia* (Philadelphia: The Library Company of Philadelphia, 2015), 5, librarycompany.org/about/AttheInstance2015_98709140764695.pdf.

9. Dale Dougherty, "The Maker Movement," *innovations* 7, no. 3 (Summer 2012): 11.

10. Mark Hatch, *The Maker Movement Manifesto: Rules for Innovation in the New World of Crafters, Hackers, and Tinkerers* (New York: McGraw-Hill, 2014), 5–6.

11. Chris Anderson, *Makers: The New Industrial Revolution* (New York: Crown Business, 2012), 18.

12. Kimberly M. Sheridan et al., "Learning in the Making: A Comparative Case Study of Three Makerspaces," *Harvard Educational Review* 84, no. 4 (Winter 2014): 509.

13. Jannette L. Finch and Renée N. Jefferson, "Designing Authentic Learning Tasks for Online Library Instruction," *The Journal of Academic Librarianship* 39, no. 2 (March 2013): 186–87.

14. Seymour Papert, "Situating Constructionism," in *Constructionism: Research Reports and Essays, 1985–1990*, ed. Idit Harel and Seymour Papert (Norwood, NJ: Ablex Publishing, 1991), 1.

15. R. David Lankes, *The New Librarianship Field Guide* (Cambridge, MA: MIT Press, 2016): 23–42; R. David Lankes, *The Atlas of New Librarianship* (Cambridge, MA: MIT Press, 2012): 15, davidlankes.org/rdlankes/Publications/Books/OpenAtlas.pdf.

16. Nicholas Schiller, "Hacker values ≈ Library Values," *TechConnect* (blog), ACRL, November 13, 2012, acrl.ala.org/techconnect/post/hacker-values-≈-library-values.

17. Steven Levy, *Hackers: Heroes of the Computer Revolution* (New York: Penguin, 2001), 40–41.

18. Richard Stallman, "On Hacking," Richard Stallman, accessed July 30, 2019, stallman.org/articles/on-hacking.html.

19. American Library Association. "Library Bill of Rights," American Library Association, accessed July 30, 2019, www.ala.org/advocacy/intfreedom/librarybill.

20. Hatch, *The Maker Movement Manifesto*, 14–15.

21. Mark Bieraugel and Stern Neill, "Ascending Bloom's Pyramid: Fostering Student Creativity and Innovation in Academic Library Spaces," *College & Research Libraries* 78, no. 1 (January 2017): 38, dx.doi.org/10.5860/crl.78.1.35.

Chapter Two

Building an Accessible and Inclusive Makerspace

Carli Spina

Makerspaces have the potential to teach new skills, introduce innovative tools, and unlock creativity for everyone who visits them. They can ignite an interest in new technologies and an innovative spirit in people of all ages. Many participants discover unknown talents and passions and may even come to see themselves in a whole new light. However, without careful planning and design, makerspaces can become exclusive places that attract the same homogeneous group of people time after time while appearing off-limits to other members of the community. This limits the impact of the makerspace and contributes to a greater sense of exclusion for those who do not feel that their needs, skills, interests, and circumstances are understood, accommodated, or celebrated.

To build a truly inclusive community at a makerspace, it is vital to focus on ensuring everyone will have the ability to participate and will be supported in their work while there. This requires conscientious planning that centers user needs, while focusing on accessibility and empowerment for all makers, regardless of their needs or interests. But these efforts can have significant benefits. As Vecchione et al. have argued, "By casting a broad net of inclusion for all types of individuals, a makerspace can radically embrace and help them find their place in the makerspace and begin to identify as makers."[1] The best practices presented here will help to create an environment that offers support and inclusion to everyone.

CODES OF CONDUCT

To create a supportive and inclusive environment, it is vital to set ground rules to ensure that the community remains comfortable and welcoming for all. One way to make a powerful statement about acceptable behavior is by creating and publicly displaying a code of conduct that explicitly states the behaviors that are desired and those that will not be tolerated. These can take different formats at different institutions. At Innovation @ the Edge at the University of Oklahoma, both a Credo and a Code of Conduct are posted on the wall. The Credo serves as a statement of purpose for the space and features their mission statement, which includes a statement that "it is open, free and accessible to everyone."[2] The Code of Conduct, which is based on one designed by Code{4}Lib, prohibits harassment and refers users to the student conduct website for the wider institution.[3] At the Miami University Libraries, the Co-Lab makerspace has references to the campus-wide policy prohibiting harassment and discrimination posted in the space, included on the website, and referenced in training materials.[4] The space also has a clearly posted Safe Zone sign,[5] which designates it as "a safe and affirming space for LGBTQ people." Though the language differs, each of these posted notices publicly demonstrates the commitment of the teams to support inclusive and diverse use of the spaces.

When posting a code of conduct, it is important to consider the consequences for violations. This might fall under the purview of other segments of the institution, but no matter who will enforce the rules, it is important that there be a means of enforcement. The key is that the document have an enforcement mechanism to serve as a demonstration that harassment and exclusionary behavior will not be tolerated. This signals to visitors that the makerspace will welcome them and can serve as a helpful tool for dealing with any negative interactions that occur.

ACCESSIBILITY

The design of a makerspace can have a critical impact on the audience that will be drawn to the space and the community that can form there. Many makerspaces unintentionally send signals about who is welcome by providing equipment that requires physical dexterity, failing to offer assistive technologies, or offering inaccessible safety and training documentation. Even work surfaces are often high-top tables that offer a lab aesthetic but limit who can use the amenities. For disabled individuals, the physical space can immediately signal that their needs have not been considered and therefore create the impression they are not the intended audience for the space.

This means that all aspects of the makerspace, including physical features, the web presence, and all instructional content, must be readily accessible to disabled individuals. A good starting place is ensuring the space meets any applicable legal requirements, such as the Americans with Disabilities Act in the United States. While in some situations it may seem easier to offer assistance as a work-around for inaccessible components (for example, offering to operate inaccessible equipment on behalf of users), these accommodations do not offer disabled makers an opportunity to use the space on the same terms as their peers. This risks alienating them from the community and limiting their ability to learn new skills and achieve their creative potential. As Brady et al. note, makerspace staff "should strive to design our stations such that people with a variety of disabilities would be able to participate fully without any facilitator 'doing' for them."[6] This independence is a fundamental element of the making experience.

It is not enough that the larger institution, such as the library as a whole, offer accessible alternatives; rather, the makerspace itself should offer accessible furniture and workspaces so that disabled users are able to work side-by-side with their peers. For the same reason, the makerspace must offer access to standard assistive technologies and should allow users to bring their own assistive technologies to use in the space whenever possible. Unfortunately, this is particularly rare, according to Brady et al., who note that "while many public libraries offer assistive technologies for individuals with hearing and visual impairments, assistive technologies are typically not made available in library makerspaces."[7] Without the ability to make use of these tools, individuals who use assistive technologies will never be able to be meaningfully included in the makerspace's activities.

True accessibility and inclusion often necessitates moving beyond minimum legal requirements. Instead, when designing a makerspace, it is worthwhile to think about how the space can best serve the needs of disabled makers. Answering this question should involve input from disabled individuals in the community. On college campuses, partnering with the office responsible for providing disability services can be a helpful first step toward gathering expert and user data. Any participatory design or user experience testing should include individuals with a variety of disabilities to ensure that their needs and feedback are being taken into account. As she plans for the new C+I Makerspace, Sarah Nagle, creation and innovation services librarian at Miami University Libraries, is taking both of these steps. In the design of the space, she has worked with the Student Disability Services office to make sure it is accessible, both physically and in terms of online materials such as tutorials.[8] She also has plans to conduct focus groups to collect student feedback on a variety of issues, including accessibility and inclusion.[9]

Even flexible and well-designed spaces may not be accessible to everyone. Each disabled user will have unique interests, goals, and needs, as with any other user, so it is vital to have a clear process for users to ask questions and request accommodations and a clear plan for how staff will respond to such requests.

INTEGRATING UNIVERSAL DESIGN AND INCLUSIVE DESIGN

In addition to considering accessibility standards and requirements, it is important to center the needs of users and consider how the design of the space, the selection of the equipment, and the development of programs can meet the needs of all users. This level of inclusion requires a conscientious focus on user-centered design. Applying the principles of both universal design and inclusive design in the creation of a makerspace will make it a place where all members of the community can come together to collaborate in new ways and develop their skills.

Universal design is a concept that is credited to Ron Mace, an architect and designer who defined the term to mean "the design of products and environments to be usable by all people, to the greatest extent possible, without the need for adaptation or specialized design."[10] In 1997, he led a team that created the seven principles of universal design, which are:

- equitable use: usability by individuals of varying needs and abilities;
- flexibility in use: adaptability to accommodate different preferences and approaches;
- simple and intuitive use: easy to understand and operate;

- perceptible information: information is conveyed in a widely understandable manner regardless of sensory ability or knowledge;
- tolerance for error: minimizes the impact of incorrect use;
- low physical effort: efficient and requires minimal physical ability to operate; and
- size and space for approach and use: appropriate size and with appropriate clearance on all sides to allow easy operation regardless of the stature, size, or mobility level of the user.[11]

These principles address the major aspects of design that prevent people from using a product, space, or service. Examples of universal design in makerspaces are practically endless, including stocking tools with ergonomic grips designed to make them easier to hold and use, selecting adjustable furniture, offering instructions in multiple formats (such as digital, physical, and illustrated), and ensuring significant clearance around equipment so that people using assistive devices have a clear avenue of approach.

Inclusive design is a closely related concept that has arisen, at least in part, as a response to universal design. Though definitions vary, the Inclusive Design Research Centre of OCAD University has defined it as "design that considers the full range of human diversity with respect to ability, language, culture, gender, age and other forms of human difference," which they argue is in contrast to universal design, which they believe "has become associated with disabilities and a fairly constrained categorization of disabilities" and therefore more narrow than it was at its origin.[12] Whereas universal design aims to create a single solution that is adaptable and flexible enough to meet the needs of the widest possible group of people, inclusive design argues that "most individuals stray from the average in some facet of their needs or goals. This means that a mass solution does not work well. Optimal inclusive design is best achieved through one-size-fit-one configurations."[13] It therefore aims to find solutions that can be customized to meet needs that arise for each user. In the context of a makerspace, inclusive design means offering highly customizable content in multiple formats, particularly for digital materials such as tutorials, documentation, and instructional content, which will permit each user to find a solution that meets their needs. It also points to the need of keeping flexibility as a goal for all design work, whether this is a physical space or project design. Applying these design concepts in the context of designing a makerspace will impact everything from the layout of the workspaces to the equipment selected and will have a significant impact on how inclusive the space is.

DIVERSE PROGRAMMING TAUGHT BY DIVERSE INSTRUCTORS

It can be easy to fall into a pattern of repeating popular programs, and it can be even easier to fall into the trap of thinking that merely offering programs in response to patron requests will automatically serve your community. However, this is not always the case. While popularity and patron requests can be evidence that a specific program serves at least one segment of the community well, it is important to assess whether there are other, less vocal groups not being served. Makerspaces should strive to remain responsive to the interests of those who show up frequently while also considering how the user base can be expanded and what the current user base says about the community forming around the space.

At the North Carolina State University Libraries, the desire to attract a more diverse group of patrons prompted the staff to introduce new topics into their programming. Lauren DiMonte, director of research initiatives at the River Campus Libraries of the University of Rochester, who previously worked as an NCSU Libraries fellow at the NCSU Libraries' makerspace, notes that initially they saw the same homogeneous group of patrons all the time, but introducing e-textiles programming served as a "great bridge builder."[14] This new topic attracted new participants to workshops and programming and allowed them to partner closely with NCSU's Women in Science and Engineering on a workshop that specifically targeted women interested in STEM fields.[15] To further attract and support a diverse maker community, NCSU Libraries launched an event series entitled "Making Space," which "aims to confront bias and systemic barriers to inclusion in the STEM fields by presenting the experiences and perspectives of underrepresented groups in science and technology, including people of all identities and abilities."[16] These programs demonstrate a commitment to diversity and attract the interest of community members who may have never considered makerspaces in the past.

Beyond the topics covered, it is also important to recruit a diverse group of staff, student workers, and peer instructors, who bring their own interests and expertise to the space. At many makerspaces, the staff have a huge influence on the activities done and the skills taught. As part of their efforts to create an inclusive environment, the University of Oklahoma Libraries have paid particular attention to recruiting women to the Emerging Tech Librarians team and to teach workshops, such as the Software Carpentries courses.[17] Ensuring diversity among student workers and peer volunteers can also have a huge role in helping newcomers to see themselves as makers and to identify with those who are already succeeding in these fields.

It is also important to offer programs for individuals with varying budgets. In his research into barriers to participation in makerspaces, DiMitri Higginbotham found that "cost creates a barrier for many underserved communities who may be intimidated by any kind of financial obligation, no matter how small."[18] It is therefore vital to control costs and eliminate fees whenever possible. If some programs have a registration fee, others should be offered free of charge. Even at libraries that have the budget to cover the costs of materials, it is worthwhile to teach activities that can be done at little or no cost. Some patrons may not be interested in investing time and effort learning skills that they know will be expensive to pursue outside of a single library workshop. Demonstrating that making need not be an expensive pursuit can help to attract and retain these makers.

OUTREACH IS KEY TO BUILDING AN INCLUSIVE COMMUNITY

Because so many makerspaces do not offer inclusive environments, it is important to center these features during outreach. Without promotion, makers may assume that your makerspace is as exclusionary as others they have encountered in the past. When Brady et al. contacted representatives from United Cerebral Palsy (UCP) for advice while designing an accessible makerspace at the District of Columbia Public Library, the UCP representatives noted that "because so many such spaces are not fully accessible yet, potential makers with disabilities may feel excluded and may not show up at all. They also mentioned that, for example, some people with disabilities found travel more difficult and they might be unwilling to just drop in and see if a space had something to offer them."[19] Though the transportation concerns may be unique to some people with disabilities, the assumption that an unknown makerspace will not welcome them may influence the participation of members of other marginalized groups as well.

To counteract these assumptions, it is important to make inclusivity explicit in outreach materials, for example by:

- ensuring images used in outreach materials feature diverse groups of patrons and demonstrate the accessibility of the makerspace;
- reaching out to relevant community groups for both recommendations and marketing assistance;
- adding information to all outreach materials about the process for requesting accommodations, offering feedback, asking questions, or reporting harassment;
- creating promotional content that is both accessible and multilingual;
- highlighting the makerspace's code of conduct; and
- advertising varied programs that appeal to a range of skills, interests, abilities, and needs.

These outreach efforts will spread the word beyond the usual makerspace visitors to a wider segment of the community while helping to solicit feedback from those who may not have visited in the past. Members of the community need to see that inclusion is a key part of the makerspace's ethos in order to choose to become active participants in its programming. An effective outreach campaign that focuses on communicating these values is key to making this inclusive community a reality.

Creating an accessible and inclusive makerspace requires thoughtful design of not only the space itself, but also the programming, activities, and community associated with the space. Though this represents a significant and ongoing effort, it is an essential component of ensuring that the makerspace will achieve its promise of introducing participants to a new and exciting set of skills and abilities.

NOTES

1. Amy Vecchione, Deana Brown, Gregory Brasier, and Ann Delaney, "Encouraging a Diverse Maker Culture," in *The Makerspace Librarian's Sourcebook*, ed. Ellyssa Kroski (Chicago: American Library Association, 2017), 54.
2. Carl Grant, e-mail message to author, June 26, 2019.
3. Ibid.
4. Sarah Nagle, e-mail message to author, June 27, 2019.
5. Ibid.
6. Tara Brady, Camille Salas, Ayah Nuriddin, Walter Rodgers, and Mega Subramaniam, "MakeAbility: Creating Accessible Makerspace Events in a Public Library," *Public Library Quarterly* 33, no. 4 (2014): 336.
7. Ibid., 334–35.
8. Nagle, e-mail message to author.
9. Ibid.
10. "About UD," The Center for Universal Design, accessed July 21, 2019, projects.ncsu.edu/ncsu/design/cud/about_ud/about_ud.htm.
11. "The 7 Principles," National Disability Authority, accessed July 21, 2019, universaldesign.ie/What-is-Universal-Design/The-7-Principles/.
12. Inclusive Design Research Centre, "What do we mean by Inclusive Design?" OCAD University, accessed on July 30, 2019, idrc.ocadu.ca/resources/idrc-online/49-articles-and-papers/443-whatisinclusivedesign.
13. Ibid.
14. Lauren DiMonte in discussion with the author, May 2019.
15. "Women in STEM Build Community (and Circuits) in E-Textiles Workshop," NC State University Libraries, June 15, 2015, www.lib.ncsu.edu/stories/women-in-stem-build-community-and-circuits-in-e-textiles-workshop.
16. "Making Space Event Series," NC State University Libraries, accessed July 29, 2019, www.lib.ncsu.edu/events/series/making-space.
17. Grant, e-mail message to author.
18. DiMitri Higginbotham, "Barriers to Equity in Makerspaces" (poster presentation, International Symposium on Academic Makerspaces, Stanford, CA, August 4, 2018).
19. Brady et al., "MakeAbility," 336–37.

Chapter Three

Making an Academic Makerspace and Making Assignments by the Moment

Successes and Challenges during the First Year of Operation

Sara E. Wright, James McKee, and Camille Andrews

In the fall of 2015, Cornell University Library created a task force that investigated the campus landscape regarding design labs, fab labs, and makerspaces to gauge what was available to students and what, if any, role there might be for the library. Determining that most of what was available on campus was restricted to students and faculty who were part of particular departments, majors, courses, or clubs, the task force concluded that the library could definitely help in creating equity of access to tools, technology, and software. Additionally, the team recognized an important educational role for a library makerspace as a space to promote and engage students in digital and making literacies as well as to work with faculty on creating curricula that would require tangible application of skills learned through the makerspace. The next step was to determine what the space might look like, how it would be staffed, and what it would house so that it was capable of doing all those things.

Taking a user-centered approach and engaging with design thinking methodologies,[1] the task force embarked on an aggressive user research plan: observing other makerspaces, distributing a survey, and doing pop-up makerspace events within various unit libraries to observe student use and comfort with technology as well as to ask questions about the type of coursework and extracurricular projects that might make use of the makerspace. We also facilitated ideation workshops for library staff in which they designed their ideal makerspace.

From all these activities, we were able to develop a vision for the makerspace as a place that would be an inclusive, welcoming facility allowing for skill building and the start or continuation of projects, connecting students with expertise, providing targeted programming to help students develop literacies, as well as serving as a forum for the exchange and development of ideas.

Additionally, the makerspace would:

- be an "easy on-ramp" to making and a hub to more advanced shops on campus;
- act as an interdisciplinary space for connections and networking and the development of an encouraging community for collaboration and experimentation;
- be designed with flexibility and a sense of openness to provide "breathing room" for users to think; and

- provide the opportunity for informal and formal learning and a place to collaborate with faculty on inquiry-based, real-world projects and assignments.

With this vision, we soft-launched in November 2017, and the mannUfactory makerspace opened fully in February 2018. There were many steps between our vision and opening, and even more lessons learned in the first year of operation.

INITIAL IMPLEMENTATION: STAFFING MODELS, SERVICE OFFERINGS, AND TECHNICAL EXPERTISE

After our initial design phase, the challenges of implementation lay ahead. Our prior assessment work helped produce a nice list of equipment with which to outfit our space. Based on student responses and the frequency of campus use, we knew 3D printers are in demand. Mechanical sewing machines and a small serger are a great addition—it isn't pragmatic for college students to store or use that sort of equipment in their small living spaces. Poster printing was an existing library service, which we built upon by offering new printable media such as: polyester fabric (great for banners, foldable conference posters, and sewing) and adhesive vinyl (great for stickers, vinyl branding, and signage). Virtual reality (VR) has a relatively high barrier of entry for the average user, but we decided to experiment and offer an outlet for faculty and students to delve into immersive technologies.

As we narrowed down what we would provide, *how* we were going to do it became the next question. We had to decide how hands-on we wanted a patron's experience to be with equipment and what made sense for our team to mediate. For example, while there are definite benefits in letting patrons 3D print on their own, managing print queues becomes more challenging and potential damage to printer components increases.

Drawing from our initial needs assessment, we projected high demand for our services, which, along with our wide user base, encouraged us to pursue a mediated service–based approach, where student assistants or staff assist patrons with 3D printing through walk-up consultations. This approach minimizes equipment downtime while still giving patrons individualized attention and curated settings for their 3D models. However, offering this model also raised the bar regarding staff technical expertise and service expectations. Both the students and full-time library personnel working at the service point have to meet patrons' needs so that no one walks away with a poor and frustrating experience.

We dedicated 1.5 FTE to the makerspace, reallocating staff from our Access Services department. This was made possible through a parallel effort in the library to combine our reference and circulation desks into one service point, which allotted more dedicated staff for a new integrated Help Desk. Full-time staff working alongside well-trained and well-supported student staff was our solution to staffing the makerspace. Although student management is not a new challenge in and of itself, curating job expectations, creating reference and training documentation, developing workflows, and training the initial cohort of hires was a time-consuming task that occupied almost a full academic semester.

We hired a fantastic student crew, doing our best to hire diverse students from a variety of majors, with different skill sets that would complement one another. The training and workflows developed over the course of that initial semester enabled the student team and makerspace to operate smoothly by the start of the second full semester, with limited staff intervention. Any new student hires now have the benefit of an experienced cohort of mentors, accessible and detailed documentation, and clearly defined workflows. Our full-time staff have now shifted their time from student management to focusing on the equipment maintenance, upkeep, and other tasks that fall under the direct operational oversight of the space.

At the same time that student expectations and training were being developed, we also had to decide how to handle issues around 3D printing such as: requests from patrons to use their own filament, what and how to charge for printing, and what materials to provide. As a land-grant library that is open to anyone in the community—not just Cornell affiliates—remaining accessible to our community members was one of our top priorities. This meant that any pricing scheme had to be reasonable, financially sustainable, and transparent. We chose to charge for 3D prints based on time, poster printing pricing was based on linear feet of paper used, and buttons were based on quantity made. This allowed us to recoup the cost of our consumables and purchase more, while remaining less expensive than commercial alternatives. Currently, everything else in the makerspace is free of charge.[2]

FACULTY OUTREACH AND COURSE INTEGRATION

Our noncurricular instruction began with a consultation model but quickly transitioned to both consultations and workshops upon full opening. To encourage curricular use, outreach to faculty included: e-mails distributed by our departmental library liaisons; brochures, presentation slides, and a page for instructors on our website; and partnership with the Digital CoLab, the library's digital scholarship center. Our most effective engagement has been a tour and introductory workshop for the CoLab's Digital Humanities Fellows graduate students, starting in 2017.

After the initial workshop, one of the fellows was interested in doing an assignment for her first year writing seminar. The assignment outcomes were that students would be able to: translate a critical analysis and close reading of symbolism into a creative representation by crafting an argument in nontextual form and develop skills in using creative tools to produce a multimodal scholarly argument or creative representation. Students had to write an essay on a symbol in the works they were reading, do a creative representation of their argument about the symbol in the form of an artist's book (broadly defined), and write a short artist's statement. The instructor and librarians gave feedback on students' draft proposals to make sure they were feasible in the given time frame, met the assignment terms, and used materials appropriately. Later in the semester, there were two in-class working sessions (where students could make their projects, ask questions, and get materials and support from staff) and a final presentation. Many of the projects were displayed as examples in the makerspace and online (africanwomenwriters.omeka.net/). Though the sample size was very small, pre- and post-class surveys showed that students' level of comfort and knowledge around the outcomes increased. This course led to sessions for other writing seminars, and we have since worked with a number of other courses.[3]

Our most in-depth work has been with two courses that were awarded innovative teaching and learning awards, funded by Cornell's Center for Teaching Innovation (CTI). The Art of Math was designed to introduce non-math majors to the subject through art, architecture, music, games, and more. The professors initially consulted the makerspace to fabricate math game pieces and to investigate a possible 3D-printing assignment. After a tour and meetings with the math librarian and staff from the makerspace and CTI, the professors settled on a pre-class assignment that showed students how to search 3D model repositories and find and import 3D models into Tinkercad for modification. There was an in-class introduction to 3D printing, origami, VR, and examples of creative math projects (including knitted and 3D-printed math models). Subsequently, students were given grant funds to print their own projects. Their final assignment was to create something based on the mathematical concepts they were learning in class, through any creative medium.

Visual Communication is an approximately 150-person introductory-level required course. For the grant, the professor wanted to give her students a chance to experience VR and participate in a research project. The initial idea was to have her students and those from two Chinese universities experience full VR, learn how to make their own 3D objects, and put them in a gallery where they could comment on each other's work. Eventually, because of time and logistical constraints, this project shifted to 360 video. After instruction in shooting 360 video and circulating cameras via library staff, groups of students created one- to three-minute orientation videos introducing their universities. Then we exchanged videos. The Chinese students' videos were loaded onto Oculus Go VR headsets in the makerspace, where Cornell students (after in-person guidance or by following self-paced instructions) were able to view them. Then, they wrote reaction papers detailing what they thought the Chinese students were attempting to convey and what they received. Those reactions were then used by the professors to research intercultural communication in VR.

LESSONS LEARNED FROM THE FIRST YEAR AND FUTURE IMPROVEMENTS

This first year's work has led to a variety of successes and challenges. We've found the following useful:

- Start small, build steadily, remain flexible, and remove barriers to access.
- Base equipment purchases and service models on user research and the makerspace's vision and community.
- Hire a diverse staff with complementary expertise, provide documentation, and mentor into increasing responsibility.

- Connect with established instructional channels (e.g., fellowships and grants for innovation, writing seminars and other required courses, and teaching centers), which helps with:
    - outreach to instructors interested in innovation and pedagogy,
    - fulfillment of mandatory requirements (in a range of topics that lend themselves to making assignments), and
    - exploration of creative multimodal composition.
- Collect and exhibit project examples to serve as models for those who are interested but unsure where to start (both instructors and students). Don't forget to take photos and get FERPA releases for student-created projects.
- Provide a range of levels of curricular involvement (from listing the makerspace as a resource in syllabi to one shots to multi-session and grant-funded class projects).
- Have single-session hands-on activities that get students excited about possibilities.
- Be explicit about and proceed from learning outcomes instead of basing assignments on a specific "cool" technology. It can be useful to present maker competencies[4] to instructors as a starting point.
- Encourage draft proposals and scaffolding, especially for in-depth assignments.
- Provide flexibility in assignments and assessments (some people are more excited about and skilled with making than others) and allow people to follow their interests.

Challenges include:

- Outreach: Making instructors aware of and interested in the space; showing what's in it for them and their students and why they might want to add a making assignment. Providing channels for interaction and feedback.
- Learning outcomes: Getting instructors to think about outcomes, especially in the context of new technologies; showing them what is and isn't possible; and assessing outcomes.
- Ideation and assignment creation: Getting people to feel confident and think of ideas can be challenging, especially for those who don't think of themselves as creative individuals. Finding examples, lesson plans, and assessment tools in particular disciplines may be an issue, though projects like the Maker Literacies lesson plan repository[5] help.
- Managing expectations: Some ideas might require more time, skill, equipment, or materials than available. Timing of assignments is critical as things often take longer or are more complicated than predicted (especially with novices). Also, being explicit about who's doing (and not doing) what is important with all stakeholders; we now clarify that we don't design 3D models for people.
- Managing logistics (especially for large classes if the makerspace is small): There's only so much space, time, equipment, and materials—making sure there's enough of all of these resources at the right times is tricky.
- Staffing and expertise gaps: When not all staff have the same skills, deciding what is accomplished during one-on-one consultations vs. walk-in help and providing basic information to all library staff is important. Think about how and when to

involve liaisons and other librarians for outreach, collection development, and instruction.
- Instruction: Refining and expanding our existing workshop offerings.

To address these challenges and improve the mannUfactory to continue to meet our users' needs, we plan on, or have already implemented, the following:

- improving marketing and outreach through partnerships with other making spaces and campus units, incorporating additional user feedback, and more social media engagement;
- planning an expanded instructional support website for faculty with clearer information about possible projects, processes, logistics, and expectations—like North Carolina State University's;[6]
- deepening collaboration with instructors, including better assessment and additional grant-funded projects;
- integrating student staff as workshop instructors, which will hopefully increase basic instruction, allow more tailored course-related sessions, and enhance student staff's responsibilities and roles;
- expanding equipment offerings: including more VR headsets and a laser cutter to our repertoire;
- refining and improving internal workflows to enhance student employee autonomy;
- increased operating hours and staffing; and
- finding time to learn new software and develop skills.

Makerspaces are a continual work in progress and we look forward to seeing how our space develops in the years to come!

NOTES

1. For more information, see this poster: Camille Andrews and Sarah E. Wright, "Think Different, Design Better: Using Design Thinking to Create Evolving Makerspaces," bit.ly/312gdZh.
2. See full equipment and pricing lists at makerspace.library.cornell.edu/equipment/ and makerspace.library.cornell.edu/pricing/.
3. See full list of courses and projects at bit.ly/2K0ZrnI.
4. "Maker Competencies | Maker Literacies," accessed July 29, 2019, /library.uta.edu/maker literacies/competencies.
5. "Curriculum | Maker Literacies," accessed July 29, 2019, library.uta.edu/makerliteracies /lesson-plans.
6. "Makerspace Instruction Support | NC State University Libraries," accessed July 29, 2019, www.lib.ncsu.edu/makerspace/instructors.

Chapter Four

Intergenerational Learning and Crafting through Stitch 'n Bitch

Nancy Schuler

In the spring of 2019, Eckerd College Library implemented a maker station within the library to support the craft community on campus with resources to learn and practice needlecrafts while providing tangible ways to manage stress, improve self-esteem, provide creative fulfilment, and expose participants to craft as a means for social change. The project links an existing student-run Stitch 'n Bitch club with other members of the campus community to bring crafters from all generations together to learn about needlecrafts while providing opportunities for socializing and experiential learning. Through an internal campus grant, the library established regular joint Stitch 'n Bitch sessions, supplemented the library's academic collection with the addition of craft books, and created a Craft Exchange maker station where members of the community can freely borrow craft materials or donate any unwanted craft supplies as well. The outcome is the creation of an inclusive, supportive, and intergenerational community of crafters who take value in sharing ideas, expertise, and extra supplies.

A BRIEF HISTORY OF NEEDLECRAFTS AND THE RISE OF THE STITCH 'N BITCH MOVEMENT

The history of needlecraft, which includes knitting, embroidery, sewing, needlepoint, and crochet (which uses a hook), as well as other crafts requiring a needle, is one with origins in the domestic lives of women. Needlecrafts provide a means of artistic and cultural expression, enable financial independence, and can be used as a source of empowerment and political subversion. During the Revolution, needlecrafts were used to create "upcycled" uniforms for soldiers during America's boycott of British textiles.[1] Messages of temperance were sewn into quilts during the Reconstruction period.[2] English suffragists created outfits and accessories in purple, white, and green while the National Women's Party used purple, white, and gold to show solidarity in the movement to acquire voting rights for women at the turn of the twentieth century.[3] Sarah Corbett describes the "arpilleristas" of Chile who crafted arpilleras (small, hand-stitched pieces) to express their grief and anger over lost loved ones during the military dictatorship of Pinochet.[4] More recently, activists knitted thousands of pink pussyhats for the 2017 Women's March to show solidarity for women's rights and political resistance.[5] Techniques of knitting, quilting, embroidery, and other combinations of handicrafts are used by artists to examine issues of gender, identity, and queerness through their work.[6]

In the twentieth century, the popularity of needlecrafts fluctuated as the women's suffrage movement gained steam and leaders rejected traditionally "feminine" tasks. Needlecrafts saw another decline in the 1960s and 1970s as they were seen as a symbol of women's oppression by second-wave feminists.[7] The 1990s brought the anti-consumerist attitudes that encouraged do-it-yourself (DIY) culture to flourish. Needlecrafts once again became popular as a means to reject corporate dominance and place value in craft as a potential tool for positive change. The 2003 publication of the *Stitch 'n Bitch* book series by Debbie Stoller introduced knitting to a new generation. At about the same time, the term "craftivist" emerged, described by Betsy Greer as anyone who uses their craft to help the greater good. As the popularity of knitting and other needlecrafts increased, crafting circles thrived. At one point, stitchnbitch.org (no longer active) maintained a registry of more than 12,800 knitting groups worldwide.[8]

The reemergence of needlecrafts within our culture is something that libraries can support through the creation of needlecraft makerspaces and relevant programming. Needlecrafts require skill, knowledge, refinement, and experience to master. Creating a place for needlecrafters to convene allows for the expansion of craft, as well as the building of community, and with this, the possibility of encouraging positive change through craft.

LIBRARIES AND MAKERSPACES: EXTENSIONS OF WHAT WE DO

Eckerd College is an undergraduate liberal arts college in St. Petersburg, Florida, with a full-time student body of 1,930. As a residential undergraduate campus with more than 80 percent of our students living on-campus, patrons value our library for its comfort, technology, and quiet space, with students using the library for academic and personal uses as well. We work collaboratively with student groups on campus to ensure that our collections reflect their needs. In recent years, we created a LEGO table, where students are encouraged to create projects as part of a class, release steam, be creative, and have fun building. Our tabletop game collection invites patrons to learn new games in the library or take them home. A campus makerspace provides access to 3D printing, vinyl cutting, and other machinery to enhance student's making and creative abilities, and while this is not located within the library, we partner with the student-run MakerSpace Club to make sure relevant books and magazines are available in our permanent collection. Outreach to other student groups, like the Tabletop Club and Afro American Society, allows us to build partnerships with students to enhance our collection and create student-driven library displays. The Stitch 'n Bitch project combines our community-driven mission with the passions of librarians to support the existing maker community on campus, while creating opportunities for positive engagement with our patrons.

THE ECKERD LIBRARY STITCH 'N BITCH PROJECT

The Eckerd Library Stitch 'n Bitch project aims to unite Eckerd's Queer Straight Alliance (QSA) Stitch 'n Bitch club with other crafters across campus to learn about needlecrafts while providing opportunities for socializing and experiential learning. The project supports the development of a community of crafters on campus by combining (1) monthly Stitch 'n Bitch craft sessions open to the entire campus community, (2) a Craft Exchange station of starter supplies, and (3) supplemental books to the library's collection to help crafters learn about the social and political history of craft, while providing resources to refine their skills. A total of fourteen titles were added to the library collection including the entire Stitch 'n Bitch series by Debbie Stoller. These titles were placed in the existing stacks, mostly in the Library of Congress sections for Visual Art (N) and Technology (T).

The Craft Exchange encourages novices to try out new crafts and learn new skills, without the need to invest in supplies and starter materials. In addition, users can borrow and give back to the exchange as needed to help create a collaborative community of needlecrafters who take value in sharing extra supplies. This also helps our community reduce waste by giving new purpose to unwanted materials. The overall project helps us nurture a community of novice and experienced crafters that can provide encouragement and expertise to each other, as well as a supportive environment for interaction and learning regardless of age, ethnicity, class, or gender.

Creating the Craft Exchange

The Craft Exchange station consists of a fixed location within the library where those interested in needlecrafts can borrow craft supplies and exchange yarn and other materials. It is currently located in an open lounge area on the second floor of the library, as shown in figure 4.1. This is similar to other special collections within the library, including our LEGO station and game collection, which are located in areas of high visibility. An existing drawer unit provides storage for the station. The Craft Exchange was seeded with a basic set of needlecrafting supplies, as listed in table 4.1. The exchange includes various drawers that separate tools and materials by type of craft, each with labeled compartments to encourage organization.

BEST PRACTICES FOR SMALL MAKER STATIONS

Collaborating Across Campus

Collaboration was the key to success for this particular project. The student-run Queer Straight Alliance (QSA) formed a new Stitch 'n Bitch group in the fall of 2018, holding biweekly meetings where students would gather to work on various craft projects while discussing college life. At the same time, the library applied for an internal grant through the college's Senior Professionals group (ASPEC), which provided seed money for the project. ASPEC consists of retired and semi-retired professionals who participate in weekly classes, lectures, and social activities to stay intellectually

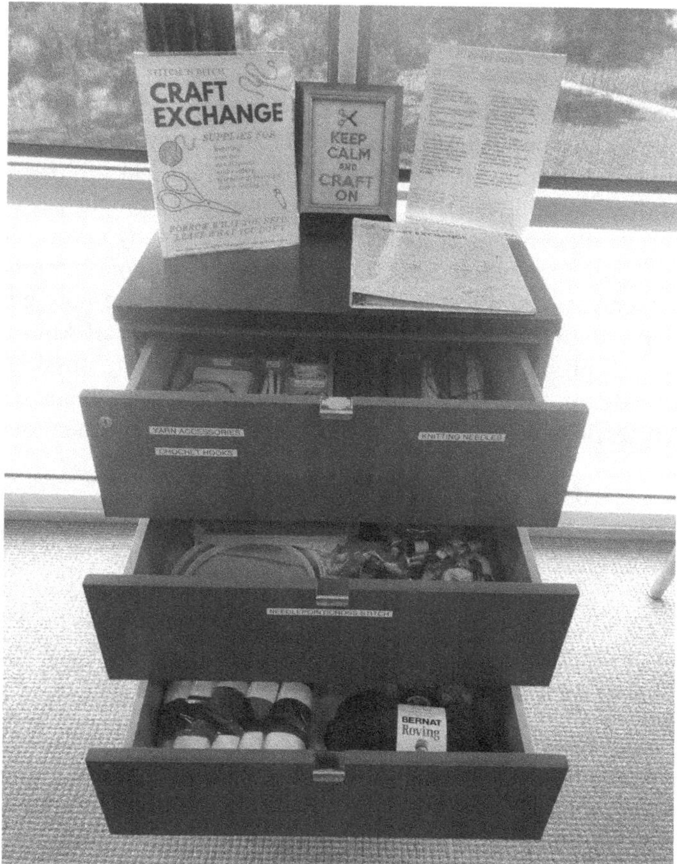

Figure 4.1. The Craft Exchange station where craft supplies and exchange yarn and other materials are stored. ***Nancy Schuler***

Table 4.1. Craft Exchange Supplies List

Yarn crafts	Knitting needles (assorted sizes)
	Circular needles (assorted sizes)
	Crochet hooks
	Needle point protectors
	Stitch markers and holders
	Darning needles
	Measuring tape
	Yarn of varying fibers, weights, and colors
Embroidery and cross-stitch	Embroidery hoops
	Embroidery thread in a variety of colors
	Embroidery and cross-stitch cloth
Other miscellaneous materials	Sewing kit
	Donation bin
	Drawer organizers

engaged and make connections. ASPEC supports campus efforts to create opportunities for members to interact with students through a $500 Intergenerational Learning Grant (ILG). This partnership brings in crafters from ASPEC to join students in our monthly Stitch 'n Bitch sessions.

Bringing these two campus groups together creates many opportunities for interaction as participants typically share a passion for crafting and lifelong learning. This blending of crafters from different generations allows us to see the skill and creativity in each other, regardless of age or gender. It also creates many interesting discussions as participants learn about each other's experiences. Common themes of discussion include school, careers, families, current events, passions, and how gender expectations have changed over time. A student-led demonstration of knitting with plarn (yarn created with plastic grocery bags) exposed many to the possibilities of using upcycled materials for craft. By providing an inclusive setting to share and learn, the Stitch 'n Bitch sessions create new opportunities for meeting others outside of one's typical circle.

Establishing Policies and Procedures to Encourage Open Participation

To communicate the purpose of the Craft Exchange, a simple mission statement was written to briefly summarize the goals of the Exchange, which has helped to guide the scope of materials included, the selection of books acquired for the collection, as well as relevant programming to support the project.

> The Eckerd Library Stitch 'n Bitch project aims to unite Eckerd College's Queer Straight Alliance (ECQSA) Stitch 'n Bitch club with other knitters on campus to bring crafters from all generations together to learn about needlecrafts while providing opportunities for socializing and experiential learning.

In addition, the following community usage guidelines (see textbox 4.1) were established to define procedures for borrowing and donating materials to the Craft Exchange. Signage created using poster templates available on canva.com, a free graphic design site, is prominently displayed on top of the station.

Internal policies and procedures also needed to be established to determine how best to organize, keep track of, and replace materials. Items in the Craft Exchange consist of crafting materials that can be borrowed, like knitting needles, as well as consumable materials such as yarn and embroidery floss that will not be returned. Cataloging certain craft tools and making them available for circulation was considered as a means to control loss; however, we decided against this due to the complexity of materials to be borrowed, issues with labeling, not wanting to discourage use, and an interest in maintaining a cooperative approach that encourages taking and giving back for long-term sustainability. This may be revisited in the future as the Exchange gets more use.

In planning for a makerspace, even a project with a small footprint requires a plan for long-term maintenance for the project to succeed. Initial funding for the project came from an internal grant program, but the long-term cost of maintaining the Craft Exchange needs to factor in the continued use of consumable materials and the po-

TEXTBOX 4.1. COMMUNITY USAGE GUIDELINES

Taking Items

- When borrowing supplies, please sign them out so that others know they are not available.
- Try to bring the item back by the date you indicated.
- If an item is lost or broken, add that to the notes.
- Yarn and floss do NOT need to be signed out. Just take it!

Leaving Items

- Items should be clean and in good condition.
- Optionally add items to the inventory list.

tential for loss. The hope is that increased use will yield some donations over time, as well as a sense of ownership with our users to maintain a useful collection for the community, but the potential for additional investments over time will be likely.

Relevant Programming: Now and into the Future

Regular programming enables us to introduce the Craft Exchange to the community of crafters on campus so they know it exists. As Theresa Willingham states in her book, *Library Makerspaces: A Complete Guide* (2018), "If you don't offer at least some Maker-style programming related to your makerspace, it's hard to introduce people to your space and the tools and resources available to them or help them see the possibilities."[9] While awareness of the Craft Exchange continues to spread as students encounter the new space, word of mouth through the Stitch 'n Bitch group and other programming will drive the continued use and long-term support of the resource.

The first year of the project established monthly Stitch 'n Bitch crafting sessions for the campus community and included anywhere from six to ten participants at each session. After a successful initial launch, we hope to expand the project through additional programming for the campus community. These might include introductory workshops for learning specific types of needlecrafts, like knitting or cross-stitch; talks by local craft specialists related to upcycling, embroidery, and other crafts of interest; and craft-related events timed with new student orientations, alumni week, finals week, and graduation. In addition, the existing Stitch 'n Bitch group could take part in an effort to craft for good, such as crocheting octopuses for premature babies or knitting protective straps for working animals. Given the small staff at the library and limited areas of expertise related to craft, this would be most successful through partnerships with expert crafters on campus or invitations to local crafters from the surrounding community to help host sessions.

OUTCOMES

The Stitch 'n Bitch project is a simple and cost-effective approach for libraries with limited space and resources to delve into the makerspace arena. The project has been well received on campus, and the experience of hosting monthly crafting sessions has been rewarding for the new connections made, crafts shared, and stimulating conversations. Patrons discovering the Craft Exchange have been elated to see the materials provided, as they often are unable to craft in school due to a lack of access to supplies. Providing crafts as a means for self-care, creative expression, and to support social causes also helps to enhance the library's efforts to be part of the campus community.

NOTES

1. Tove Hermanson, "Knitting as Dissent: Female Resistance in America Since the Revolutionary War," *Textile Society of America Symposium Proceedings* 696 (2012): 3, digitalcommons.unl.edu/tsaconf/696/.
2. Corinne Segal, "Stitch by Stitch, a Brief History of Knitting and Activism," *PBS NewsHour*, April 23, 2017, www.pbs.org/newshour/arts/stitch-stitch-history-knitting-activism.
3. Anne-Marie Codur and Mary Elizabeth King, "Women in Civil Resistance," in *Women, War, and Violence: Topography, Resistance, and Hope*, edited by Mariam M. Kurtz and Lester R. Kurtz (Santa Barbara, CA: ABC-CLIO, 2015), 401–46.
4. Sarah Corbett, *How to Be a Craftivist: The Art of Gentle Protest* (London: Unbound, 2019), 8.
5. "The Pussyhat Story," The Pussyhat Project, accessed July 17, 2019, www.pussyhatproject.com/our-story.
6. John Chaich and Todd Oldham, *Queer Threads: Crafting Identity and Community* (Los Angeles: Ammo Books, 2018), 5.
7. Hermanson, "Knitting as Dissent," 4.
8. "Stitch 'n Bitch: Find a Knitting Group Knitting Club or Start Your Own," Archive.org, last modified March 1, 2016, web.archive.org/web/20160301072149/http://stitchnbitch.org/Florida/index.html.
9. Theresa Willingham, *Library Makerspaces: The Complete Guide* (Lanham, MD: Rowman & Littlefield, 2018), 11.

Chapter Five

Constructing and Critiquing Learning Pyramids in a University Makerspace

Jasia Stuart and Dianne Cmor

Makerspaces have now established themselves as multidisciplinary spaces of student learning in many higher education institutions, many of these in academic libraries. Early literature focused on how to set up such spaces (i.e., equipment, staffing, programming)[1] and why academic libraries see makerspaces as an extension of their purpose.[2] Once a critical mass of makerspaces were up and running, scholarly attention shifted to questions of pedagogy, faculty partnerships, curriculum integration, and assessment.[3] Bieraugel and Neill put forth a cogent case for makerspaces to strive toward "ascending" Bloom's taxonomy in support of innovation goals.[4] This chapter, while acknowledging innovative potential and actualization in makerspaces, will focus on a model of learning in makerspaces where high-level innovation is not the only valuable learning pathway or destination for students.

The Technology Sandbox at Concordia University Library was envisioned as part of a larger technology program initiated alongside a major library renovation project. Initial goals were to make a variety of cutting-edge technological tools available to all and to foster experimentation and learning through on-site support and workshops. The space provides opportunities and support with 3D printing, virtual reality, multimedia creation, electronics, and more. Learning by doing, making, playing, and sharing can be observed in action on any day, at any time. With two full-time staff, part-time student support, and a growing community of volunteers, the Sandbox's on-site support and array of workshops continue to broaden and deepen.

Much of the learning that takes place in the Technology Sandbox, like other academic makerspaces, happens outside of the traditional model of an expert transmitting knowledge. This creates an opportunity to observe and examine how our environment, tools, staff, and community of learners converge to create various kinds of learning opportunities. Beyond identifying these opportunities, we also seek to describe how such a space enables students to forge diverse learning pathways.

When the Technology Sandbox first opened, we saw many first-time visitors trying out simple virtual reality (VR) experiences, observing the 3D printers at work without actually making anything, and toggling between settings on the analog synthesizer with little purpose. At some point an important shift occurred—students began modifying cell phone cases with their own designs, recording midi compositions, and using VR headsets to test applications they had built themselves. As the variety and complexity of projects happening in the space increased, we began identifying and grouping them with the hope of better understanding what brought about this shift and what underlying pedagogical principles were at play.

MAKERSPACE LEARNING PYRAMID

A scaffolded approach for technology learning or makerspace learning, like other types of learning, seemed appropriate. We used the common metaphor of a pyramid, with learning starting at a base and moving toward a summit as a general framework (see figure 5.1).

With little intent, we immediately saw parallels with Bloom's taxonomy of learning, wherein learners ascend a pyramid using skills from the previous level to climb to a higher one. Bloom's taxonomy is often used as a pedagogical tool to improve and direct learning by structuring learning outcomes in an appropriate sequence. Our goal in developing this mental model is to help contextualize the kinds of learning happening in our space, improving our ability to support it.

In the following section, we share examples for each level in our framework, with the caveat that many do not fit neatly into a single level. For clarity, we are beginning from the base of the pyramid and moving upward, even though, as will become apparent, we do not ascribe to the belief that higher levels are necessarily the goal.

Awareness

This base level, or "know it exists," was the catalyst for our thinking, as it was initially a source of frustration. When the Sandbox first opened, we spent hundreds of hours

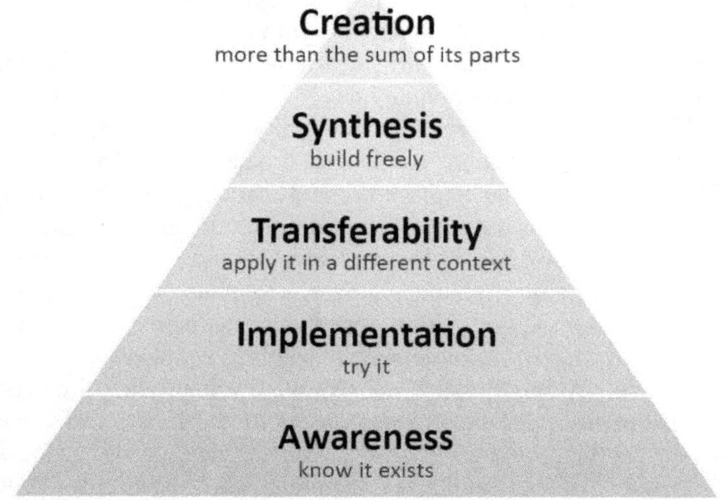

Figure 5.1. Learning pyramid. ***Jasia Stuart***

initiating students into the wonders of VR, explaining the potential of 3D printers, and extolling the simplicity of prototyping electronics. At a certain point, we began to question ourselves, as the students were simply not making things. However, the importance of this less hands-on stage of activity gradually became apparent—until users "know it exists," they cannot make use of most technology.

To get learning started in a makerspace, it is not sufficient to promote the space, the tools, and the services; an understanding of what is possible with certain technologies must be showcased in order to spark the imagination. Our strategies include a visible space that is highlighted to new students, a newsletter, and a team of staff and student workers who are always modeling maker attitudes and behaviors.

Implementation

"Try it" is one of the most important layers in our makerspace learning framework as hands-on learning is obviously significant. This step is also highly rewarding, with "I made this" being a great motivator. Some implementation activities happen independently with staff offering basic advice on appropriate tools or recommending an online tutorial to help get a project started. Workshops offer a more accompanied option, providing a structured introduction to various technological tools. For example, our Raspberry Pi workshop, entitled Cat Selfie Machine, has attendees following step-by-step instructions to connect a camera and a motion detector to a Raspberry Pi (bringing it home to test with your pet is optional). Our workshops guide newcomers through their first hands-on experience, providing all tools, instructions, and context.

Jumping in and trying something can be one of the hardest thresholds to cross. The perceived failure risk is high. Of the thousands of students that show interest in 3D printing during tours or walking by our space, only a few hundred actually attempt to print something themselves. We see that among experienced makers, there is still a lot of time spent exchanging knowledge and improving awareness before judiciously selecting their next project. This transition from awareness to implementation is a key moment.

Transferability

Transferring what was learned to a new context is a compelling technology skill, without which options are significantly limited. "Applying it in a different context" can be a difficult activity to spot; we are not always aware of the original context in which a technology was used. One student used 3D printing to make a mold for casting other materials—a clear and creative shift from how we generally teach about the printers as an additive technology.

Creating opportunities for learning transfer in a makerspace can be surprisingly simple. For example, we keep crochet hooks and a yarn bin on hand. We challenge students to consider how a crochet pattern is similar to code. Hopefully, from recognizing code outside of the digital, learners are motivated to revisit the awareness and implementation levels of our framework with an eye to recontextualizing their knowledge in new ways.

Synthesis

Synthesis is the ability to "build freely" and combine tools, examples, and ideas to achieve a goal. For example, we had a student who used a star map to build an augmented reality (AR) game. By providing a multitude of examples and projects in the space, we aim to support this synthesis level. In selecting Arduino kits, we prioritized the usability of a manual filled with examples. Various students, with no prior experience in programming or electronics, have borrowed these kits and been able to combine elements from examples in the manual in surprising ways.

In some cases, we observe a linear learning path from awareness through implementation and transfer into synthesis. However, such a clear trajectory is the exception rather than the rule. Students arrive in our space with different degrees of openness, experience, and goals. Through collaboration with a more experienced person, a student with no technical background jumped almost directly to the synthesis phase with a project using a brain-computer interface (BCI) to generate an artistic visualization. This nonlinear learning pathway is neither more nor less desirable than a linear one—it simply demonstrates that learning is an individual endeavor.

Creation

Our initial hope when our makerspace opened was for projects of pure invention. In many ways, by definition, creation happens at all levels in a makerspace. Creation is easily seen in our previous examples; however, there is a special moment where the creative act becomes "more than the sum of its parts."

While the impetus for creation is often described as mysterious and even mythologized, pure invention/creation is more likely to occur for users who have seriously engaged in other levels of our framework, not necessarily all levels and not necessarily in a particular order. They build their capabilities, take joy in new skills, playfully transpose ideas to new contexts, and are often working at a synthesis level when their activity takes on the qualities of pure invention.

As an example, what started off as one student's desire to make artwork in a VR painting software grew into a piece combining the original painted VR environments, 3D scans of sculptures, and music. The work became a platform for integrating the collaborative contributions of other artists into a virtual environment. There was no single element or clear path toward this innovative creation, but we hypothesize that the services, the community, the technology, and the constant buzz of activity all contribute. The entire ecosystem fosters an environment favorable to transitioning back and forth between levels, over a number of projects, increasing the possibility of moving into the creation level.

REFLECTING ON LEARNING PYRAMID MODELS

Bieraugel and Neill describe the differences between exploitative and explorative learning, wherein the former is about exploiting what is known in new ways and the latter explores novel and unknown areas.[5] Though allowing that the first is necessary for the second, they go on to assert that it is important to "foster the highest level of Bloom's taxonomy, that of creativity and innovation."[6] This focus on the "summit" of creative innovation may deter students from fully exploring and enjoying other learning pathways.

Our experiences and observations lead us to value a more nuanced and diverse set of goals for academic makerspaces. There is high value in the simple act of igniting curiosity and/or supporting open-ended thinking about how things work and how problems might be solved. This alone can be a worthy outcome of isolated visits to a makerspace. Creative propositions exist at all levels and throughout all experiences; providing students with an array of ways to explore and express their learning is a more inclusive model compared to pushing all students toward an innovation ideal. Tomko et al. describe "building and testing skills [as] critical for overcoming design fixation to flawed designs"[7] for engineers, but this can be generalized beyond engineering. Sheridan et al. note a "dispositional shift" that occurs for users of makerspaces wherein a more curious and open mindset is awakened.[8] Makerspaces allow students from all disciplines to posit ideas, test, see errors, rethink, and try again. Makerspaces facilitate a tolerance for error in our own thinking, facilitating resilient and open thinking. The scaffolding element of the pyramid, which illustrates hierarchy and sequencing of learning, remains valuable. However, some students follow a clear progression through the hierarchy; others forge their own.

The diverse student learning shared in this chapter (and other observed examples) lead us to question the innovation summit model of makerspace pedagogy, and though use of a pyramid model has helped us to initially chart our observations, a shift in our thinking toward a rock-climbing model may be more helpful. Such a metaphor would still value different levels of learning but would allow for various entrance and exit points, diverse learning pathways, and a variety of creative outputs at all levels.

Articulating a framework to organize the types of learning happening in our space was a powerful reflective exercise. A variety of adjacent questions have surfaced during this process, for our future consideration:

1. How do we more clearly articulate learning outcomes and assessment models for makerspaces that value individualized learning pathways?
2. What community norms explicitly value and support a range of goals, and how can we help to establish such norms in academic makerspaces?
3. How can we ensure that staff are prepared to recognize and support a multitude of desired experiences?
4. Is technology learning unique in some way to other types of learning? If so, how can makerspaces enrich this learning?

From observing our students, we have begun to better understand their learning pathways in our makerspace. In some cases, impressive innovation can occur, and in other cases, no less significant, we observe inspired application, creative problem-solving, and even simple wonder and delight. Considering the rock-climbing metaphor, we envision that some of our students will vertically move up such a wall using a variety of paths in order to summit toward creation/innovation. Others will work with less vertical propulsion, forging personal learning paths in many directions or even reworking paths in different ways again and again.

NOTES

1. Heather Moorefield-Lang, "Makers in the Library: Case Studies of 3D Printers and Maker Spaces in Library Settings," *Library Hi Tech* 32, no. 4 (November 11, 2014): 583–93, doi.org/10.1108/LHT-06-2014-0056; Kyungwon Koh et al., "Competencies for Information Professionals in Learning Labs and Makerspaces," *Journal of Education for Library and Information Science* 56, no. 2 (January 1, 2015): 114–29, files.eric.ed.gov/fulltext/EJ1073572.pdf; Thomas William Barrett et al., "A Review of University Makerspaces" (122nd ASEE Annual Conference, Seattle, Washington, June 14–17, 2015), www.asee.org/file_server/papers/attachment/file/0005/5802/A_Review_of_University_Maker_Spaces.pdf.

2. John J. Burke, "Making Sense: Can Makerspaces Work in Academic Libraries?" (paper presented at the annual meeting of the Association of College & Research Libraries, Portland, OR, March 25–28, 2015), www.ala.org/acrl/sites/ala.org.acrl/files/content/conferences/confsandpreconfs/2015/Burke.pdf; Anne Wong et al., "Making as Learning: Makerspaces in Universities," *Australian Academic & Research Libraries* 47, no. 3 (July 2, 2016): 143–59, doi.org/10.1080/00048623.2016.1228163.

3. Sofia Papavlasopoulou et al., "Empirical Studies on the Maker Movement, a Promising Approach to Learning: A Literature Review," *Entertainment Computing* 18 (January 1, 2017): 57–78, doi.org/10.1016/j.entcom.2016.09.002; Megan Tomko et al., "A Qualitative Approach to Studying the Interplay Between Expertise, Creativity, and Learning in University Makerspaces" (paper presented at the ASME 2017 International Design Engineering Technical Conferences and Computers and Information in Engineering Conference, Cleveland, Ohio, 2017), doi.org/10.1115/DETC2017-68256; Jaime Cantu et al., "Developing Student Learning Outcome Metrics for Makerspaces: A Stem Pilot Course" (paper presented at the American Society for Engineering Management (ASEM) Conference, Coeur d'Alene, Idaho, 2018), rc.library.uta.edu/uta-ir/bitstream/handle/10106/27569/ASEM_2018_311%20Final_rev.pdf?sequence=1; Aijuan Cun et al., "An Assessment Matrix for Library Makerspaces," *Library & Information Science Research* 41, no. 1 (January 1, 2019): 39–47, doi.org/10.1016/j.lisr.2019.02.008.

4. Mark Bieraugel et al., "Ascending Bloom's Pyramid: Fostering Student Creativity and Innovation in Academic Library Spaces," *College & Research Libraries* 78, no. 1 (2017), doi.org/10.5860/crl.78.1.35.

5. Ibid., 36.

6. Ibid., 50.

7. Tomko et al., "A Qualitative Approach," 4.

8. Kimberly Sheridan et al., "Learning in the Making: A Comparative Case Study of Three Makerspaces," *Harvard Educational Review* 84, no. 4 (December 1, 2014): 518, doi.org/10.17763/haer.84.4.brr34733723j648u.

Chapter Six

Collaborating across the Institution to Deliver Makerspace Services to Students

Laura Wiegand McBrayer, Adalia Hiltebeitel, Gene A. Felice II, Peter Fritzler, and Jason Fleming

Teaching and learning practices within academic institutions are increasingly integrating, both in terms of course design and classroom experience and the technologies, software, materials, and opportunities for creating and prototyping provided by makerspaces. As such, there is a growing need for such spaces and services across the institution.[1] Within any institution, there may be a variety of departments, colleges, schools, or student life divisions hosting makerspace-type spaces and services for their constituents. As academic libraries move away from traditional roles and instead toward serving as facilitators and stewards of content creation, including academic integration of "making," libraries are increasingly providing makerspaces that support both classroom use, as well as unstructured exploration for students, faculty, and the community.[2] Libraries, as multidisciplinary, democratic, highly accessible, and often highly visible spaces, are ideally positioned to provide makerspace services for the institution. Situating makerspace services and spaces within academic libraries provides students and faculty, regardless of major, discipline, or department affiliation, with access to new technologies and services.[3]

Institutions are increasingly discovering that interdisciplinary collaboration is a highly effective way to provide makerspace services and spaces to the broadest university audience. Libraries, in general, have long been engaged in collaborating across disciplines to deliver library services to students and faculty, and many are discovering that makerspaces can benefit as well.[4] This chapter will explore the various models of collaboration found in academic library makerspaces, along with recommendations for how to work with partners more effectively.

At the University of North Carolina Wilmington (UNCW), Randall Library and the Technology Assistance Center (TAC) began collaborating in 2016 to create, furnish, equip, and staff a 500-square-foot makerspace. While operated separately in terms of funding, staffing, and organization, there has always been a synergy between the two units based on shared space in the library and the shared mission of providing access to emerging technology and technology assistance to students. The collaboration began with the managers of the TAC and the Library Information Technology Department envisioning ways to enhance the current technology and services available in the library so as to contribute to the campus interest in enhancing digital literacy. At the time, the technology and services consisted of media editing stations in addition to traditional desktop computing. The result is the Digital Makerspace, which initially consisted of virtual reality, 3D printing, a 3D scanner, a 360 camera, and high-end computing. Responsibilities in terms of staffing and operations were divided between the two units (TAC and library). With the exception of the addition of funding a student worker budget, no additional staff were hired at the start-up. A third partner, the Department of Art and Art History, joined the collaboration and utilized the makerspace facility and staff to house and operate the equipment needed to serve its own curriculum, adding a laser cutter and a secondary type of 3D printer. In exchange for space and support, the department allowed use of its equipment and shared its faculty expertise with TAC and library staff, benefiting all students in a way that would not have been possible if the equipment had been located within the department's space.

In an exploration of the types of makerspace collaborations at other institutions, we discovered that there are a wide range of collaboration models. The most common model for makerspace operation often is not collaborative in nature, instead housed and resourced through one unit such as a library or an academic program. However, we did find that even when operated by one unit, these types of makerspaces often engage in less defined collaborations. Other partners participate in grants or campus funding initiatives, provide advisory input, assist with marketing and outreach, partner on applied learning opportunities, provide space for equipment, or even simply utilize the space for classes and projects. In large units such as libraries, the collaboration witnessed may be internal, such as library information technology departments providing technical support for the equipment and other public service units providing organizational or programmatic services. At some institutions, we found a model of partial collaboration where one unit is the primary operator, but other units contribute funding, space, equipment, or services.

On the more collaborative end of the spectrum, a common model for delivering makerspace services that is similar to the collaboration found at UNCW is where the library and campus IT partner to deliver services. Often there is already a strong collaboration between these two units, more so than other campus units. Many libraries have some sort of campus technology presence in their space and so collaborating to deliver services can be natural. Lastly, the strongest and most complex model of collaboration we found is when a network of makerspaces across campus are organized to provide a wider range of technologies and services to the broadest audience. Akin to "makerspace franchises," these networked makerspaces are often operated by individual units but collaborate to deliver a seamless experience for students, partnering with each other to meet shared needs like outreach, staffing, and instruction.

In addition to our own experiences with collaboration at UNCW, for this chapter we interviewed and surveyed a number of institutions regarding how they approached collaboration and their lessons learned. The following discussion brings together what we learned from these institutions.

Based on our experience and the experience of our interviewees, the benefits of collaborating across the institution to provide makerspace services are numerous. Especially during start-up, it can spread out the cost of creating, equipping, and staffing the space. Collaboration makes the most of resources across campus and helps to avoid duplication of services, fostering overall efficiency. In our case, it allowed us to distribute the workload of adding a new service across two units without (at the time) adding additional staff beyond student work assistants. We were able to harness the existing technology management skills and strong student workforce found in the TAC in conjunction with library funding opportunities and expertise in delivering course-related instruction, programs, and events. This knowledge sharing and leveraging of existing expertise is another benefit of collaboration commonly cited; it helps bring a wide range of skill sets to the table that may not exist within one unit. Information technology staff, librarians, faculty from various disciplines, and student life staff bring various strengths, skill sets, and perspectives that are needed to pull together the various components of a successful makerspace, such as technology, operations, support, and outreach. Collaborating can offset the need to build those skills within one unit. Lastly, if potential or existing makerspaces on campus are able to join forces, students benefit with increased access to a greater variety of makerspace services.

Of course, collaboration introduces many difficulties as we and others have experienced. It makes the process more complicated as the vision, needs, and resources of multiple units have to be taken into account in delivering services and planning for the future. It is more time-consuming to involve additional people or units in operations or decision-making. For example, coming to consensus about who funds what—or what should even be funded—can add an extra layer of complexity. At the most fundamental level, there are challenges if leadership of the various partners do not share the same vision for the future of the makerspace, making it more difficult to move forward. Collaboration can lead to unclear roles and concerns about "stepping on toes" or a lack of feeling ownership. Depending on the complexity of the collaboration, there can be issues with communication; situations can develop where not all team members get looped in or information is not shared equally. Like most relationships, collaborations require constant negotiation and attention to stay effective. In our situation, the most difficult aspect of collaboration was that our model was created without additional staff, so there was a little bit added to everyone's plate without a single person being responsible for coordinating the makerspace. Eventually we were able to address this issue through the creation of a new position in the library. Putting this coordinator within the library's organizational hierarchy will by nature alter the balance of our existing collaboration but will also lead to more coordinated services.

To mitigate these problems and others, a number of steps can be taken. First, before entering into a collaboration to deliver makerspace services, carefully assess the collaboration fit and potential both within your own organization as well as with any potential partners. There are a number of assessment rubrics, such as the "Collaboration Assessment Tool" analyzed by Marek et al.,[5] that can be used to evaluate whether a collaboration will be successful, as well as to assess its functioning when under way. These rubrics also give clues as to how to organize an effective collaboration. Investing ahead of time in the review of in-depth resources outlining how to plan for and assess collaborations, such as the publication by Taylor-Powell et al.,[6] can yield long-term benefits if the collaboration is begun based on established best practices.

Beyond such formal tools, we and our interviewees recommend that if possible, start by picking partners that you already have a good working relationship with.

Piloting a project with a potential collaborator that is short-term or allowed to fail could prevent larger failures down the road. Have conversations around vision and goals to make sure all partners, including the leadership of those partners, will be able to agree on future directions. Clearly communicate with potential partners about funding and resources allocation expectations. When requesting funding, especially from administrators who may not be familiar with the makerspace, be prepared to thoroughly explain the educational benefits of investigating emerging technologies. Also, keep in mind that most projects require more resources than originally planned for, and have a plan for how to deal with unanticipated needs. Collaborations are about relationships and flexibility to move in new directions.

Once a collaboration has been formed, there are a number of best practices that should be followed to ensure success. Foremost, mentioned by most every interviewee, is creating a memorandum of understanding (MOU), which, at its most basic, outlines the purpose and scope of the collaboration, roles and responsibilities of partner members, and funding and resource allocation expectations. MOU templates vary and can be easily found online. Library-related examples include the *Memorandum of Understanding Workbook*[7] developed by the University of Texas and the MOU components listed by Walters and Van Gordon.[8] All of the stakeholders and partner leaders should participate in and approve the MOU as the first stage of collaboration. The MOU should be a flexible living document, revisited, consulted, and updated as necessary, and written in a way as to support the work of an operations group who will be implementing the daily work in line with the MOU.[9]

In addition to creating and frequently reviewing a MOU, we suggest other best practices to ensure an effective collaboration. Establishing clear leadership, even if shared leadership, is necessary for understanding how decisions will be made and who will make them. No matter the amount of planning, there will be unanticipated situations where existing policies or processes cannot answer an immediate issue about delivering makerspace services and so understanding who has the authority to make decisions is crucial. If possible to do so, it is empowering to all partners to ask about major decisions or additional work before committing. Each partner unit, and each member within the units, should understand what their roles and responsibilities are so that they can contribute effectively. Ideally these roles and responsibilities should be documented in a shared location so that all team members can understand their relationship to their teammates. To overcome problems with communication, the team should decide early in the process on a transparent, accessible, shared communication vehicle and establish expectations around communication. In addition to regular, planned check-ins and group meetings, utilizing platforms such as Slack or Microsoft Teams is invaluable to making sure that the members of the group stay in coordination and that all partners have access to information. Additional recommendations from our interviewees include identifying new ways to collaborate each year with existing partners to keep forward momentum and clearly establishing at the front end who will get credit for what and when so that all parties feel properly valued for their contributions.

The final thought about collaboration shared by many of the institutions we interviewed was that it is important to be willing to explore and try. While in the end more intentionality is needed to be successful, at first it is necessary to simply say "yes" to opportunities for collaboration. Ultimately, whether they succeed or fail, attempts at collaboration can create other opportunities for support and increased networks. Our recommendation is to seek out collaboration that supports makerspace services but also carefully implement collaborations using best practices to deliver effective services to students and faculty in support of teaching and learning.

LIBRARIES INTERVIEWED

Cameron, Ryan. Western Carolina University—Technology Commons. Interview by Dali Hiltebeitel. Personal Interview. July 2019.

Ferrill, T. J. University of Utah Library—Creative Spaces. Interview by Peter Fritzler. Personal Interview. July 2019.

Romito, David. UNC Chapel Hill Kenan Science Library Makerspace. Interview by Dali Hiltebeitel. Personal Interview. July 2019.

Schell, Justin. University of Michigan Libraries—Shapiro Design Lab. Interview by Gene Felice. Personal Interview. July 2019.

Thompson, Emily. University of Tennessee at Chattanooga Library—Studio. Interview by Peter Fritzler. Personal Interview. July 2019.

Wharton, Alyssa. University of North Carolina at Greensboro—Digital Media Commons. Interview by Jason Fleming. Personal Interview. October 2019.

NOTES

1. Vince Wilczynski, Aubrey Wigner, Micah Lande, and Shawn Jordan, "The Value of Higher Education Academic Makerspaces for Accreditation and Beyond," *Planning for Higher Education* 46, no. 1 (2017): 32, search.proquest.com/docview/2008824527?accountid=14606.
2. Robert Curry, "Makerspaces: A Beneficial New Service for Academic Libraries?" *Library Review* 66, no. 4 (2017): 210, dx.doi.org.liblink.uncw.edu/10.1108/LR-09-2016-0081.
3. Rebekah Lee, "Campus-Library Collaboration with Makerspaces," *Public Services Quarterly* 13, no. 2 (2017): 109, doi.org/10.1080/15228959.2017.1303421.
4. Ibid., 111.
5. Lydia Marek, Donna Brock, and Jyoti Savla, "Evaluating Collaboration for Effectiveness: Conceptualization and Measurement," *American Journal of Evaluation* 36, no. 1 (2015): 77, doi.org/10.1177/1098214014531068.
6. Ellen Taylor-Powell, Boyd Rossing, and Jean Geran, *Evaluating Collaboratives: Reaching the Potential (G3658-8)* (Madison: University of Wisconsin–Extension, 1998), cdn.shopify.com/s/files/1/0145/8808/4272/files/G3658-08.pdf.
7. Rafia Mirza, Brett Currier, and Peace Ossom Williamson, *Memorandum of Understanding Workbook* (Arlington: University of Texas, 2016), rc.library.uta.edu/uta-ir/handle/10106/25651.
8. Mary C. Walters and E. Van Gordon, "Get It in Writing: MOUs and Library/IT Partnerships," *Reference Services Review* 35, no. 3 (2007): 391, doi.org/10.1108/00907320710774265.
9. Ibid., 392.

Part II

CONNECTING TO THE CURRICULUM

Chapter Seven

Applying Design Thinking, Collaboration, and Makerspaces to Encourage Innovation in the Classroom

Thomas Mays

Collaboration and innovation are critical aspects in our modern world, and students should engage in activities that foster proficiencies in these areas. This project integrates collaboration and makerspaces with the design thinking process, providing students with the opportunity to engage in human-centric innovation while working on a team. While this project is intended to serve as a semester-length project in a course on innovation, it can be modified to fit shorter time frames as well as other disciplines.

The design thinking process is an iterative and human-centric approach to innovation that matches well with the rapid prototyping possibilities makerspaces offer. Many makerspaces maintain laser cutters/engravers, 3D printers, and CNC machines in their facilities. Additionally, some makerspaces have audio and video production studios, robotics capabilities, and other technologies to broaden the creative and development options available to students. The iterative process encourages students to complete multiple cycles of data collection, design, and testing, and the makerspace is a key tool in the process.

The goal of the Design Thinking Makerspace Team Project is for students to collaborate through the design thinking process as they explore the versatile tools and expertise offered at makerspaces. Before starting the project, several foundational subjects should be covered, including defining success and failure, exploring the various forms of innovation, and the design thinking process. Project deliverables include a final prototype or design as well as a final report that documents the team's processes and activities completed during the project time period. Individual reflection essays are also encouraged. The following sections provide possible project outcomes, foundational learning for before beginning the project, and tools and approaches that can be applied to support the design thinking process.

PROJECT OUTCOMES

The suggested student learning outcomes for the Design Thinking Makerspace project include the following:

1. Apply the design thinking process to generate solutions for a customer problem.
2. Engage in team activities to encourage working together in problem-solving, creative thinking, and innovation processes.
3. Use makerspace resources to engage in product prototyping/development and testing.
4. Generate a final team report describing the team's processes and results.

Foundational Topics for Review Prior to Starting the Project

For a project of this magnitude, it is essential to set the stage for students in terms of the activities, definitions, processes, and expectations. In a senior-level college course on innovation, we begin our focus on defining success and failure. Next, students learn about innovation with specific attention to the forms of innovation outside of radically new products. Finally, students learn about the design thinking process. Each of these is briefly described below and may be altered to fit different teaching situations.

How Do You Define Success and Failure?

Success and failure are often seen as two ends of a spectrum instead of as a part of a process. Small business owners, entrepreneurs, and inventors often understand that failure isn't necessarily an ending, but merely a step from which one builds and continues. Failure is often a vital part of the process. Thus, discussing this distinction is essential for students who are preparing to embark on an iterative design and innovation process. Through discussion, students often find that failure should not be the end but the start of a new direction.

What Is Innovation?

There are many ways to define innovation. People often think of innovation as a radically new product or advancement in technology. While this does describe a form of innovation, it is not inclusive of other innovation types. For this project, innovation is broadly defined as we consider two ways to think about innovation. First, innovation can be viewed from the perspective of the focus of the innovation (product or service, process, or business model). Second, we can consider the degree of innovation (incremental to radical).

Product innovation is straightforward and what often comes to mind when first discussing innovation. It is the use of innovation to create a new product or to improve an existing product. Process innovation involves improving manufacturing or business processes and can be thought of as improvements "behind the scenes." Business model innovation consists of changing an organization's approach to conducting business, for instance, a company changing from brick-and-mortar storefronts to online retailing.

Radical innovations are also known as *disruptive* innovations. Disruptive innovation "describes a process by which a product or service takes root initially in simple applications at the bottom of a market and then relentlessly moves up market, eventually displacing established competitors."[1] Disruptive innovations are what most people think about when discussing innovation—a brand-new, revolutionary product. With this mindset, students may feel overwhelmed when asked to innovate, thus the importance of understanding the variety of innovation possibilities.

Joe Dwyer defines innovation in this way: "Innovation is the process of creating value by applying novel solutions to meaningful problems."[2] With this definition, all kinds of new ideas and approaches can be considered instead of the commonly thought of "brand-new" product. When the concepts of incremental innovation, as well as process and business model innovations, are considered, our creative universe expands. Furthermore, while makerspaces may often be thought of as new-product laboratories, they can also support other kinds of innovation, especially with the expanded creative tools many makerspaces offer.

What Is Design Thinking?

According to IDEO, design thinking is human-centered, meaning in part that the end-user experience should be central in the problem-solving and innovative thinking. It is an iterative process that involves empathy, ideation, and experimentation. In other words, the process relies on perceiving the world through another's eyes (empathy), idea generation driven by those perceptions (ideation), and testing through prototyping.[3] John Spencer and A. J. Juliani note that "design thinking isn't a subject, topic, or class. It's more a way of solving problems that encourages positive risk-taking and creativity."[4]

Tim Brown describes the personality traits reflected in design thinkers, including empathy, integrative thinking, optimism, an experiential nature, and a collaborative attitude. With these traits in mind, Brown described innovation as "powered by a thorough understanding, through direct observation, of what people want and need in their lives and what they like or dislike about the way particular products are made, packaged, marketed, sold, and supported."[5] It is also an iterative cycle where design thinkers alternate among the areas of inspiration, ideation, and implementation.[6]

Design thinkers can develop empathy through activities, including observation and interviews. Next, brainstorming or other open-minded, team-based idea generation activities can be used to ideate based on what was learned during the empathy activities. Job mapping can also be beneficial. Additionally, teams can use some basic makerspace resources at this stage. Working with Play-Doh, construction paper, and pipe cleaners may help spark new ideas. After ideation, the design thinkers engage in prototyping. The process returns to the empathy stage where the team gathers data from users about the prototype.

Design thinking focuses on the human side of the customer or user. While empathy and understanding the person's perspective are critical in design thinking, experimentation and prototyping help bring those perspectives alongside new and innovative ideas. Students learn about focusing on the human experience, creative problem-solving, and engaging with others in an iterative development process with support from the makerspace.

PROJECT DETAILS

Now that we have covered the foundational concepts, we can review how the project can proceed. The main steps include forming teams, identifying a client or problem to study, and beginning the empathy, ideation, and prototyping iterations. As a reminder, the project can be modified to fit a specific course. For example, instructors can require a certain number of iterations with each one due during a specified time period. Also, depending on the team's project focus, the central human component could be a user, a customer, a client, and so on. As we proceed, the word "user" is used and should be considered within the context of the topic or problem chosen by the teams.

Getting Started

While individuals can complete the project, one of the objectives of this project is collaboration. After forming teams, it is a good idea to have students engage in an ice-breaker activity centered on a creative thinking exercise. Instructors may want to coincide this activity with a tour of the makerspace that student teams will have access to for the project.

After getting to know one another, the teams should discuss various problems, situations, or topics that they would like to explore regarding innovation. Teams should select something in which they have a keen interest. The following are ideas that teachers can share as examples. These ideas also have several dimensions and directions that teams could follow.

1. Café: While keeping their minds on being human-centric, teams can investigate either the customer experience or the employee experience. Since cafés are public locations, teams can collect data through observation and, with permission, interview customers or employees.
2. Not-for-profit organization: There are several paths for teams at not-for-profits, including the experiences and activities of employees, volunteers, donors, and beneficiaries. While a new or updated product may not be applicable, process and business model innovations can apply as can website development, social media strategy innovations, and video or audio productions.

Design Thinking: Generating Empathy

Observation can be an essential tool for gathering data about people, problems, or phenomenon. There are several things to consider when observing. Merriam and Tisdell recommend that observers pay attention to the physical setting, participants, activities and interactions, conversations, subtle factors, and the observers' own behavior. It is also suggested to describe the physical environment, including who is there and what they are doing. A key factor is recognizing how the observer may be influencing the environment. Thus a reflection on what these impacts could be is also important.[7] With this project, observations that focus on these areas can help shed light on the user's experiences and what new or different products, services, processes, and so forth may help them.

Interviewing people can provide invaluable insight into their thoughts and perspectives on interacting with products and services. Michael Patton suggests several types of interview questions. Foci include experience and behavior questions, opinion and values questions, feeling questions, knowledge questions, sensory questions, and background and demographic questions. Patton suggests also considering the time frame, including past, present, and future.[8] After collecting observational and interview data, teams can proceed to the ideation stage.

Design Thinking: Facilitating Ideation

A good start to ideation is through brainstorming. While the ideas generated during brainstorming can be powerful, sometimes guidance or focus can be beneficial. After brainstorming, teams can use a more structured approach like customer-centered job mapping to focus on specific aspects of the user experience and spark new innovative directions.

As noted by Bettencourt and Ulwick, "The goal of creating a job map is not to find out how the customer is executing a job—that only generates maps of existing activities and solutions. Instead the aim is to discover what the customer is trying to get done at different points in executing a job and what must happen at each juncture in order for the job to be carried out successfully."[9]

It is critical to note that the word "job" is defined loosely. Returning to the café example, we describe the customer's job as buying a cup of coffee. A job map walks us through each stage of what the customer needs to do to complete the task. While purchasing a cup of coffee may seem trivial, the job map can reveal opportunities to improve the human experience.

The customer-centered job mapping includes these areas: define, locate, prepare, confirm, execute, monitor, and modify.[10] Table 7.1 uses our café example.

Table 7.1. Design Thinking Café Example

Step	*Customer job*
Define	Customer decides to buy a cup of coffee
Locate	Considers where to buy the coffee and travels there
Prepare	Orders coffee
Confirm	Receives coffee
Execute	Consumes the coffee
Monitor	Decides if the coffee was good
Modify	Considers if will return in the future
Conclude	Disposes of the cup

When we consider areas to improve the customer experience, we may want to focus on the prepare and confirm stages. Can customers place mobile orders beforehand and pick up later? How can we improve product pickup or delivery? Can any products, services, or processes be added or improved? Considering the interview and observational data collected in the empathy stage, some of these answers may already exist, and job mapping is a way to organize that data.

Keep in mind that every scenario will be different, and in some cases, one or more areas may be more important than others. However, teams can find ways to innovate at each stage of the customer job. Teachers considering using the customer-centered job map should conduct additional research in this area to take advantage of its full potential.

Design Thinking: Development and Prototyping in the Makerspace

Experimentation is key. Teams should understand that the process is iterative in that returning to the empathy and ideation stages is a critical element. Thus "failure" is turned into an opportunity for improvement. As teams work with the results of the ideation phase, they should collaborate with makerspace staff on equipment access and safety concerns. Furthermore, staff may also have suggestions and recommendations on tools or processes that best meet the team's needs. Additionally, teachers should consider the learning curves necessary to use not only the makerspace equipment but also design tools such as CAD software.

Product development or improvement is not the only option. Sometimes a documentary, podcast, mobile app, website, or social media innovation is what is required. Some makerspaces have resources to help with these alternatives to traditional product prototyping. Aside from that difference, the process remains the same with scripts, storyboards, and visual mockups created for review.

After teams complete the empathy, ideation, and design/development stages, the user reviews the project. This is the start of the next iteration, where teams gather data through interviews and observations regarding how the user interacts with and responds to the prototype, and the teams make adjustments and continue with the iteration.

PROJECT WRAP-UP

At the end of the project, the teams should submit their final report and individual reflections. Another option is to ask teams to present their projects to demonstrate their final product, service, or other innovation. Additionally, soliciting feedback from students about their project experiences may help teachers improve the project experience for future students.

NOTES

1. Clayton Christensen, "Disruptive Innovation," accessed July 3, 2019, claytonchristensen.com/key-concepts/.

2. Joe Dwyer, "What Is Innovation: Why Almost Everyone Defines It Wrong," Digital Intent, accessed July 4, 2019, digintent.com/what-is-innovation/.

3. "What Is Design Thinking," IDEO U, accessed July 1, 2019, www.ideou.com/blogs/inspiration/what-is-design-thinking.

4. John Spencer and A. J. Juliani, *Launch: Using Design Thinking to Boost Creativity and Bring Out the Maker in Every Student* (San Diego: Dave Burgess Consulting, Inc., 2016), 52.
5. Tim Brown, “Design Thinking,” *Harvard Business Review* 86 (2008): 86.
6. Ibid., 88–89.
7. Sharan Merriam and Elizabeth Tisdell, *Qualitative Research* (San Francisco: Jossey-Bass, 2016), 140–43.
8. Michael Patton, *Qualitative Evaluation and Research Methods* (Newbury Park, CA: Sage Publications, 1990), 290–94.
9. Lance Bettencourt and Anthony Ulwick, “The Customer Centered Innovation Map,” in *On Innovation* (Boston: Harvard Business School Publishing Corporation, 2013), 48–49.
10. Ibid., 46–47.

Chapter Eight

3D Printing in a Senior Seminar Fashion Course

Bernadette Smith Mirro, Julia Ravindran, and Mason Hongqiang Yang

The integration of 3D printing in academia is well established in physical sciences, health sciences, and IT fields. However, there is a lack of information regarding 3D printing in fashion design programs. This is surprising given the increased presence of 3D-printed materials in various fashion markets including garments, shoes, and accessories. Incorporating 3D printing into fashion curricula, involving the basics of 3D design, the printing process, and 3D's use in innovative design, will give students a competitive edge in the industry.

Academic literature is sparse in regard to incorporating 3D printing into fashion design curricula. This is potentially due to the cost of 3D printers, which ranges from a few hundred dollars to well over a million dollars, and the specialist knowledge of 3D-modeling software that can present a challenge for smaller universities. Nevertheless, evidence of 3D printing in curriculum is apparent; a review of course offerings at the Fashion Institute of Technology revealed a certificate program launching in fall 2019 in 3D printing and design,[1] and Parsons's catalog included 3D printing in courses such as jewelry design.[2]

These factors led us to incorporate 3D printing in the AA 408 curriculum by creating a fully fashioned look focusing on the interaction of the body with space, form, volume, and movement. This project allowed students to demonstrate the ability to design and construct a garment using more difficult materials and creatively solve structural problems when it came to assembling the 3D-printed aspect of the design.

FASHION DESIGN AND 3D PRINTING

The fashion industry continues to evolve and cater to shifting trends, and an increasing number of designers are turning to newer technologies, such as 3D printing, for both practical and artistic needs. 3D printing has not only become more accessible for use by fashion designers and fashion houses, but will likely continue to grow in scale due to its affordability, accessibility, reduction of environmental waste, and viability due to evolving techniques.

The importance of designers considering the affordability of their products cannot be overstated. Students need to understand these price and time constraints prior to entering the industry. When designing jewelry and other fashion accessories, partnering with a third-party vendor in order to get professional molds created can cost thousands of dollars.[3] Combine that with the time spent creating prototypes and modifying designs, and the traditional production process is lengthy and expensive. However, by utilizing 3D printing, this can all be done in house, at the pace of the designer's work hours, limited only by the speed of the 3D printer and the designer's imagination. Designers are now able to experiment and create pieces at the mere cost of electricity and plastic filament cartridges. Despite the fact that not all fashion designers can afford large-scale 3D printers like those utilized at major fashion corporations, 3D printing now comes in various sizes and scales, in order to cater to different creators and needs. By incorporating 3D printing on smaller-scale printers in our fashion curriculum, we provide an opportunity for students to understand the printing production process related to the fashion industry, gain knowledge on 3D-modeling software to create innovative objects and designs, and explore various ways 3D printing can be applied to garment making. Students are encouraged to use critical thinking and problem-solving skills when it comes to the creativity of assembling their designs due to the limitations posed by the smaller-scale 3D printers.

Reducing environmental waste is a goal of the fashion industry, and 3D printing can be responsibly utilized to reduce environmental waste.[4] AA 408 deepens the understanding of sustainability, then engages students in critical thinking to find ways to incorporate what they learn into the development of their garment designs by making mindful choices that have a positive impact to the environment, such as promoting recycled fabrics and repurposing scrap waste. The materials that 3D printers use can be recycled from the more than nine billion tons of plastic that have been produced since the 1950s, or they can be newly created and customized to fit a specific task.[5] Several major companies have already successfully implemented environmental waste reduction by utilizing 3D printing. Nike's Flyprint 3D-printed shoe requires less pieces to assemble and therefore produces less manufacturing waste than traditionally designed sneakers.[6] Adidas's AlphaEdge shoe is environmentally friendly because the 3D-printed materials utilized can be melted down and recreated from the same materials over and over therefore eliminating plastic waste.[7] In addition, the use of 3D printing has made it financially feasible for both Nike and Adidas to manufacture sneakers in the United States, cutting down on the environmental impact of shipping when production occurs overseas and allowing them to fill customized orders quickly.[8]

3D printing is a technique, and the 3D printer is a versatile tool that keeps expanding the possibilities of the imagination. For example, Nike's Flyprint shoe is designed for each specific athlete to improve performance. Under Armour has been designing 3D-printed athletic shoe prototypes that they hope to apply to aerospace, opening up a new market.[9] In fact, 3D printing has been praised as "nothing short of a new industrial revolution"[10] and "part of the 4th industrial revolution that focuses on technology."[11] A 2019 Plunkett report on market research and trends in the apparel, textile, and fashion industry cites the importance of 3D printing as it relates to the ability to create custom-ordered items that can be produced in the United States as reasons that the 3D printing market will remain strong.

CURRENT DESIGNERS UTILIZING 3D PRINTING

Fashion Designer Zac Posen recently incorporated 3D printing at the 2019 Met Gala event in New York City. Posen collaborated with GE Additive for the engineering and Protolabs for the printing to create a range of innovative 3D-printed garments, embellishments, and accessories. One of the dresses was made specifically to the mold of the celebrity to create a custom fit and printed on a stereolithography machine, which can cost up to $10,000. It was sanded and sprayed with a clear coat to give it a glass appearance. The printing and finishing of the bustier took more than two hundred hours.[12] Another piece designed for the event was a collar accessory with pearlescent purple palm leaves draped over the shoulders and attached to the tulle gown at the neckline. This piece took fifty-six hours to print and finish on an SLA machine. SLA technology allows designers to print complex designs and shapes with less handwork construction.[13]

Dutch designer Iris Van Herpen has been utilizing 3D printing and technology with couture craftsmanship for more than a decade. She made her first 3D-printed dress in 2009 when flexible materials weren't available. By creatively assembling the non-flexible 3D panels, she was able to construct the dress with no restrictions in movement. It took seven days, twenty-four hours per day, to print the dress.[14] Ten years later, Van Herpen 3D prints delicate leaves and foliage directly onto semi-transparent fabrics, not restricting any of the movement while wearing the dress. Van Herpen has also been known to collaborate with architects, sculptures, and artists.[15] One thing that's noticeable about the creations from these designers is that they may have an idea, but it is not always brought to life in 3D form all on their own; it takes a team of people who also share that vision to bring it to life.

Julia Daviy is a 3D-printed clothing designer and clean-tech specialist who went into 3D-printed fashion design to find sustainable and waste-free ways of producing clothing.[16] She typically prints her pieces in two to four parts using industrial large-format Fused Deposition Modeling 3D printers using thermoplastic polyurethane materials.[17] In 2017 Daviy devoted an average of ten to fifteen hours a week just learning and experimenting with the printer and sometimes having her printer going twenty-four hours per day. Her practical knowledge comes from everyday experimentation, researching books and magazines on 3D printing, and hundreds of mistakes. When Daviy creates customized pieces for clients, she will use 3D-scanning applications to get the client's body measurements and silhouettes, which involves little to no material waste.[18]

IMPLEMENTATION OF 3D PRINTING IN A FASHION DESIGN CLASS

The process of integrating the library's 3D-printing resources with the fashion curriculum started organically. The professor teaching AA 408 contacted the fashion liaison librarian about including 3D printing in her assignment and arranged a time for her class, typically composed of ten students, to visit the library to learn about 3D printing. The electronic services librarian, who had the expertise in 3D printing, the fashion liaison librarian, and the teaching faculty member pooled their collective knowledge, and a partnership was born!

Designers and educators that do not have funding to experiment with large-format technology typically use smaller-scale printers, which require more time for printing, cutting/sanding, and assembling their pieces because the bed of the printer is smaller. When Daviy prints her designs on large-format printers, she is able to bypass having to hand sew and glue her pieces together.[19] Our library's MakerSpace hosts three consumer-level 3D printers. These printers come with different build volumes, ranging from 6 × 6 × 6 inches to 8.9 × 5.8 × 5.9 inches. Printing capabilities are important to consider when designing an assignment. It's reasonable to expect students to print an accessory, as opposed to an entire 3D-printed garment. Consumer-level 3D printers can limit a student's capabilities due to their size. However, this can also foster creativity when designing pieces that either stand alone or are assembled into one larger cohesive piece.

The course integration started in fall 2017 with students visiting the library for a 3D-printing workshop. They were given an overview of the 3D-printing process. This included demonstrating the basic mechanics of 3D printers, introducing various software options, and explaining how the library can support their 3D-printing projects. The students were given a handout created to outline the learning objectives of the workshop and give a holistic view of the process. This holistic view included: graphic design, 3D design and modeling, 3D printer operation and maintenance, and parts assembling and processing. During the workshop, students had a chance to see how a design file was created online using Thingiverse.com, a user-friendly 3D-printing tool for novice designers. They also observed how a 3D printer read the modeling file and started the printing process. In order to help them to have a more realistic view, the electronic services librarian shared several 3D-printing tips and lessons with students during the printer warm-up and printing process, such as the usability and print quality of different 3D printers, the max size of print output, impacts of air flow and temperature, incidents of 3D printer falling down onto the floor, and so on.

After the initial workshop, the electronic services librarian engaged in one-on-one support to ensure student designs were compatible with the printers and to work through the process. This initially resulted in five printed pieces. Figure 8.1 shows one of the more elaborate designs. The student printed four pieces of a crown using transparent material. She then assembled all four pieces together with a thin metal wire and spray painted the assembled product a deep red to match the full garment it was designed to accompany. The final product, the crown, became an integrated part of the garment for her final portfolio. An unanticipated challenge with this course was the relatively small number of students that sought assistance 3D printing from the librarians. Coincidently, the students that did not visit the library for help were enrolled in a physical sciences lab and managed to 3D print their pieces with the assistance of a science faculty member. In the end, all students did incorporate a 3D-printed piece in their final garment, making the first iteration of the project undoubtedly a success.

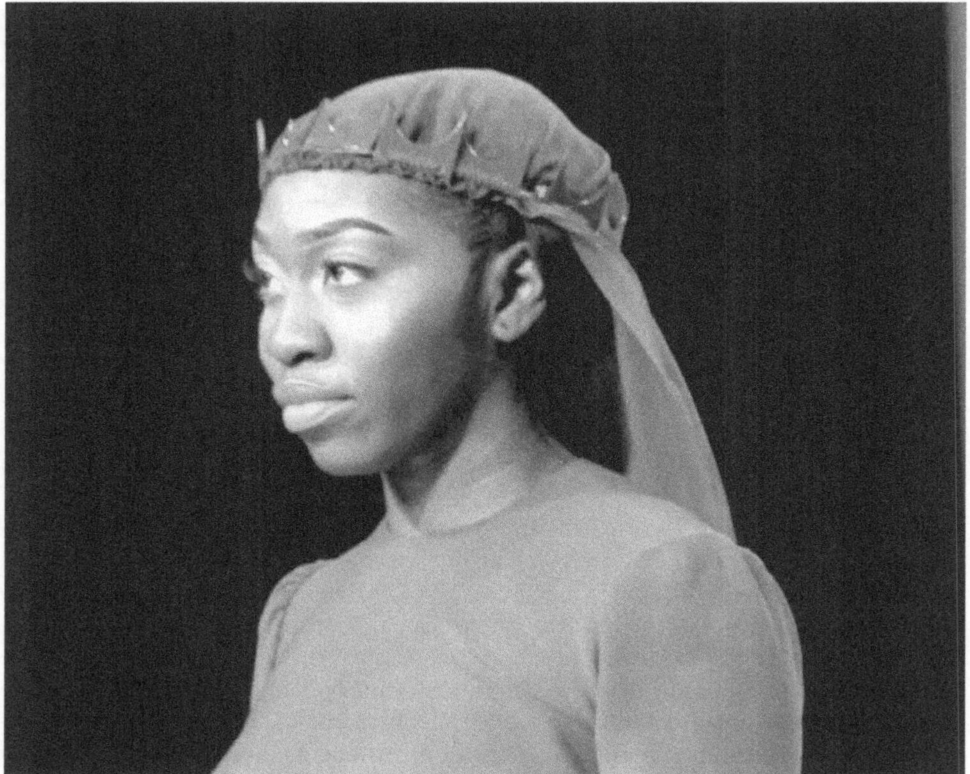

Figure 8.1. Chris Radcliffe Photography. Garment and crown designed by Odalis Ihrig. 2018, color photographic print. *Bernadette Smith Mirro*

AA 408 runs only in the fall semester, so in 2018 we had the opportunity to expand on the initial session. The fashion liaison librarian purchased print materials on designers who were using 3D printing, albeit on a much larger scale, in their designs. These books were laid out for students to review when they came to the library session. In addition, a curated YouTube playlist of fashion shows and designer interviews featuring 3D-printed garments was playing in the background. We repeated the same demonstration of the 3D printers and the design software, but students were much more engaged in the process after seeing the potential and seeing how 3D printing was being used in the industry. A challenge of the session was the level of familiarity with 3D printing as several students had used 3D printers in high school and others were brand new to the process. By creating a series of step-by-step handouts on the 3D printers as well as the software, we were able to mitigate this knowledge gap and create a session that was engaging for students. A particularly noteworthy product of the second session was a handbag made up of six parts (see figure 8.2). Three solid panels were developed for the front, back, and bottom of the bag to create stability, and the two side panels and the top flap have a lightweight mesh texture designed for added movement and mobility. When designing the bag using 3D software, the student included small holes on all sides of each printed panel in order to facilitate sewing the pieces together by hand. In addition, the student was able to find silver thread to match the color of the handbag. Lastly, she sewed a strap made of silver tulle to the bag in order to create a finished piece. The featured pieces were included in the student's final portfolio of garments and were featured in the annual Portfolio in Motion event. Portfolio in Motion is a student-run fashion show that has occurred at Marymount University annually since 1989.

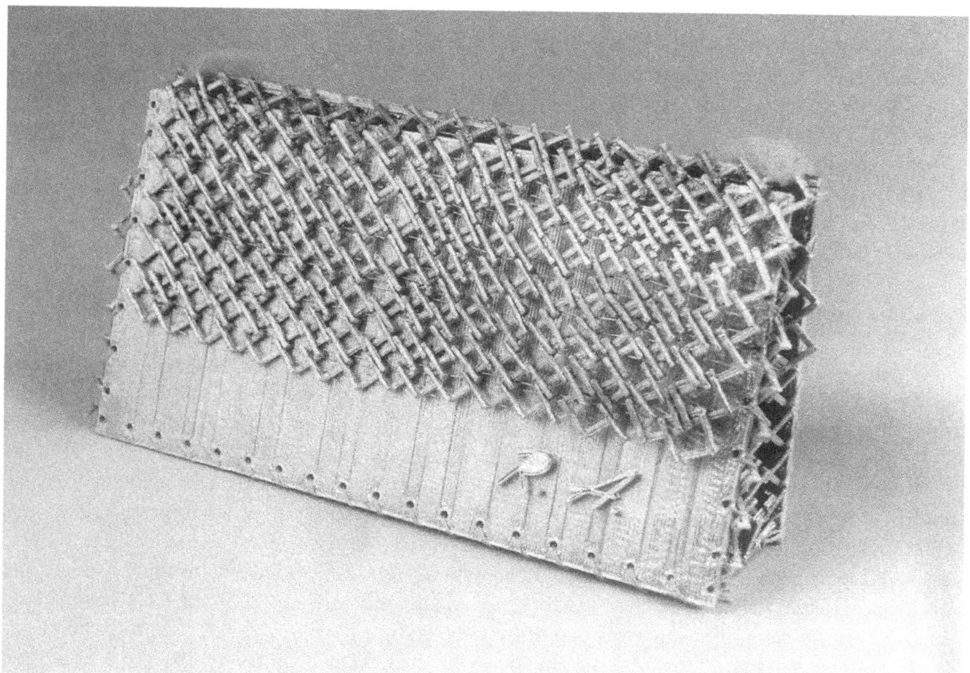

Figure 8.2. Professor Joseph Hicks. 3D-printed handbag designed by Rebecca Moreno. 2018, color photographic print. ***Bernadette Smith Mirro***

It is extremely important to continue enhancing fashion curriculums with the most updated information on 3D printing in order to prepare our students for future market changes and the technology-driven industry they will be entering. In future AA 408 classes, we plan to seek feedback from the students about the process and adjust our approach accordingly; consideration for dividing students with prior 3D-printing knowledge from beginners to provide a more appropriate introduction session is a possibility. In addition, there is potential to streamline the production of student designs by forging a partnership with other departments on campus that are incorporating 3D printing in their curricula. By preparing students with the basics of 3D printing and giving them hands-on opportunities to practice designing and producing a 3D-printed piece, students will have the confidence and knowledge to enter the industry. In addition, this knowledge will encourage students to think about 3D design not as a solo process but to consider collaborating with architects, engineers, and artists in the future on large-scale industry printers. We want them to continue to push boundaries.

NOTES

1. "Certificate Programs," Fashion Institute of Technology, accessed July 2, 2019, www.fitnyc.edu/ccps/certificate-programs/index.php.

2. "The New School Course Catalog," The New School, accessed July 2, 2019, courses.newschool.edu/courses/PSOF3040/.

3. Alex Crease, "The Economics of 3D Printing," Markforged, last modified October 18, 2016, markforged.com/blog/economics-of-3d-printing/.

4. "Can You Recycle 3D-Printed Objects?" RecycleBank, last modified December 12, 2017, livegreen.recyclebank.com/column/because-you-asked/can-you-recycle-3d-printed-objects.

5. Robert Ferris, "The World Has Made More than 9 Billion Tons of Plastic, Says New Study," CNBC, last modified July 19, 2017, www.cnbc.com/2017/07/19/the-world-has-made-more-than-9-billion-tons-of-plastic-says-new-study.html.

6. "3-D Printing and Robotics Revolutionize Manufacture of Shoes and Fabrics," Plunkett Research Ltd., last modified April 26, 2019, www.plunkettresearchonline.com/ResearchCenter/Trends/display.aspx?Industry=23.

7. "Nike Flyprint is the First Performance 3D Printed Textile Upper," Nike News, last modified April 17, 2018, news.nike.com/news/nike-flyprint-3d-printed-textile.

8. Ibid.

9. Roopinder Tara, "Under Armour Implements Autodesk's Generative Design to Engineer the Perfect 3D-Printed Shoe," last modified March 24, 2016, www.engineering.com/3DPrinting/3DPrintingArticles/ArticleID/11747/Under-Armour-Implements-Autodesks-Generative-Design-to-Engineer-the-Perfect-3D-Printed-Shoe.aspx.

10. Pascal Morand, "What 3D Printing Means for Fashion," Business of Fashion, last modified July 27, 2016, www.businessoffashion.com/articles/opinion/3d-printing-technology-disrupt-fashion-and-luxury-pascal-morand.

11. Herbert Sim, "3D Printing in Luxury Fashion: Revolution Or Evolution?" *Forbes*, last modified December 3, 2017, www.forbes.com/sites/herbertrsim/2017/12/03/3d-printing-in-luxury-fashion-revolution-or-evolution/#60f3a9b53f20.

12. Natalie Wilson, "How Zac Posen 3D Printed Dresses Took Over the 2019 Met Gala Event," WTVOX, last modified May 9, 2019, wtvox.com/fashion/zac-posen-3d-printed-dresses-met-gala-2019/.

13. "Zac Posen X GE Additive X Protolabs Unveil Breathtaking 3D Printing Collaboration at the Met Gala," Business Wire, last modified May 7, 2019, www.businesswire.com/news/home/20190507005386/en/Zac-Posen-GE-Additive-Protolabs-Unveil-Breathtaking.

14. Mark Holgate, "Meet Iris Van Herpen, the Dutch Designer Boldly Going into the Future," *Vogue*, last modified April 28, 2016, www.vogue.com/article/iris-van-herpen-dutch-designer-interview-3d-printing?verso=true.

15. "Iris Van Herpen," Iris Van Herpen, accessed June 20, 2019, www.irisvanherpen.com/.

16. Carlota V., "Designer Julia Daviy on Disrupting and Bringing Sustainability to the Fashion Industry," 3D Natives, last modified May 28, 2019, www.3dnatives.com/en/julia-daviy-280520194/.

17. Julia Daviy, "3D Printed Clothing Designer Julia Daviy Debuts First Ever 3D Printed Collection for Women within the U.S. that is Wearable Day-to-Day at NYFW," PRN News Wire, last modified September 10, 2018, www.prnewswire.com/news-releases/3d-printed-clothing-designer-julia-daviy-debuts-first-ever-3d-printed-collection-for-women-within-the-us-that-is-wearable-day-to-day-at-nyfw-300709512.html.

18. "3D Clothing Designer: Julia Daviy," Made Lokal, last modified April 30, 2018, www.madelokal.com/blogs/news/julia-daviy-ecologist-3d-clothing-designer.

19. Julia Daviy, "3D Printed Clothing Designer."

Chapter Nine

Sculpting Synesthesia

Using the Makerspace to Develop Creative Writing and Creative Minds

Eric Melbye

In my Introduction to Creative Writing class at Miami University Middletown, one issue students express about the creative writing process is so-called writer's block. Students feel stuck, either with how to begin writing a story or poem or with how to continue once their work has reached a point where there are too many options—or seemingly no options. However, after some engagement with this issue in the classroom, I believe the issue doesn't lie with any sort of writer's block. It lies more with students' adherence to convergent thinking, a mode of thinking that students are accustomed to use in addressing a wide variety of other writing opportunities, from basic five-paragraph expository essays to long, inquiry-based research essays and beyond, but which doesn't always lend itself to creative challenges, such as crafting a story or poem. I have approached this issue from several different directions, with varying results. One approach, using the concept of synesthesia in writing exercises, has had encouraging but limited success. Nonetheless, I wonder if the use of synesthesia as a pedagogical technique, combined with the opportunities of our university's makerspace, might guide my creative writing students through the block of convergent thinking and into a mode of divergent thinking that is more conducive to creative activity.

CONVERGING ON DIVERGENT THINKING

When my students express frustration with "writer's block"—the difficulty of how to begin or continue a creative writing project—I like to share a commonly cited quotation by author and screenwriter John Rogers: "You can't think yourself out of a writing block; you have to write yourself out of a thinking block." I like the way this quotation cleverly turns the problem of writer's block on its head, positing it as a disruption in thinking rather than a problem in the writing process and equally cleverly proposing that the way out of not feeling able to write is to write.

Yet while discussing this idea alongside strategies for writing through blocks seems to inspire my students in the classroom moment, it doesn't consistently yield positive results for them once they're alone with their work again. The students who discuss Rogers's quotation and seem to find inspiration and writing strategies from it still express frustration at not knowing how to start writing or how to continue once they have some writing completed. In their creative writing, I often read opening paragraphs that introduce characters and plot, as though Rod Serling or Alfred Hitchcock were informing the readers of what exactly is taking place. And while that is certainly a viable option for beginning a story, it's usually a sign that students are falling back on previous writing experiences with composition and expository writing models in order to complete a new creative writing challenge. In short, students are approaching the messy chaos of the creative process as an equation to be solved or a riddle to be answered rather than a process in which to engage.

Consequently, I believe the real issue is not necessarily with the creative writing process, or the common problem students face of where and how to begin or continue any piece of academic writing, though that's certainly a challenge for some students whose previous course work hasn't required them to utilize creative thinking techniques. The real issue is developing an approach to a writing task that does not rely purely on convergent thinking, in which there is one problem or issue and one single solution. When students dive into the creative process, especially for the first time, and meet with any kind of frustration or problem, their inclination is to fall back on what they are familiar with to help them through the problem. Usually, that means falling back on convergent thinking techniques they learned in elementary or secondary school to find their way through anything from a mathematical equation to a research essay: identify the problem, identify the proper solution, and implement the solution to solve the problem. But when working through the often messy, confusing creative process, divergent thinking is often more productive. Using a divergent thinking approach, a problem, question, or issue has many possible solutions, and writers explore and select the most effective solution as they move through the process of generating their work. For example, in the first week of class, I engage my students in a simple exercise: I write "What is one half of thirteen?" on the board, and ask the class for the answer. Students are always quick to respond with a correct answer: six and a half. But what other ways might there be to answer the question, or to ask the question? After some discussion, students develop other possible answers such as "thir" and "teen," "1" and "3," and "XI" and "II." Depending on the context and the circumstance, one of these answers will work best, but to start with, they are all possibilities.

In an effort to guide students out of a convergent thinking approach to creative writing, I've used a writing exercise that employs synesthesia. Loosely defined, synesthesia involves the combining or confusing of our five senses in unexpected ways—describing sunlight as fuzzy, for example, or the color green as chilly, the letter B as shiny, or wallpaper as noisy. As a psychological condition that many people are born with, synesthesia can be an artistic blessing or a daily curse. As a teaching tool, though, it can help writing students to "short circuit" the logical, convergent brain and fully engage the creative, divergent faculties of our brain, which in turn can encourage students to think about their writing projects in creative, divergent ways that bypass their convergent thinking–related issues. For example, as an in-class writing exercise, I invite students to complete a fill-in-the-blank "survey" about the fiction and poetry they have recently begun writing. Surveys might include questions such as "If your story was an animal, it would be a ___," or "If your poem was a food, it would be

___." I ask students to complete each blank with several possibilities, then pick the one answer that captures their attention for any reason and write about why—why is the story they're writing a giraffe or a snail or an eagle? Why is the poem a banana? Because this exercise forces students into a very unfamiliar way of thinking, I have to keep at it patiently and ask for the students to keep pushing at it with some patience, too. Eventually, interesting and useful things happen. I don't ask students to share the results of the survey right away; instead, I ask them to respond in writing to further questions: "What color is your story?" "What does your poem taste like?" And again, I ask them to write out explanations for their responses.

One of the most interesting parts of this exercise in synesthesia is what happens when I ask students to share and try to explain their responses. Sometimes conversations develop to explore whether the color yellow is sweet or savory or whether letters of the alphabet have individual smells. And when I ask students how any of this might help them think through their questions, frustrations, and issues with their creative work, they quickly develop ideas. If a student describes her poetry as blue, for example, the student can reflect on what blue means for her and whether blue is really the color she wants her poetry to be. These are often very strange, wonderful, and productive conversations and revelations.

However, once students get back into the mental and physical work of writing, the conceptual knowledge they may have gained through classroom discussion and synesthesical writing exercises seems to disappear, as students continue expressing frustration at being stuck in the writing process just as they were before. When students engage in peer-review writing workshops or ask me privately for guidance, it's very clear to me that they are still approaching creative writing as a problem to be solved through a prescribed method of writing or thinking. In other words, they're still thinking about the creative process in a convergent way, looking for a single, correct solution to a problem.

SCULPTING SYNESTHESIA

Encouraged nonetheless by the minor successes of synesthesical writing exercises and discussions, I have developed a new project to: (1) engage students in divergent thinking more effectively in a writing-based class; (2) guide them through the whole writing process, step by step; and (3) possibly generate creative work that is more imaginative or experimental than a rote, "by the numbers" creative work might appear. The exercise makes use of a makerspace in our local library and invites students to extend the writing exercises they did with synesthesia into a physical, tangible object that can be utilized in a variety of ways. By creating a physical, sensory object that students can hold and examine, and possibly revise alongside the fiction and poetry they are writing, I believe the use of synesthesia as a pedagogical tool combined with the library's makerspace can become an effective way for students to guide themselves through the sometimes challenging labyrinth of composing fiction or poetry for the first time. In addition, this method could strengthen students' abilities to generate more imaginative or experimental work.

The basic idea for the makerspace project is simple, though there are several ways to modify it for use in a variety of different writing situations. The basic idea is to invite students to use the makerspace to generate a three-dimensional object that represents their creative work and then use their makerspace object as a tool for inspiration, for reflection, or for revision, all the while continually employing the use of synesthesia to help them think about their work using divergent thinking, rather than linear, convergent thinking.

As one hypothetical example: After a student begins his creative work, he engages in the in-class exercise described above that employs divergent and synesthesical thinking about his work. Working with the notion that his story is green, plastic, twisted, and too large (for example), the student is then challenged to use the makerspace to create a physical, tangible representation of his story using the results of the synesthesia writing exercise. The student may decide to use a 3D pen, 3D printer, or any other means and materials at hand to transform the abstract concepts of story, green, plastic, twisted, and too large into something the student can hold, feel, turn in his hand, and examine. He can give it a sniff or, if he's truly bold, give it a taste. This object is his story—at least what he thought of it while brainstorming, what he thinks of it now, or maybe (or maybe not) what he wants his story to be.

Now that he has the object in his hands, there are many ways for the student to use it that can push him to think more divergently and guide him through the common frustrations of where to begin writing or how to continue. If, for example, the student is unhappy with the beginning of his story or the way his plot design is unfolding, he can engage in free-writing activity that focuses on why his story is so green or so twisted. The synesthesical nature of the writing activity immediately forces his brain out of convergent thinking mode, which would focus on distinct, clearly delineated solutions to beginning the story or structuring its plot, and into more "free-form" territory, which he is invited to explore, wander, wonder, interrogate, reflect, and eventually resolve. His story is green because it's a sci fi story and green is the color of the alien in the story. Its plot is twisted because the student wanted to create an elaborate plot structure to keep his readers engaged and guessing what will happen next. But with his makerspace object in hand and the exploratory writing he's just completed, the student realizes that the story is not just green; it's also red because there is both bloodshed and a budding romance between two characters. The student hadn't seen that before, but now realizes it was holding back his writing process. In addition, the student sees that while he initially wanted a convoluted plot, such a plot structure is more confusing than necessary.

Consequently, the student may decide to modify his makerspace object—add a thread of red 3D ink, experiment with straightening out the structure, or even start over with a completely new design with new materials. The makerspace object becomes a crucial element of the writing process because it's an immediate, tangible representation that can be interpreted in a variety of ways through writing exercises and also reshaped, recast, and revised in ways as the student continues working through the vagaries of the creative process.

To be clear, this is just one example of how synesthesia as a pedagogical tool combined with the potential of a makerspace can guide students through a writing challenge and invite them to approach such challenges with a productive, divergent mode of thinking. The synesthesia writing exercise and the makerspace product could be used as generative tools to brainstorm a writing project, to work through the writing process itself, to aid in writing revision, to reflect on a writing project, or any combination thereof. The makerspace object is a vital key, though, because it invites students to transform their abstract concepts about their work into tangible, experiential, and even malleable objects that help them understand and engage in their work in novel, productive ways.

Chapter Ten

The Makerspace as a Place for Social Justice Learning

Emily Lelandais, Donna Femenella, and Antoaneta Tileva

American University (AU) in Washington, D.C., has a strong dedication to social justice inside and outside of the classroom, and our students are recognized as the most politically active students on U.S. college campuses according to Princeton Review.[1] Social equity, and supporting the change-making work of student, faculty, and staff in using scholarship to address the most pressing issues facing our local, national, and global communities, is one of four areas of strategic focus for our university.[2] The commitment to social justice learning is apparent in both university-wide programming, such as AU's Explore DC program,[3] and in course offerings such as Dr. Antoaneta Tileva's ANTH-215: Sex, Gender and Culture course. In this class, students explore social justice themes, including the topic of menstruation and its intersection with issues of race, class, and place.

In addition to our university's dedication to social justice, AU is also committed to experiential education as a way for students to connect their course curriculum to their experiences in local, national, and global communities. Experiential education is an important way for students to understand how what they are learning, in ANTH-215, for example, applies to issues faced by women, minorities, and the homeless in Washington, D.C. The AU Library Makerspace is a place where students, faculty, and staff can translate their dedication to social justice into activities that supplement traditional classroom learning.

The AU Library Makerspace opened in its current location in the spring of 2018.[4] Until that time, 3D and large-format printing were mostly offered on-demand through our lower-level Technology and Course Reserves service point. With a dedicated space, we were able to expand our services and divide them into three workbenches: Digital Creation, Craft Fabrication, and 3D Production. Our Digital Creation workbench includes a large-format printer and a range of high-end audio-visual equipment. The 3D Production workbench includes 3D printers, a Carvey (a 3D carving machine), and 3D "Doodle Pens." Lastly, the Craft Fabrication workbench includes sewing machines, a vinyl cutter, a button maker, and various hand-crafting tools.

Collaborating with Dr. Tileva and her class was a new experience for the AU Library Makerspace staff. Previously we spoke with faculty who asked, "How can I use the Makerspace in my class? What sort of projects can we do in here?" The Makerspace has no dedicated instructional designer, and many times we would respond, "You can use the Makerspace however you want!" (This is still true, more on that later!) When Dr. Tileva came to us with interest in having her students craft creative projects to connect to what they were learning in her Sex, Gender, and Culture class, we were eager to support her. So how do you connect the themes of social justice taught in liberal arts college courses to the Makerspace? Additionally, what did we learn from the experience? Here's our story.

CONNECTING WITH ANTH-215: SEX, GENDER, AND CULTURE

In September 2018, Dr. Tileva attended the inaugural AU Library Makerspace Open House. Dr. Tileva said, "Once I saw the space, I fell in love with it, and I knew that I had to be back." For Dr. Tileva, the ethos of DIY and encouraging her students' creativity to connect with course objectives is reflected across her syllabus: "You are invited to do a final research paper or a creative project, which can be a zine, a photo essay, a documentary, a podcast, a protest poster."[5] One objective in bringing her students to the Makerspace was to introduce them to what the Makerspace has to offer and the possibility of creating something that could fulfill course requirements in her and other classes.

Fortuitously, an excellent opportunity came up during the class discussion about periods, including the topics of menstrual suppression, period shaming, the pink tax, the tampon tax, and how inaccessible period products are to homeless and low-income people. One of Dr. Tileva's students had previously made reusable menstrual pads and brought up the idea of making them in the makerspace as a way to (1) connect with the curriculum and issues of consumerism and environmental sustainability and (2) be potentially packaged up for distribution in period kits for the D.C. community. "I really liked the idea [of using the makerspace] and wanted to extend our classroom discussion and create space for further discussion, as well as give students something they could take home with them," Dr. Tileva said. She proposed the idea to her class, and after a vote, they decided to use the Makerspace to make the reusable menstrual pads. Thus, the Pad Project was started.

After her class agreed on the project, Dr. Tileva e-mailed Makerspace staff to see if we would be willing to sponsor the Pad Project by purchasing materials and coordinating time in the Makerspace for her class to meet. Excited for the opportunity to connect the Makerspace to the classroom, we agreed. In preparation for her class visit, we showed Dr. Tileva how to use the sewing machine and made sure we had all the necessary hand tools (such as scissors and sewing chalk) to make the project a success. Students came to the Makerspace on the agreed-upon date and began cutting patterns and fitting all of the layers together. During that time, they discussed period activism, as it related to assigned course reading, but also as it connected to larger issues within the Washington, D.C., community.

The success of the Pad Project depended on the entirely volunteer nature of it. Students did not feel pressured to participate and knew they had other opportunities to connect with course topics. No one should be forced to create something. Usually when creativity is forced, it doesn't end up working out too well. See figure 10.1.

Figure 10.1. Students in the AU Library Makerspace working on the Pad Project. *Emily Lelandais*

As previously mentioned, Dr. Tileva also gave her students the opportunity to do either a makerspace project, an ethnographic project, or a paper as their final project for the course. Immediately after the Makerspace Open House, we heard from Dr. Tileva that some of her students had already reached out with final project ideas. In the end, many students took Dr. Tileva up on the opportunity to do a creative project. She received a photo essay on women's relationship with hair, a project about shaving one's armpits, several vision boards, a podcast about periods, and a sex education comic book.

LESSONS LEARNED

How can incorporating creative projects into course syllabi be successful? It's about allowing for flexibility and for students to make choices about how they want to connect to the curriculum. The makerspace is a place of equity where students in all disciplines can benefit from a more hands-on engagement with their learning. Using "science projects" to support course objectives does not have to stop in secondary school and can certainly be used outside of traditional STEM (science, technology, engineering, and math) courses or supporting STEM learning objectives. Creating is a chance for students to be in charge of their learning both literally and figuratively.

Another common concern is: how do you grade projects such as these? Dr. Tileva graded based on effort. If she saw that something had meaning to the students and that they were excited about it, she graded it with high marks. It is hard to grade creativity; instead, one really grades passion and whether the person took steps to move the project forward. Some students gave up on the creative tasks and did a paper instead. They did not feel like it was a "waste." They enjoyed the process. Allowing for this flexibility is integral to incorporating creativity into the classroom.

Though Dr. Tileva was successful in incorporating creative projects into her ANTH-215: Sex, Gender, and Culture course, there was a limit to just how "free flowing" her class could be. When she suggested a new class to the powers that be with a more democratic assessment process than traditional, it did not go over particularly well. The syllabus stated that the first day of class, students would get to vote on the kinds of assessment measures they wanted to have for the class. But the department at the time was reluctant to give this less-structured approach a try, citing "lack of comfort with the assessment methods." Another concern is that the students themselves might consider creative projects a sign of lack of class rigor. Dr. Tileva thinks this is a reflection of the preoccupation with grades, especially as a gauge of rigor, that is quite prevalent at all levels of the education system. At this time, the compromise, it seems, is a mix of assignments with the option for creative projects and traditional assessment.

One of the biggest struggles for the AU Library Makerspace has been to show that what we do and have to offer is a legitimate way to connect with the curriculum. We are asked, "What's the benefit of a makerspace?" "Why are we spending so much money building up this space when we could be buying databases?" The short answer: because this type of hands-on, experiential learning is important, too. Experiential education allows students to practice critical thinking, problem solving, and decision making in a hands-on way, providing them with the opportunity to enhance their curricular knowledge through creative engagement.[6] The AU Library Makerspace does not have the traditional support of a large STEM makerspace. As previously noted, there is no designated instructional designer, and all full-time staff that support the Makerspace work in other library departments as well. As such, one of the most important aspects of our Makerspace is the community we create—a community where students feel comfortable learning through collaboration, learning through connecting, and learning through making mistakes. Dr. Tileva agrees; for her, the collaborative nature of making is an integral part of the social justice activist community.

Working with Dr. Tileva taught us a lot about what it looks like to incorporate makerspace learning into a college class. Fear of allowing space for creative flexibility can make it challenging to incorporate into a class. This pedagogical approach chips away at the emphasis on assessing students based on how well something is *completed*. Remember when we said faculty can do whatever projects they want in the makerspace? Using the makerspace in a college class is not necessarily about one project all of the students do that will be graded based on doneness, but rather, about allowing students freedom to creatively connect with weekly themes in a way that resonates with them.

Our job in the Makerspace is to offer the tools for students to explore and challenge traditional modes of learning and show that experiential education has a place alongside traditional assignments, such as research papers. Our tips for faculty? You do not necessarily have to come up with a single project for students to do. Allow students to take the themes of the course and suggest hands-on ways they can connect to those themes; what types of projects can they do that will contribute to them remembering what you've discussed in class? Exploring this will let students make more meaningful connections to the curriculum and form relationships outside of the classroom.

Apart from offering physical tools and instruction, the role of the makerspace in supporting social justice is to be a place where collaboration can happen; social justice activism is inherently a collective action.[7] In our experience, students who know about and use the makerspace for a class returned to it as a place to create items, such as posters and buttons, that do not have an academic objective. For a school as dedicated to social justice activism as American University, connecting with the curriculum in a hands-on way bridges the gap between classroom learning and what is happening in the college, local, and national communities.

Incorporating the AU Library Makerspace into Dr. Tileva's ANTH-215: Sex, Gender, and Culture class and allowing her students to work on creative projects had implications outside of the classroom. In spring 2019, one of Dr. Tileva's previous students reached out to her. This student, Taylor Whittington, is the founder of AU's "The Menstrual Mission," an organization on campus that prepares and donates period kits to homeless shelters and domestic violence shelters in the Washington, D.C., area. The student saw there was extra fabric from the class project and asked Dr. Tileva if she could use it to make more reusable menstrual pads to include in the period kits assembled by the Menstrual Mission. The student and other volunteers returned to the Makerspace and made more reusable pads. These pads were accepted for donation and distributed to area shelters in the spring.

SELECTED READINGS FROM ANTH-215: SEX, GENDER, AND CULTURE

Bobel, Chris. "Feminist Engagements with Menstruation." In *New Blood: Third-Wave Feminism and the Politics of Menstruation Book*, 28–41. New Brunswick, NJ: Rutgers University Press, 2010.

———. "The Emergence of Menstrual Activism." In *New Blood: Third-Wave Feminism and the Politics of Menstruation Book*, 42–64. New Brunswick, NJ: Rutgers University Press, 2010.

Gunman, Jessica Shipman. "'More Natural but Less Normal': Reconsidering Medicalisation and Agency through Women's Accounts of Menstrual Suppression." *Social Science and Medicine* 71, no. 7 (October 2010): 1324–31. doi.org/10.1016/j.socscimed.2010.06.041.

Sagner, Ema. "More States Move to End 'Tampon Tax.'" *NPR: Business*. March 25, 2018. www.npr.org/2018/03/25/564580736/more-states-move-to-end-tampon-tax-that-s-seen-as-discriminating-against-women.

Siebert, Valerie. "Nearly Half of Women Have Experienced 'Period Shaming.'" *New York Post*. January 3, 2018. nypost.com/2018/01/03/nearly-half-of-women-have-experienced-period-shaming/.

NOTES

1. "Most Politically Active Students," Princeton Review, accessed June 26, 2019, www.princetonreview.com/college-rankings?rankings=most-politically-active-students.

2. "AU's 5-Year Strategic Plan: Changemakers for a Changing World," American University, accessed July 10, 2019, www.american.edu/about/strategic-plan/.

3. AU's Explore DC Program allows students to learn about Washington, D.C., by participating in volunteer experiences within one of five social justice issue areas.

4. Visit the AU Library Makerspace at bit.ly/aumkrspace.

5. Antoaneta Tileva, "ANTH-215: Sex, Gender, and Culture" (syllabus, American University, Washington, DC, Fall 2018).

6. Sara Jose, Patricia G. Patrick, and Christine Moseley, "Experiential Learning Theory: The Importance of Outdoor Classrooms in Environmental Education," *International Journal of Science Education, Part B: Communication and Public Engagement* 7, no. 3 (2017): 270.

7. Andrea Smith, "Social-Justice Activism in the Academic Industrial Complex," *Journal of Feminist Studies in Religion* 23, no. 2 (Fall 2007): 144.

Chapter Eleven

City of Galadriel

How It Is Used to Explore Understanding Surface and Groundwaters

Tammie L. Gerke

Upper-level college classes should incorporate, when applicable, activities focusing on improving students' ability to problem-solve using a wide-range of knowledge, that is, learn how to connect seemingly disconnected information into a comprehensive understanding of a given problem. These classes should also incorporate learning experiences that focus on developing necessary life skills needed to succeed in the work force such as: understanding the needs of potential clients, how to develop well-thought-out proposals used to bid for work, strong technical writing skills, and how to present findings to a client in written and oral presentations.

Ideally an activity would incorporate the development/improvement of all of these skills. The project would need to have a clearly defined problem, data, and the need for research outside of the class setting and would require students to draw from their understanding of key concepts being presented in the classroom for it to achieve this goal.

Thus a semester-long project was developed to simulate real-world work experiences based on a notional city (the city of Galadriel, also referred to as the City) that was experiencing drinking-water source contamination. The learning goals for this activity included: development of critical thinking skills by connecting a range of concepts learned in this and previous classes into a succinct interpretation of data provided; the ability to convey clearly in written and oral formats and understand the importance of professional communication via e-mail and in person; and knowledge of how to present and conduct oneself in meetings and open forums, how to show respect for competitors, and how to work effectively as part of a team. Another goal was to help the students to learn to "think on their feet" as they did not know what question might be asked and how fast the questions would be asked. I wanted the students to learn that you do not have to have all the answers, but rather there is a very professional way to acknowledge that you do not have that information and yet still present yourself as a competent scientist.

MAKERSPACE

Makerspaces allow for students to design and build different types of visual aids, such as examples of unconfined and confined aquifer models to supplement the project. This project is designed to allow the students to be creative using a makerspace, which is necessary for them to learn to develop a comprehensive understanding of the project. At Miami University Middletown, the students used the TEC Lab in the Gardner-Harvey Library (GHL) (www.mid.miamioh.edu/library/makerspace.htm). In the beginning of the semester, a staff member of the GHL came to class to inform students on what was available for use in the TEC Lab, how to gain access to the facility, and what costs there were for using the TEC Lab. This allowed students to begin designing models for their projects early in the semester.

THE PROJECT

The project was designed for students preparing to work in the environmental sciences, but the acquired skills are applicable to a wide range of careers. The learning goals for the project included but were not limited to: inspiring and encouraging student learning, stimulating students to think critically, and creating opportunities for reflection and action.

In this scenario, the city requested proposals for five key concepts: protection of surface water, groundwater, wetlands, and drinking water and the development of an educational program for the citizens of the city. Students were grouped into companies and allowed to choose one of the key categories the city needed addressed. Each company had to write a proposal on how they would address all of the criteria listed in the call for bids including: company name, list of previous experience their company had to support qualifications, design for the model to be used to explain the issue of choice to city officials, budget, and timeline. Each company was given a budget of $50 to build a model that would to be utilized in their plan on how to address their topic and to explain it to city officials and citizens of the city. Purchasing of supplies was coordinated with the city budget officer (the instructor) and establishing use of supplies in the TEC Lab at GHL were coordinated with the city's library representative (GHL staff member). These interactions were designed to allow the students to learn how to interact with other professionals just as they would in the work force.

Following proposal submissions, biweekly progress reports and a final report were submitted by each company. Written reports were edited for content and grammar, and feedback was provided to the teams. Students used the TEC Lab in the GHL to construct their models. Models were built from a range of materials, including plastic or plexiglass pieces and tanks, sand, pebbles, and plastic tubing. Funding for supplies for the models was obtained from funded proposals and teaching awards. All supplies were allowed to stay in the TEC Lab during final construction, and the laser cutter, soldering iron, and glue guns were the primary TEC Lab equipment used by the students.

A mock public forum open to campus students, staff, and faculty as well as the general public was held in GHL at the end of the semester. The forum provided an opportunity for students to dry-run their presentations, answer questions, and make modifications without the pressure of being graded. Formal presentations were given by each company the following week. Colleagues, staff, and external community members comprised the city officials and concerned citizens of Galadriel.

INSIGHTS FROM IMPLEMENTATION OF ACTIVITY

Challenges with Project

Overall, students' writing skills were very weak. Students were provided extensive feedback on every submission, some of which was applied, but most groups were not able to take the feedback and apply it to the following submission. A colleague from the English Department was willing to work with the "companies" to try to help address their writing skills. All companies were provided the opportunity to obtain help with their writing for a per-half-hour consulting fee that was deducted from their operating budget. Most companies, however, did not see the benefit to working with this colleague.

Presentations were minimal; students only presented the basics of the list of requirements and the presentations were not very inventive. Also it was clear that the students were not able to critically think and see "big picture" concepts. Students initially were very excited about this opportunity but became more stressed as the term progressed; however, they did not request additional help. Students did not seem to learn that it is OK to not know an answer but there is a good and bad way to deal with this. Also the two groups that presented on the second day did not seem to "learn" from questions/ issues brought up in the presentations on the first day. Also in just about all groups one person was "driving" the project.

Students did use the TEC Lab; however, because of their challenge with time management, they all produced similar water models and were not respectful of others using the space. Though the GHL staff were very kind about the matter, it did cause issues.

Such a project required many different faculty and staff to make it successful. One would want to confirm the support of all to be involved prior to the use of such a project in their class. If support can be found, it is amazing what the students, regardless of the weaknesses, are able to develop and present.

Modifications to Project

In the future, more detail on what is expected should be provided. Students need more writing activities in lower-level classes to help them improve their basic writings skills so this activity in the future can focus on helping develop technical writing skills. These skills are needed to be successful in the work force. Also one needs to explore how to help the students be more creative and learn to go beyond the "basics of the assignment." In addition, one needs to determine a way to get all students in each group more engaged in the overall process. Leaning to be an effective member of a team is a critical skill for being successful in the work force; thus one needs to establish a way to ensure all members are participating more in each company. Future use of this activity should also incorporate very strict rules on use of a makerspace, and if groups do not follow those, then they would be denied access for the rest of the semester.

Chapter Twelve

Little Shop of Horror

Wes Smith and Ethan Mills

Are you afraid of the dark? What does horror teach us about the meaning of life and death? How can we appreciate the deeper philosophical and religious aspects of popular culture, particularly horror, as well as ways in which popular culture can shape our understandings of philosophy and religion? These questions were asked in two sections of PHIL 2350: Popular Culture, Religion, and Philosophy during the fall of 2018. These students were taking part in a brand-new class developed by Dr. Ethan Mills to provide an introduction to the study of philosophy through popular culture. The class offered the usual tenets of undergraduate work such as readings, group presentations, and papers, but Dr. Mills strived to have his students do something more than just apply these philosophical concepts on paper. He hoped students would be able to apply their unique perspectives to the bodies of thought in another medium. Dr. Mills encouraged students to showcase their creative talents while applying philosophical ideas to a film project. He wanted to utilize a film project as a hands-on method of teaching to help students engage in digital authorship, allowing them to become active creators rather than passive consumers of digital media.[1] This desire to engage in digital authorship led Dr. Mills to seek out the University of Tennessee at Chattanooga (UTC) Library Studio to discuss incorporating filmmaking into his course.

MULTIMEDIA AT THE UTC LIBRARY STUDIO

The UTC Library Studio is an emerging multimedia space that focuses on helping students, faculty, and staff engage with media literacy, media production, and innovative technologies. Since its opening in 2015, the UTC Library Studio has worked to address the growing technological and access needs across campus. The UTC Library Studio includes a virtual reality space, an audio production room, and a green-screen production room. A collection of cameras, tripods, development kits, and accessories are also housed in the UTC Studio. This space functions as a computer lab with a wide array of creative software like the Adobe Creative Cloud and CAD software such as Autodesk suite on twenty-four high-powered computers, Macs and PCs. The UTC Library Studio is staffed by three tenure-track librarians and three staff members who specialize in instructional design and an element of either video, audio, graphic design, or 3D modeling. Six student employees also serve as assistants in the studio.

CREATING A FILM ASSIGNMENT

Dr. Mills sought the expertise of the UTC Library Studio to give himself and his students the support needed to execute the assignment he envisioned. The film assignment was created in collaboration with Dr. Mills and studio librarian Wes Smith. Dr. Mills approached the UTC Library Studio and described his vision of students creating a horror film to showcase the philosophical concepts they would learn during the semester, such as existentialism and double consciousness. We structured this assignment to provide enough scaffolding to limit student anxiety related to this nontraditional assignment but with enough freedom to allow students to feel unconstrained by limitations. The UTC Library Studio first helped Dr. Mills establish baseline expectations for the assignment. Limiting the duration of films to three to five minutes allowed for the students to focus on the quality of what was being showcased rather than working toward a duration. Next, we planned sessions to support students throughout the semester both in class and in the UTC Library Studio. These instructional sessions focused on storyboarding, scriptwriting, camera techniques, watching commercial horror films, and readings on philosophical topics.

While the focus of the assignment was the creation of a film, the primary grading component was not the film itself but the other deliverables. The deliverables included an outline, a script, a three- to five-minute film, and a group reflection. The outline summarized the specific requirements the groups needed to move forward with the assignment. These requirements included drafting a general description of their film, creating rudimentary drawings, developing a timeline until completion, and forming a specific plan for the contributions of each member of the project group. We wanted students to predict the difficulties that they envisioned experiencing while creating their project so we could provide additional scaffolding to address specific problem areas. During this process, we emphasized the key aspects of their outlines were written in sand rather than stone. We wanted students to have ideas down on paper to move forward but not to feel constrained by their earlier ideas. We added criteria for revising ideas midway through by adding that if their film differed greatly from their outline, students needed to write about the changes they made in their reflection. Once the storyboard outline was graded and reviewed, the students could move on to crafting their script.

Defining very few parameters concerning the script allowed students to utilize their own creativity. A few requirements were included to ensure students had clarity and direction, such as including at least "one character with speaking lines, although you'll probably need at least two characters so there can be some sort of dialogue" and using some element of horror. The script also needed to contain a paragraph describing the philosophical content of the script. We left the opportunity open for those who chose to have a silent horror in the instructions, opening the door for no lines but a description of scenery and character reactions (we had a few projects with limited lines).

HELPING STUDENTS DEVELOP TECHNICAL SKILLS

Students are often viewed as adept technology users who can utilize any new software or hardware. Faculty members can often make assumptions when assigning projects such as this. However, if we want students to succeed, we need to provide support with utilizing software, handling hardware, and generating ideas. During the collaboration with Dr. Mills, the UTC Library Studio provided students access to cameras, tripods, lights, microphones, and backdrops. Along with the access to the equipment, we provided hands-on training for students to effectively use Adobe Premiere, TechSmith's Camtasia, and iMovie, which gave students a wide range of technological tools to choose from. This selection of software provided a foundation for students who wish to continue their filmmaking pursuits outside of this assignment. Discussion sessions were also provided by a community partner at the local television station who discussed tips and tricks of lighting, camerawork, and scriptwriting. Students received support through scheduled class time, scheduled one-on-one appointments, and drop-in hours.

SCREENING THE FILMS

A distinctive feature of the class was that students would not only be producing their own horror films but also screening their work at an event called Horrific Thoughts: Halloween Philosophical Horror Film Fest. The film fest included a panel of jurors from across campus and the community, free food and drink, and prizes for the best films. Dr. Mills obtained funding from his department and from an on-campus grant for experiential learning. The prizes for the best films were given by the jurors and the audience. The screening was a unique opportunity to connect campus and community in a showcase of students' work. The films that were presented ranged from artistic one-camera shots to more complicated motion graphics and music. The event was deemed a success by the students and the department with around 120 to 130 attendees from the campus and the community.

DEVELOPING A FOUNDATION OF PHILOSOPHY WITH FILMS

Dr. Mills has used films in philosophy courses for years to make abstract philosophical ideas more concrete. For instance, clips of *The Matrix* help dramatize external-world skepticism in Descartes or Vasubandhu (how do we really know the world is as we perceive it to be?) or a clip of *The Good Place* helps foster discussion of the trolley problem (should you divert a runaway trolley to kill one person rather than let it continue on a track to kill five people?). Films help students who are unused to abstract philosophical thinking by giving them a foothold so instructors can guide them to understanding.

The class spends the first unit covering fiction and film in conjunction with philosophy. This shows students how to scratch beneath the surface to find underlying philosophical concepts. For instance, Mary Shelley's novel, several film versions of *Frankenstein,* and Jennifer McMahon's article "The Existential Frankenstein" help students to unearth deeper issues about authenticity and the denial of death.

OUTSIDE OF PHIL 2350

While philosophy courses involving watching and discussing films are relatively common, philosophy courses in which students are required to make their own films are still rare. Dr. Mills recently asked philosophers via Twitter, "Philosophers, do you know anyone who teaches a philosophy class in which students are required to MAKE films, rather than just watch them and write about them?" He found nine examples of other courses in philosophy and related disciplines that incorporate filmmaking in some way.[2] There have been in-depth discussions of incorporating filmmaking in philosophy courses in several other venues.[3]

We have published a blog post about this course on the blog of the American Philosophical Association, the largest association of professional academic philosophers in the United States.[4] This post is intended to generate discussion among a national and international audience of academic philosophers about including filmmaking in philosophy courses.

While incorporating filmmaking remains uncommon in philosophy courses, there is a small movement toward doing so. We hope that our own efforts can contribute to the discussions surrounding this movement.

STRENGTH OF THIS TYPE OF ASSIGNMENT

One major strength of this project was that the assignment was fun! It was fun for us to see how students brainstormed ideas and incorporated the philosophical material in their own filmmaking, and it was fun for students to make the films.

This project introduces students to the fundamentals of filmmaking, although of course not at the same level of depth as a course dedicated exclusively to filmmaking. Just as philosophy courses can cultivate students' interests in philosophy (even if they may not have known they had such interests in the first place), a project like this can cultivate students' nascent interests in filmmaking.

Dr. Mills successfully applied for the next iteration of the course to be on a university-designated list of courses that contain experiential learning outcomes. Going forward, the course will focus even more on the experience of filmmaking. Students will be given more time to complete the film assignment, and students will independently reflect on the assignment instead of completing this component as a group. One of the subtler yet profound benefits of incorporating filmmaking into a philosophy course is that it encourages students not just to *find* philosophy in fiction and film, but to *do* philosophy through the medium of film. For instance, the film that won the first prize at the film festival demonstrated how the students were thinking through the concept of absurdity both conceptually and aesthetically in a somewhat surreal campfire discussion.[5] The second-place film explored Du Boisian double-consciousness through the experience of a woman in an abusive romantic relationship.[6]

One major debate within African philosophy has been whether philosophy must be textual or if it could be oral. Likewise, one might wonder whether philosophy could be done in other media such as film. We'll let readers judge for themselves, but we believe the results of this class demonstrate the potential for a positive answer at the undergraduate level.

Another benefit of filmmaking is that it encourages students to think more critically due to an unfamiliar medium in the context of most academic courses. It's not a direct translation from paper to script to film, and there's a bit of the unknown in the process. Making this a successful project requires some creativity and critical thinking on the part of both the students and the instructor.

STUDENT FEEDBACK

The most common critical feedback from students, both in person and on course evaluations, was that they wished they had had more time to complete the project. For instance, one course evaluation suggested, "You should implement more class time in the studio and have someone go through the general steps of editing so that way if students have no editing experience they will not be at such a disadvantage." Another student said, "I think I would start it a little earlier in the semester than only having 30 days to complete it. It is really difficult to meet with other classmates that have full time jobs and go to school full time in order to film."

Aside from these and other similar comments, the reaction to the project was overwhelmingly positive. One evaluation said, "The film project was fun, and I wish I could retake this course." Another student wrote, "I loved the horror theme of this class and it made me appreciate horror movies and literature much more now that I understand more about the philosophical impact."

HOW LIBRARIANS CAN ENGAGE WITH FACULTY IN MULTIMEDIA

Partnering with faculty is a great way to explore new ideas and forge lasting relationships both professionally and personally. Finding the right faculty member to work with on experimental projects such as film assignments is rewarding but can be difficult. Not every assignment will translate fluidly across the curriculum. If you are a librarian with liaison duties, working with the current faculty members in your department will give the best starting point for unique assignments such as this. If your college or university has an interdisciplinary research group, you may be able to identify faculty members who are interested in cross-disciplinary research. One of the first things to look for is compatibility in your current scholarship.

This project was conceived at an interdisciplinary group meet-up. In crafting the group film project, we both had a personal and professional interest in filmmaking, which allowed for clear and open dialogue about what we both thought should be included in the assignment. If you work in a space like UTC Studio but do not have the instructional design skill set, bringing in another university partner, such as a teaching and learning center, can make crafting assignments like this easier. Finally, when working with faculty members in crafting unique experiences for your students, start out small with projects such as creating infographics or flyers and work your way up to larger projects such as film projects.

MOVING FORWARD

The strength of this assignment was grounded in the fact that Dr. Mills made it the forefront of his class and provided students the time (albeit not as much as they wanted) and resources to complete it. It is important to remember that projects like these are not a replacement for traditional work, such as papers or exams, so a straight assignment swap might not yield the intended results. Plan for your intended outcomes and seek feedback from students to improve your projects. And do not forget to have fun!

NOTES

1. Chareen Snelson, "Video Production in Content-Area Pedagogy: A Scoping Study of the Research Literature," *Learning, Media and Technology* 43, no. 3 (2018): 294.
2. Ethan Mills (@Ethan_Mills_42), Twitter, July 22, 2019, twitter.com/Ethan_Mills_42/status/1153406877872656387.
3. Nathan Anderson, "Filmmaking in the Classroom: Illustrating the Examined Life," *Teaching Philosophy* 33, no. 4 (2010): 375; Angela Bolte, "Syllabus Showcase: Unicorns, Vampires, and Aliens: Philosophy & Speculative Fiction," Blog of the APA, July 17, 2019, blog.apaonline.org/2019/07/17/syllabus-showcase-angela-bolte-unicorns-vampires-aliens-philosophy-speculative-fiction/; Leigh M. Johnson, "Philosophy's Next Generation of Auteurs," *ReadMoreWriteMoreThinkMoreBeMore: politics, technology, culture, & philosophy . . . deconstructed* (blog), December 11, 2013, www.readmorewritemorethinkmorebemore.com/2013/12/philosophys-next-generation-of-auteurs.html?m=1; Leigh M. Johnson, "Postmillennial Public Service Announcements," *ReadMoreWriteMoreThinkMoreBeMore: politics, technology, culture, & philosophy . . . deconstructed* (blog). May 25, 2019, www.readmorewritemorethinkmorebemore.com/2019/05/postmillennial-public-service.html?m=1.
4. Wes Smith and Ethan Mills, "Horrific Thoughts: Incorporating Student Film-Making in a Course on Horror and Philosophy," *The Blog of the APA*, May 2, 2019, blog.apaonline.org/2019/05/02/incorporating-student-film-making-in-a-course-on-horror-and-philosophy/
5. UTC Philosophy and Religion Department (@UTC_Rel_phil), "This week we're posting some of the films made by students in Popular Culture, Religion, and Philosophy. This film, 'Both Light and Dark Are Blinding,' won FIRST PLACE . . . ," Twitter, November 14, 2018, 9:37 a.m., twitter.com/UTC_Phil_Rel/status/1062716079628267520.
6. UTC Philosophy and Religion Department (@UTC_Rel_Phil), "This week we're posting some of the films made by students in Popular Culture, Religion, and Philosophy. This film, 'To Stay,' won second . . . ," Twitter, November 14, 2018, 9:35 a.m., twitter.com/UTC_Phil_Rel/status/1062715543214608384.

Part III

PUBLIC LIBRARIES AND COMMUNITY OUTREACH

Chapter Thirteen

Growing a Maker Community

Planning and Implementing a Local Community Maker Fest

Tracy Paradis, Debby Emerson, and Michelle Costello

The first annual Geneseo Maker Fest was designed to bring a major maker event to our rural region in western New York. The idea for this event grew out of a collaboration between the education and community engagement librarian at SUNY Geneseo's Milne Library and the director of Geneseo's public library, Wadsworth Library. The two had worked together on prior events to the benefit of both campus and community. This partnership met a goal for both libraries. Milne, an academic library, wanted to interact more closely with members of the community, and the public library wanted to utilize more fully the resources available through the SUNY Geneseo campus. Our event was modeled after the Mini-Maker Faire,[1] which takes place in nearby Rochester, New York. We wanted to offer a similar experience for residents in our more rural community. We felt strongly that all of our exhibits should be interactive. Rather than simply observing things, we wanted our audience to be doing or making. In talking with schools and other educational organizations in our area, we quickly determined that nothing like this had been done locally.

FIRST STEPS

We needed a group of individuals with a range of skills, connections, and experience to map out our event. We first turned to the digital collections and archives librarian at Milne Library, as her extensive experience with curating exhibits and event programming was essential. In this initial meeting, we identified other areas of expertise that were needed to make a workable plan. This included SUNY Geneseo's coordinator of student leadership, volunteerism, and service; a professor from the School of Education at SUNY Geneseo with close ties to Geneseo Central School; two library STEAM specialists from the Genesee Valley Educational Partnership; and one of the cochairs of the Rochester Maker Faire.[2]

Initial planning meetings were focused on defining the scope: making the event interactive, regional, open to all ages, and free to attend. We also considered logistics such as when and where to hold the event and how we would fund it. We thought our project was too large to plan and implement in under a year, taking into consideration the potential schedules of the families we hoped would attend and the students we would rely on as volunteers. When we were able to secure an ideal venue for a date only seven months out, we accelerated our timeline.

The team determined that a one-day festival, running from 10 a.m. to 3 p.m. on a Saturday, would be best for a family event. This would be a full day for people who were volunteering their time and energy. It was important to avoid conflicts with other major events in the community so people would be available to attend.

We wanted a location that was easily accessible and where people would feel comfortable. Cost was a factor since we did not yet know how much funding we would be able to secure. One of our planning groups had close ties to the town's school, allowing us to secure space there free of charge. This was ideal since many families would feel comfortable attending an event at the school and there was ample parking available.

We needed to obtain funding for the event. The Rochester Regional Library Council, a multi-type library system serving a five-county area surrounding Rochester, New York, had a grant program that was ideal for our needs. The Harold Hacker Fund for the Advancement of Libraries[3] supports innovative projects, and our proposed Maker Fest easily met the criteria for this funding. Two planning committee members with extensive successful grant-writing experience prepared our application. Wadsworth Library was the lead applicant since that library could most easily manage the incoming and outgoing payments. We were awarded $3,700 for our project titled *Growing a Maker Community*.

Under the terms of the grant, items purchased specifically for the Maker Fest (such as a green screen and two iPads) would become the property of Wadsworth Library following the event.[4] The library would continue to make these items available to the public in addition to future Maker Fest events.

DEVELOPMENT

We needed to recruit a diverse range of makers including students, community members, faculty, and local business owners able to implement stations or workshops that aligned with our goals. Since this was our first Maker Fest, we didn't have an established pool of known makers to pull from, so we needed to be thoughtful in our recruitment process. In order to guarantee attendees a variety of experiences, the committee seeded the event with three core stations: cardboard creation, green-screen video production, and tile painting.

We used an online application form[5] with questions informed by our project goals, asking the makers to provide a description of their station or workshop to ensure they included the interactive element. We wanted to expose students to STEAM opportunities and the maker movement, so we offered financial assistance for their supplies or materials. We recruited twenty makers, including community members and high school and college students.[6] Managing our makers was as important as recruiting them. This included determining their technology and space needs, creating their schedules, and relaying logistical information about the event. We assigned a group of volunteers to act as liaisons with a specific maker in order to assist them with any issues that might arise throughout the day. Most of the makers met our goals and objectives. We attribute this to several factors: asking detailed questions in the application form, maintaining consistent communication prior to the event, and providing them with assistance during the event.

Having a large group of committed student volunteers would meet campus goals focused on advancing the public good, give students a chance to connect with the larger community, and increase the success of the Maker Fest. We created an online application for volunteers[7] to make sure that they fully understood our expectations and to give us an idea as to their motivation for volunteering. The form linked to a document[8] detailing the volunteer roles and duties so students could indicate which role they would be interested in filling. We recruited approximately thirty-five volunteers. A large percentage of the students were education majors so this event gave them the unique opportunity to connect with parents and children and put into practice what they learned in their coursework.

One of our biggest concerns in developing the Maker Fest was attracting a robust audience, so creating a comprehensive marketing plan was important. We created a website that described the purpose of the event and displayed the event schedule and program.[9] In addition to our website, we promoted by using direct e-mails, listservs, social media, and flyers targeted to our collective institutions, local businesses, and schools. We approached a student intern from the college campus to assist with the social media piece, which not only helped us but gave her experience she could take forward in her career. She used Facebook, Instagram, and Twitter as vehicles to market the event and to inform the community about the maker movement. We also used an optional registration form to monitor our attendee numbers and increase our marketing as needed.

We were fortunate to secure a venue that included a committed and generous set of partners at the high school. They provided floor plans, organized the event space, promoted the event, and provided personnel, supplies, and equipment. Additionally, the school's Arts Booster Club provided the refreshments for the event. We recommend tapping into resources like this as we benefited from not having to purchase and sell refreshments and they were able to fund-raise for their club. School personnel sought opportunities for their students to make and have a venue to display their projects. This event aligned with those objectives and benefited them as well as our committee. We were especially excited to have a high school student apply to be a maker to showcase his board game design project. While others may not find a venue with such a dedicated staff, with consistent communication and a clear plan, it is still possible to have a successful event.

IMPLEMENTATION AND LESSONS LEARNED

The first annual Geneseo Maker Fest took place on March 30, 2019. More than three hundred participants, makers, presenters, student workers, and committee members attended. The event opened with a keynote speaker to inspire attendees and impart the importance of making. Volunteers at the registration and information table welcomed attendees and provided maps, schedules, and other event information. We offered sixteen maker stations including calligraphy design, music composition and production, cardboard creation, and woodworking, as well as five workshops: virtual reality, puppet making, Makey Makey, green-screen video creation, and an escape experience. Fixed-booth stations ran continuously in a large cafeteria while the workshops took place in a nearby smaller cafeteria. The stations ran smoothly, and we only needed to make minor adjustments. Volunteers staffed all event spaces, stations, and workshops, allowing makers to remain focused on their stations. Two volunteers served as photographers to record the event, which also benefited them since they could add these photos to their portfolios of work. All Maker Fest committee members assisted throughout the day of the event, which was an important factor in its success. We felt that it was important to provide refreshments for the makers, volunteers, and committee members, but refreshments were outside of the scope of the grant. We secured separate funding from the college to provide food and highly recommend this practice.

We hoped to attract several makers from our area college and secondary student populations. Since we were requiring each maker to have an interactive element to their station, we wanted to ensure that the expense for materials used during the event was not a roadblock to students who wished to participate. We decided to use the bulk of our grant money to subsidize makers purchasing materials. We had anticipated requests outstripping funds and were surprised when only three of our twenty makers requested funding. The total amount requested was under $100—well under the amount we had available.

We were frugal in our spending for supplies. We purchased two iPads, door prize gifts for attendees, and supplies for the stations we programmed. While having fancy virtual reality units, 3D printers, and building electronics is certainly a popular area of making, we felt it was important to demonstrate that making doesn't require expensive equipment and materials. We wanted to support local businesses, use recycled materials, and keep this project sustainable. We found three local nonprofits who sell recycled materials at deeply discounted prices and also support local worthy causes: Craft Bits & Pieces,[10] Greenovation,[11] and Repurpose & More.[12] This was good for the budget, easier on the environment, and great for teaching kids to imagine new possibilities!

We had T-shirts printed for committee members so we could be easily identified by attendees. All of our printed promotional materials, posters and flyers, were done in-house, and we relied on personal appeals to targeted, high-interest groups known to the committee members and with whom there were established relationships. After totaling all of the administrative expenses for the event, nearly half of the grant monies remained unspent. With the permission of the grantor, we rolled these funds over for use in the next iteration and will be purchasing a first aid kit and supplies for at least two more stations provided by us. We will consider providing funding assistance to all makers, not just to students.

While committee members were not assigned specific tasks, all circulated and participated throughout the day. This allowed us to continuously monitor the event and make necessary adjustments. We had used a floor plan of the area to design our layout, but once the attendees arrived, we saw ways to take better advantage of the physical environment. For instance, the cardboard station was set up at the entrance to the cafeteria, directly in front of the doors. We hoped it would grab the attention of kids and draw them into the rest of the space. This strategy was so successful that the creation area expanded throughout the day as more children and parents got involved. We had to stay on top of maintaining a walkway so that people could enter and exit. In the future, we will allot a much larger area for this workstation that will be set back from the entryway.

We furnished a video creation station and a collection of props where attendees could use Do Ink's Green Screen app[13] on an iPad to make videos or still shots. Initially we set this up in the small cafeteria to allow more space for users, but this hid it from a lot of attendees who simply didn't leave the main space. We moved the station into an open area of the larger room where it immediately began getting used. In doing this, we realized that we had lost an opportunity to draw people in simply by placing one or two of the stations outside of the cafeterias in a very wide hallway. Next year we will place the virtual reality and green-screen booths there, as they are both high-interest.

We considered signage needs throughout the event space and printed several signs to post on the walls and tables to indicate the various stations. We purchased colorful balloons that were placed at entrances and stations to give visual cues. The path from the school entry to the cafeterias' location wasn't immediately intuitive, and our signage ended up being inadequate. We will remedy this with larger signs that we will display on easels to make them stand out. We will distribute a floor map that clearly shows the location of all stations to make navigation easier.

Volunteers were absolutely essential to the success of our event. Since the idea for a maker event arose from seeking opportunities for the School of Education students to engage with kids using their classroom knowledge, we knew that we had a healthy pool from which to draw. While setup was much easier than anticipated, the cleanup was more challenging. We scheduled too many volunteers early and too few for the end of the day. We needed to better communicate our expectations of volunteers with a list of specific tasks; for example, at a painting station, having the volunteer actively engage and interact with attendees by offering tools, materials, and examples as opposed to hanging back and only answering direct questions. In the future, we will provide training for our volunteers.

We felt we had clearly communicated our expectation of an interactive element for all stations in our instructions, but some stations did not function as expected. One maker submitted a proposal, but then handed off the responsibility to a second person without giving us their contact information. The new person missed all of the follow-up communications and was ignorant of important details. In our next iteration, we will include a statement explaining that if the registrant is handing off their responsibilities to another individual, they must provide that person's contact information to us so that we can be sure all participants are getting the most up-to-date information, not only in the call for makers but in all subsequent communication.

Following the initial promotions for the Maker Fest, we very quickly realized the need to make it clear up-front that it was designed as a family event where parents interact with their children as opposed to a situation where children would be dropped off and unsupervised. While we made every effort to have a safe environment, we felt uncomfortable being responsible for unattended children.

As planning evolved, we spoke with more local connections and learned of two new maker ventures in nearby communities: Makacademy[14] and the Little Lakes Community Center.[15] Both groups participated as makers, but seeing that the event was only a few weeks out, we elected not to include them in the current organizing phase. We will ask them to be part of the planning process next year. Furthermore, we will be including students in the committee to encourage more student involvement.

We made plans for a formal assessment from the inception of the project. Obviously, the first metric would be the number of attendees, but we also created a survey for attendees and volunteers. Response to the event was overwhelmingly positive. From the smiles and excited roar of all the participants throughout the day to the enthusiastic verbal comments received by organizers from attendees and school staff, there is no doubt that our Maker Fest was a success. Everyone involved is excited to see it happen again next year.

Counting attendees was problematic for several reasons. First, due to other events going on at the school concurrently and our event taking place in multiple rooms connected by a hallway, we couldn't be certain of the participation of each person moving through the shared area. Second, we were happily surprised to find that many families ended up staying at the event for several hours and moving between all three of our areas, but this made it difficult to know whether or not someone had previously been counted. We realized that we should have assigned an individual to keep a regular count, so we started taking a snapshot count of people in each of the rooms every hour, which we then estimated to result in about three hundred attendees.

We created a ten-question digital survey[16] to follow up on the experiences of attendees and volunteers. Due to technical issues, distribution was extremely restricted and, in turn, led to few responses. While the collected responses are extremely positive, it's difficult to draw meaningful conclusions from such a small sample. Next time, we will set up an iPad with the form and provide paper surveys at the exit with clear signage and a volunteer to encourage attendees to complete the survey before exiting. Additionally, we failed to follow up with our makers for feedback and will include them in the survey as well. Finally, we debriefed with all committee members, where we analyzed survey results, shared anecdotes and concerns gathered from attendees, and discussed our overall impressions. We are using this information to improve the design and implementation of the next Geneseo Maker Fest.

We were surprised with how easily this event fell into place. The key to its success was finding the right people with the needed skills and experience, as well as securing an appropriate venue. You will likely find that there are already creative people making in your communities and already providing maker programming, so canvas your area to see who else is looking to create either makerspaces or maker events and take advantage of their established efforts. Based on our experience and the positive responses received, we believe that producing this type of event is possible with thoughtful planning.

NOTES

1. New York State Association for Computers and Technologies in Education, "Maker Faire Rochester Home Page," Maker Faire Rochester, accessed September 2, 2019, rochester .makerfaire.com/.

2. Geneseo Maker Fest, "Geneseo Maker Fest Supplemental Documents," last modified October 9, 2019, 2, drive.google.com/open?id=1l009TwRbw1-QJn0YMtEqxySr1w81_i6.

3. Rochester Regional Library Council, "Harold Hacker Fund for the Advancement of Libraries," RRLC, accessed September 2, 2019, rrlc.org/services/grant-opportunities/harold -hacker-fund/.

4. Geneseo Maker Fest, "Geneseo Maker Fest Supplemental Documents," 3.

5. Ibid., 4.

6. "Makers and Station Descriptions," Geneseo Maker Fest, accessed September 2, 2019, sites.google.com/view/geneseomakerfest.

7. Geneseo Maker Fest, "Geneseo Maker Fest Supplemental Documents," 12.

8. Ibid., 15.

9. "Geneseo Maker Fest," Geneseo Maker Fest, accessed September 2, 2019, sites.google .com/view/geneseomakerfest.

10. Fairport/Perinton Senior Living Council, Inc., "Craft Bits & Pieces," Senior Living Council, accessed September 2, 2019, seniorlivingcouncil.org/craft-bits-pieces.

11. Greenovation Facebook page, accessed September 2, 2019, www.facebook.com/Roch esterGreenovation/.

12. Child Care Council, "Repurpose & More Store at Child Care Council," Child Care Council, accessed September 2, 2019, childcarecouncil.com/repurpose-more-store/.

13. DK Pictures, Inc., "Green Screen Documentation," Do Ink, accessed September 2, 2019, www.doink.com/support.

14. Makacademy, LLC, "Makacademy Home," Makacademy, LLC, accessed September 2, 2019, makacademy.net/.

15. Little Lakes Community Association, "Little Lakes Community Association—Old Hemlock School," accessed September 2, 2019, www.littlelakesny.org/.

16. Geneseo Maker Fest, "Geneseo Maker Fest Supplemental Documents," 17.

Chapter Fourteen

I Saw It on Pinterest

A Choose Your Craft Adventure

Cara Bolley

In order to bring awareness to the new library MakerSpace at the Defiance Public Library System's main location, classes featuring the use of MakerSpace equipment were hosted. One particular event that was popular was called I Saw It on Pinterest. In this event, the public was able to vote for which class they would like to attend and at which location, with the winning classes being presented at each respective location.

DEFIANCE PUBLIC LIBRARY SYSTEM

DPLS is a library system that provides service across the Ohio county of Defiance with locations in Defiance, Sherwood, and Hicksville. The main library opened a makerspace in the fall of 2018 with the mission to provide every user with the opportunity to learn something new, strengthen their skills, and grow as a person. DPLS's MakerSpace is free and open to all ages, skill levels, and interests as long as they have a library card and sign a MakerSpace agreement. Library cards are free to all Ohio residents aged five and up. Patrons under eighteen must have their MakerSpace agreement signed by a parent or guardian. MakerSpace users under ten must be accompanied by an adult. Exceptions exist for programming.

Patrons can either set up an appointment to use the MakerSpace or visit during one of the scheduled Open Make times. Assistance with the technology and equipment is provided as needed during both appointments and Open Make. Patrons are asked to supply their own paper, vinyl, and so on or use the scrap materials that have been donated or left behind. Some fees exist for using some of the library supplies. These are only to cover the material costs and keep the space free for everyone to use. Fees are 10¢ per gram of 3D print filament as estimated by the Makerbot print software, 50¢ per page on the color printer, and 50¢ per button from the Badge-a-minit button maker.

In January of 2019, DPLS began offering programs at the three county locations to showcase the equipment and possibilities the MakerSpace could offer the public. These programs are either free or have a small materials fee to help cover supply costs. Programing is open to the community regardless of whether the participant has a library card or not. Participants are also not required to fill out a MakerSpace agreement before attending any programming. The library's goal is to give the community a chance to be involved in the maker movement without costing them a significant amount.

DEVELOPING THE CLASSES

Choosing the Nominees

Class options were chosen based off of popular Pinterest ideas. While choosing the classes, the available supplies and cost of the needed supplies was considered. Some of the class choices would be supported by donations of craft supplies from the public if they were to be chosen. We concentrated on what supplies we had accessible and focused on an end product participants would be excited to take home. Each class involved using at least one of the MakerSpace tools to help expose the partakers to the new equipment from the MakerSpace.

Options given to the public to vote among were personalized mugs, wooden keychains or necklaces, giant paper flowers, personalized iron-on tea towels, and bow hair ties.[1] Patrons were also asked to make any suggestions they had for future classes, so that we may provide programming of interest in the future.

Voting

Voting was made available to patrons both through social media and on paper in the library. Patrons were asked to circle the program they were interested in attending on the paper ballots. The online community was asked to comment on the social media posts related to the event with their vote and library location. Voting was open for a two-week period the month before the planned program dates. The winning crafts were giant paper flowers (Hicksville), iron-on tea towels (Defiance), and personalized mugs (Sherwood).

Class Prep

Registration was set up for the iron-on towels and mugs events due to limited supplies being available. No registration was set up for the giant paper flowers since we already had an abundant supply of paper for the class. This series of classes was budgeted for a total of $50. Expenses remained under budget with the use of existing supplies and donations, helping to keep this set of classes free. Heat transfer vinyl material and blank white tea towels were the only materials that needed to be purchased in order to host our classes.

All three classes utilized the Silhouette Cameo 3 to cut out materials. Ideas were obtained from Pinterest ideas and image searches, and cut files were created using the Silhouette Studio. For the towel and mug, about five premade cut patterns were produced. Participants would have the opportunity to choose from these premade patterns or to create their own cut files. For the paper flowers, cut patterns were utilized from Jennifer Maker's free resource library.[2] Samples were made of all three crafts, and twelve sets of the paper flowers were precut. Each location displayed the samples for patrons to see what they could make at the event. Photos were shared of the samples on social media to create interest. See figure 14.1 for samples used.

SUPPLIES

All classes need a cutting machine and design software compatible with the cutting machine.

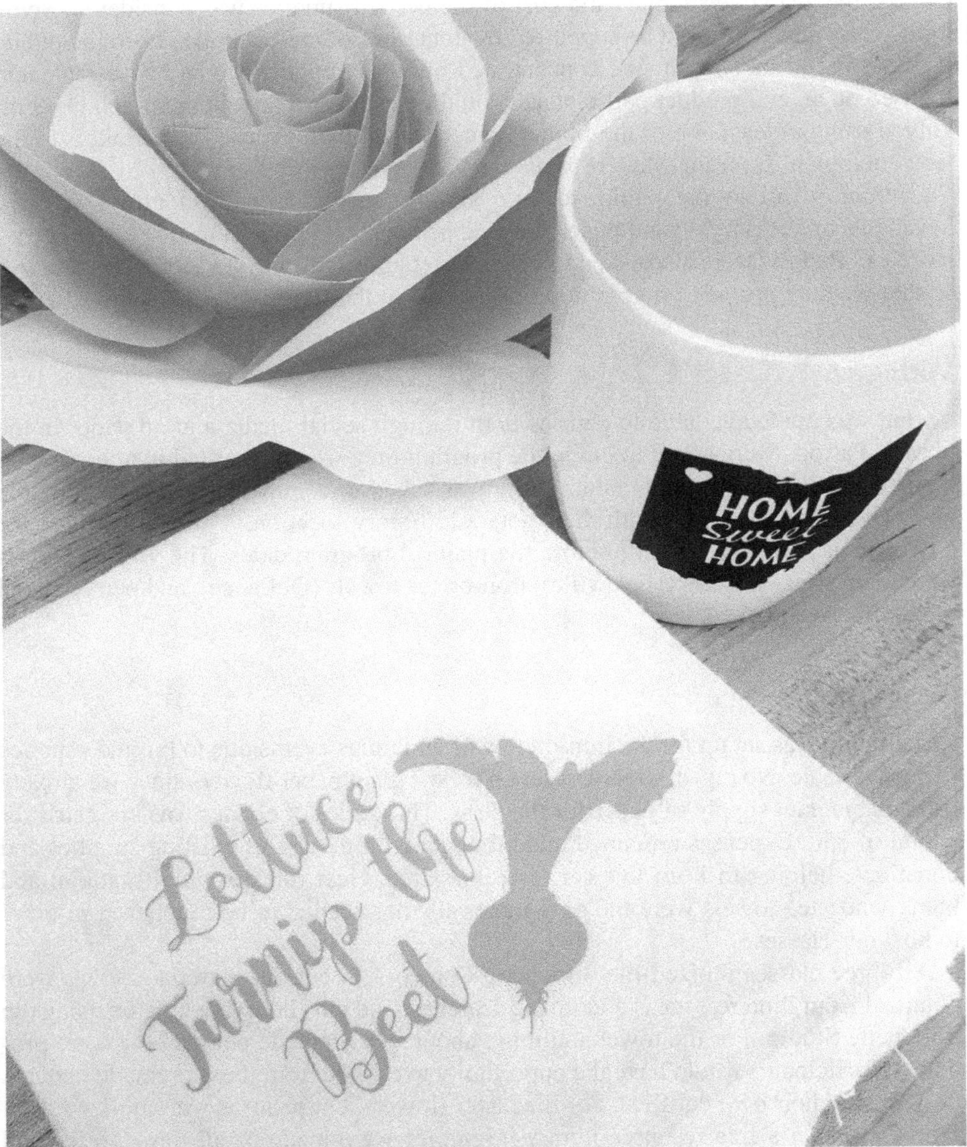

Figure 14.1. Samples of Pinterest crafts. ***Cara Bolley***

Giant Paper Flowers

- colored paper (eight sheets per flower, can be cardstock or copy paper)
- pattern from Jennifer Maker
- hot glue gun and glue sticks

Tea Towels

- heat transfer vinyl material
- iron (set to in-between cotton and linen)
- plain white tea towels or flour sack towels
- weeding tools

Personalized Mugs

- plain mugs (we used white, but other colors can be used)
- permanent vinyl
- weeding tools
- application tool (empty gift cards work well for this)
- transfer tape (contact paper is a cheaper alternative)

CLASS IS IN SESSION

We hosted our Defiance location tea towel class in the MakerSpace, where participants were allowed to use the three computers we had available to choose their patterns or create them. Participants were then able to choose what colors they wanted, and the patterns were cut out for them using the Silhouette. Each pattern was cut out in reverse since the heat transfer vinyl needs to be flipped due to having plastic backing on the outside. After that participants weeded the patterns, by removing the extra pieces of unneeded heat transfer vinyl. The towels were then ironed to heat up the fabric for about ten seconds in the location desired to have the pattern applied. Patterns were then placed on the towels and then ironed for fifteen to twenty seconds while making sure to move the iron to heat all portions of the pattern. To protect fingers and to let the image adhere to the towels, the patterns were left to cool down a few seconds. When cooled, the plastic backing was then removed. If the design didn't let go easily to the backing, it was ironed again for about ten seconds, cooled, and tried again. Finally, the pattern was ironed over one last time for about ten seconds to make sure the pattern was fully set.

Our branch location events were hosted in each of their respective community rooms. At Sherwood, we started with the participants deciding on what they wanted to put on their mugs. Then the participants decided on the color or colors they wanted to use. The cut designs were then set up in the Silhouette Studio and divided into each color to be cut. Each pattern was cut as they were finished to keep participants from having to wait too long. Intricate cuts and big designs can take quite some time with the Cameo. After the patterns were done being cut, the excess vinyl was trimmed to be saved for future use. Participants were then shown how to weed the vinyl by removing the pieces not needed for their creation with a weeding tool. When the design was weeded, contact paper was placed on top of it and pressed down using an application tool. The backing was then removed from the vinyl and contact paper so that the vinyl was picked up by the contact paper. The vinyl was then applied to the mug using the contact paper. Finally, the application tool was used to press the vinyl onto the mug and the contact paper was removed leaving the design behind.

The giant paper flowers were made using the instructional video from Jennifer Maker[3] and hot glue. The precut petals were rolled on markers and bottom tabs were glued to give them more shape. Then the petals were glued in order of size to the round base piece. The middle rosebud petals were rolled upward and glued together in a vertical direction. This middle piece was then glued into the middle of the rest of the glued petals to finish the paper flower.

OUTCOME

Overall the set of classes was a success. Both the tea towel and mug classes were well attended with nine participants at each one. The paper flower event, despite having great interest expressed, had no one in attendance. From this result, we decided that all MakerSpace events, particularly those held at the branches, will require registration. This way if there is no committed interest, the event can be canceled to help save staff time and library resources. Compared to previous programs for the MakerSpace, this event was our best-attended program, in part due to the registration and in part due to the interest created by community involvement and a finished product that was of great interest.

Based on this program format, the library also hosted a constellation necklace class where the participants could choose which constellation they got to make. The registration format worked well with this class and is proving to remain the format that will be used for future programs.

FUTURE PROGRAMS

Keeping the use of registration and giving participants the ability to take home an interesting item, the MakerSpace continued planning programs for the rest of the year. A few future programs include 3D-printed wax seals, Vinyl School Update, and Halloween goodie bags. In the 3D-printed wax seals, class patrons can design their own wax seal using Tinkercad, an online software that allows you to make 3D models for free. Participants are not able to take home the seal the same day and will have to pick them up after they are printed, but will have a chance to practice with sample wax seals and take home their practice pieces. In the Vinyl School Update event, we will once again be using the Silhouette Cameo 3 to cut vinyl. This time attendees will be able to decorate their back-to-school gear and make their own décor for the classroom or dorm room. Finally, the Halloween goodie bag class will also use the Silhouette and give participants the chance to cut out and assemble their own goodie bags for Halloween candy and prizes.

As the MakerSpace grows and new equipment is added, new programs will be adapted, but there will always be a place for the creation of Pinterest-inspired crafts. In the coming year, we hope to replicate the program to continue to give patrons the chance to choose their crafts and see what projects interest them. Furthermore, we will continue to expand our classes and projects to whatever new crafting websites, software, or projects are trending. By providing classes of interest, we can better showcase our library's resources for the community's maker needs.

NOTES

1. Elizabeth and Liz, "Hair Tie Bow Tutorial," Simple Simon and Company, last modified February 27, 2019, www.simplesimonandco.com/2019/02/hair-tie-bow-tutorial.html/.
2. Jennifer Marx, "Giant Flower: Spellbound Rose—Every Petal is Unique!—Jennifer Maker," JenuineMom.com, last modified June 3, 2017, jennifermaker.com/giant-flower-spellbound-rose-every-petal-unique/.
3. Jennifer Marx, "How to Make a Giant Flower: Spellbound Rose Tutorial," Jennifer Maker, June 4, 2017, video, 19:09, youtu.be/iDN9R4U5e34.

Chapter Fifteen

Moving beyond Craft Programs

Encouraging Creative Confidence in Adult Learners

Sarah Nagle and Amber R. Cox

According to a landmark longitudinal study by George Land, creativity peaks in early childhood, dropping drastically as we grow older.[1] Ninety-eight percent of children aged four to five score at the genius level on creativity assessments, yet by age fifteen, only 12 percent still scored at this level. When the assessment was given to adults, that number dropped to just 2 percent. These statistics support a trend that library professionals have witnessed—today's adults have a much harder time than children with tinkering, playing, and using their imaginations. This trend is concerning because creativity was predicted to be the third most important employable skill by 2020.[2] As emerging technology transforms the landscape of work, the success of individuals and society will depend on creative thinking. We must adapt programming to fit these new needs because—as discussed in Audrey Barbakoff's book—"through play, the library can encourage the flexible education that adults need in the modern workforce, developing skills like creativity, critical thinking, and resilience."[3]

Yet when it comes to creative projects, adults are afraid of trying new things. They fear failure and have forgotten how to experiment and play without a set outcome in mind. David and Tom Kelley refer to this as "*creative confidence:* the ability to come up with new ideas and the courage to try them out." According to the Kelleys, "Creativity is a natural part of humanity, but the fear of social rejection often keeps adults from trying out creative ideas."[4] In essence, adults experience creative block. Consequently, adults often come to library programs expecting step-by-step instructions, to be told exactly what to do. While there's merit for these types of crafting programs, their lack of experimentation, exploration, and personalization reduces the opportunity for participants to learn translatable skills.

BUILDING CREATIVITY

Encouraging adult learners to move beyond crafting to making and tinkering is key to helping adults tap into their inner creativity. As shown in figure 15.1, crafting, making, and tinkering represent a hierarchy of engagement whereby makers ascend toward more meaningful, self-directed creation. Keep in mind that the medium or type of making is not as important as the process. It doesn't matter whether your attendees are knitting, paper crafting, or working with robotics; what's important is the process and level of engagement. For example, in an origami crafting program, participants follow specific directions to make an origami frog. Participants learn a specific skill (in this case, basic origami folds), but they haven't experimented or embraced uncertainty because they knew what the end product would be before they began. With making, however, the end product is less defined, and the process involves iteration, creative license, and collaboration. As Megan Egbert explains, "Essential to the heart of making, and critical to the maker mindset, is the ability to choose for yourself how you will express an idea or produce a product."[5] We might encourage making in the origami program by giving attendees options for customizing their project—different types of paper, patterns for different animals, or markers and glitter glue to decorate their project.

Tinkering, the highest level in the engagement hierarchy, involves exploring and playing with a variety of materials and crafts without a specific end product in mind. According to Wilkinson and Petrich, "[Tinkering is] fooling around directly with phenomena, tools, and materials. It's thinking with your hands and learning through doing. . . . It's also about making something, but for us, that thing reveals itself to you as you go."[6] In the origami example, tinkering might mean experimenting with various origami folds to make completely original works of art or attempting to fold a frog without using a pattern. The end goal matters less than the process. Fortunately, while many adults have unlearned the ability to tinker and play, Colleen and Aaron Graves suggest that "tinkering is a skill and a habit,"[7] something that redevelops over time with effort. Without doing away with craft programs, changes can be made incrementally that begin challenging adult learners in new ways. By nudging adult learners to

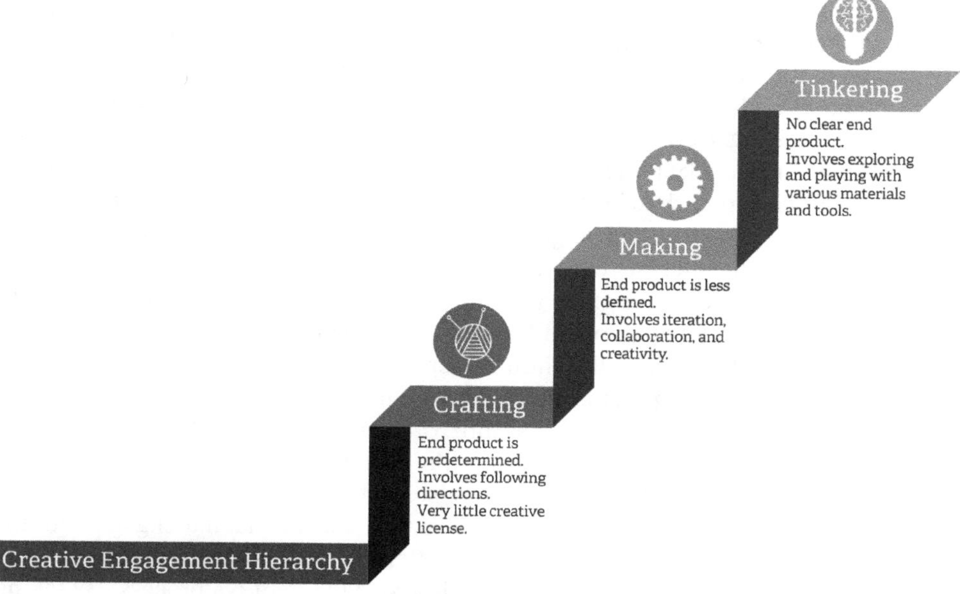

Figure 15.1. Creative engagement hierarchy. ***Sarah Nagle***

make, tinker, and play in our programs, we can help them flex creative muscles, let go of inhibitions, and make amazing things.

ADULT LEARNING

In *Maker-Centered Learning*, Clapp et al. suggest maker-centered learning is a new type of hands-on pedagogy "that encourages community and collaboration (a do-it-together mentality), distributed teaching and learning, boundary crossing, and responsive and flexible teacher practices."[8] These elements play out through redirecting authority (students and teachers alternate roles); emphasizing collaboration and troubleshooting (tinkering and iteration); fostering a sense of agency (self-directed learning); and cultivating a sensitivity to the world around us.[9] While Clapp et al. focused their three-year research project on the learning process of younger students in classroom settings, the research can be extrapolated to adults when viewed through the lens of adult learning. Many theories relate to adult learning, but TEAL Center (Teaching Excellence in Adult Literacy)[10] identifies andragogy, self-directed learning, and transformational learning as the most prominent.

Andragogy contrasts from pedagogy because it focuses on adult learners. In his research on andragogy, Malcolm Knowles identified traits of adult learners, positing that learning is self-directed, built upon accumulated life experiences, problem-based (with a desire for immediate application), and intrinsically motivated.[11] Breaking down these concepts a bit further, TEAL Center explains that adults learn by doing, "need to know *why* they are learning something," and learn best when solving real-life problems.[12] These traits have close ties with active learning, project-based learning, and constructionism, which all argue that participation in activities like making and creation solidifies concepts and helps people learn better.[13]

A component of andragogy, self-directed learning consists of individuals taking ownership of the learning process by identifying personal learning needs, setting goals to reach those needs, locating resources, forming a plan to reach identified goals, and assessing/evaluating learning outcomes.[14] While self-directed learning traditionally takes place in informal learning settings, it has strong ties with student-centered learning, which is "an approach to learning in which learners choose not only *what* to study but also *how* and *why* that topic might be of interest."[15] Student-centered learning can be a powerful tool in a library setting, working best when staff take a facilitator role in place of leading; focus on designing real-life tasks that involve collaborative, inquiry-based learning; and allow the role of teacher to shift between participants and staff.[16]

Transformational learning, the third major adult learning theory, is defined by TEAL Center as "learning that changes the way individuals think about themselves and their world, and that involves a shift of consciousness."[17] Transformational learning connects closely with Clapp et al.'s maker-centered learning concept of "sensitivity to design" in which "the exercise of looking is a starting point" that "encourag[es] curiosity and stimulat[es] a desire to understand and engage with the world."[18] In relation to making and tinkering, transformational learning can be used to find alternate ways to problem-solve and improve the iterative process. By taking a project-based learning approach to solving a problem, attendees can collaboratively discuss solutions and form new ways of thought through exposure to each other's suggestions and ideas.

Costello, Powers, and Haugh explain that "maker education is a learner-driven process" in which, much like Clapp et al.'s maker-centered learning classroom,[19] "the line between 'student' and 'teacher' starts to blur through collaboration and mutual participation in projects." This type of learning space creates loosely structured, controlled chaos. But it's important to remember that it is structured with an overarching teaching strategy, which "gently guide[s] students to discover, question, experience, and understand the concepts they are intended to absorb."[20] Thinking about your craft programs, reflect upon these learning theories and identify ways that current programming can be shifted to better support andragogy, self-directed learning, and transformational learning.

IMPLEMENTATION

With these learning theories in mind, how can you encourage adults to regain the creativity lost since childhood? A good first step is analyzing the purpose of your current programs. Ask yourself what outcomes you want to achieve with your programs and why. Examine what impressions, experiences, and skills your patrons are taking with them when they leave. This activity can be made easier by utilizing a framework such as the lesson planning worksheet created by Costello, Powers, and Haugh. Their four-step process identifies (1) program structure and target audience, (2) purpose/goals, (3) learning outcomes, and (4) action plans.[21] By spending time considering these elements, you will better organize your thoughts while ensuring that adult patrons feel comfortable, encouraged, and empowered in your programs.

In our experience, adult learners have the most difficulty with uncertainty—not knowing what the end product should be. Starting with a pre-made object and reworking it is often less intimidating for adult learners than starting from scratch. Keeping andragogy's principles in mind, seek activities that incorporate problem-based learning and tie the project into real-life problems. Adults frequently purchase garments that do not fit correctly, and rather than finding a tailor, the items sit in the closet. If your library provides sewing machines, consider implementing backward design in a sewing class to *deconstruct* clothing rather than constructing it. Instead of starting with a pattern and walking students through the project step-by-step, ask students to start with a finished or store-bought item and review its construction. Analyzing the garment would determine what steps and sewing techniques were used to make it. Then, students deconstruct the piece and decide whether to reassemble, alter, or create a pattern template for something new. If patrons use the 3D printers in your makerspace to print ready-made objects downloaded from Thingiverse or similar repositories, consider utilizing transformational learning to alter an object with 3D modeling. Ask program attendees to examine a pre-made 3D object from Thingiverse such as an octopus and experiment with adding hinges to make the tentacles articulate as they would naturally. These activities result in patrons gaining skills, such as sewing or

3D modeling, but more importantly, they provide opportunities for patrons to analyze objects and think more deeply about them.

Program goals don't need to be lofty; patrons can build upon initially modest outcomes through skills hierarchies or tiers. Harris and Cooper outline tiers of engagement in which patrons move from "users" to "innovators" and ultimately to "makers," where they "build or create new things, concepts, and theories" and collaborate with others, often even teaching others what they have learned.[22] Vecchione et al. similarly discuss "tiered levels of engagement" as a means of providing accessible entry points for patrons to feel comfortable engaging creatively regardless of prior skills or knowledge.[23] When thinking through your lesson plans, consider how patrons in a low tier of engagement (no prior knowledge of the tools or activity) may experience the program differently from those in a higher tier. Then think through how your program makes it possible for patrons to climb the tiers of engagement and build creative confidence.

Consider circuitry. On its own, circuitry can be a very intimidating concept for patrons with no prior experience. Yet when it is combined with something patrons already know well, such as sewing, it creates a new tier of engagement—e-textiles. E-textile programs bridge the gap and provide a way for patrons to move up the skills hierarchy from basic hand-stitching to complex embroidery and finally to introductory circuitry concepts. This opens the door to a whole new level of makerspace projects, introducing concepts such as simple parallel and series circuits, sewable microcontrollers, and even computer coding. Depending on your desired outcomes, this exact program could be flipped, using e-textiles as an entry point for higher-level circuitry students to learn how to sew. E-textiles could also be used as a social connector for sewists and circuitrists, redirecting authority to encourage student-centered learning and creating a platform to teach one another while collaborating on a large project. E-textiles provide an accessible entry point for students to move up the tiers of engagement and become comfortable exploring a topic that might have previously been intimidating to them. For more information on the topic, read about Fields and Lee's university course titled Craft Technologies 101, which used sewing and fiber art as an entry point for students to learn about circuitry and microelectronics.[24]

Putting adult learners into open-ended situations is often the best way to push them into making and tinkering. Drawing upon self-directed learning, Pikes Peak Library District's East Library Makerspace provides a drop-in watercolor painting program in which participants are given watercolor supplies and library books with watercolor examples and left to create at their own discretion. In the early days of this program, patrons were visibly uncomfortable with the open-ended activity. Used to the library's crafting programs, patrons expected to be walked through a series of steps by an instructor. But by talking with attendees one-on-one, staff were able to connect attendees' interests with available library books and encourage them to explore different techniques and projects. Now that this program has been ongoing for some time, longtime attendees have moved up the skills hierarchy to become mentors to other new attendees, often helping them to get started.

Adding making and tinkering to your programs doesn't have to be a huge undertaking. It can be as simple as altering one step of the process in a maker project. Give patrons basic instructions, but leave room for customization. Generally, a good rule of thumb is to consider the overall number of finished products with unique elements. If everyone is walking out of your programs with the exact same creation, there is definitely room for incorporating making and tinkering. As you plan future programs, utilize a lesson planning worksheet to assess existing programs and consider ways to incorporate opportunities for self-directed learning, project-based learning, and troubleshooting. Start small with incremental changes, and before you know it, your patrons will regain their creative confidence!

NOTES

1. George Land and Beth Jarman, *Breakpoint and Beyond: Mastering the Future Today* (New York: Harper Business, 1992), 153.
2. "The Future of Jobs," World Economic Forum, last modified January 18, 2016, www.weforum.org/reports/the-future-of-jobs/.
3. Audrey Barbakoff, *Adults Just Wanna Have Fun: Programs for Emerging Adults* (Chicago: ALA Editions, 2016), xiii.
4. David Kelley and Tom Kelley, *Creative Confidence: Unleashing the Creative Potential Within Us All* (New York: Crown Business, 2013), 6.
5. Megan Egbert, *Creating Makers: How to Start a Learning Revolution at Your Library* (Santa Barbara, CA: Libraries Unlimited, 2016), 6.
6. Karen Wilkinson and Mike Petrich, *The Art of Tinkering: Meet 150+ Makers Working at the Intersection of Art, Science & Technology* (San Francisco: Weldon Owen, 2016), 13.
7. Colleen Graves and Aaron Graves, *The Big Book of Makerspace Projects: Inspiring Makers to Experiment, Create, and Learn* (New York: McGraw-Hill Education, 2017), 1.
8. Edward P. Clapp et al., *Maker-Centered Learning: Empowering Young People to Shape Their Worlds* (San Francisco: Josey-Bass, 2017), 4.
9. Ibid., 40, 52–54, 105.
10. TEAL Center, *Adult Learning Theories: Fact Sheet No. 11* (Washington, DC: U.S. Department of Education, 2011), 1.
11. Malcolm Knowles, *The Modern Practice of Adult Education: Andragogy Versus Pedagogy*, rev. and updated ed. (Englewood Cliffs, NJ: Cambridge Adult Education, 1980), 44–45, 55.
12. TEAL Center, *Adult Learning Theories*, 1.
13. Laura Costello, Meredith Powers, and Dana Haugh, "Pedagogy and Prototyping in Library Makerspaces," in *The Makerspace Librarian's Sourcebook*, ed. Ellyssa Kroski (Chicago: ALA Editions, 2017), 31–33.
14. TEAL Center, *Adult Learning Theories*, 2.
15. TEAL Center, *Student-Centered Learning: Fact Sheet No. 6* (Washington, DC: U.S. Department of Education, 2010), 1.
16. Costello, Powers, and Haugh, "Pedagogy and Prototyping," 31–32.
17. TEAL Center, *Adult Learning Theories*, 2.
18. Clapp et al., *Maker-Centered Learning*, 110.
19. Ibid., 41.
20. Costello, Powers, and Haugh, "Pedagogy and Prototyping," 36.
21. Ibid., 42.
22. Jennifer Harris and Chris Cooper, "Make Room for a Makerspace," *Computers in Libraries* 35, no. 2 (March 2015): 5–9.

23. Amy Vecchione et al., “Encouraging a Diverse Maker Culture,” in *The Makerspace Librarian’s Sourcebook*, ed. Elyssa Kroski (Chicago: American Library Association), 55–57.

24. Deborah Fields and Victor Lee, “Craft Technologies 101: Bringing Making to Higher Education,” in *Makeology: Makerspaces as Learning Environments*, ed. Kylie Peppler, Erica Rosenfeld Halverson, and Yasmin B. Kafai (New York: Routledge, 2016), 139–56.

Chapter Sixteen

Design Thinking in a Goal-Oriented Makerspace

Amanda Sweet

Fiction empowers people to imagine things that don't yet exist. The helicopter, cell phone, submarine, liquid-fueled rocket, and mechanical hand were all inspired by science fiction.[1] Makerspaces dare people to dream big, then provide the tools to make it happen. This chapter is about closing the opportunity gap and providing adults with the tools and resources to solve real problems in the world. To accomplish this, we will progress through three sections most relevant to making and choosing relevant tech for your makerspace:

1. design thinking,
2. technology concepts, and
3. identifying technology needs.

For makers, design thinking is a process to ensure technology is built with intent to solve real, human-centered problems in the world. As makerspace designers, we should have a clearly defined goal to suit the needs of makers. We cannot make technology if we don't know it exists. This chapter will cover the major technology concepts identified by the World Economic Forum, along with how to simplify the learning process. The chapter will wrap up with a conversation-style approach to identifying which technology your community wants to explore. This all draws from experience of a team setting up makerspaces in more than twenty libraries across Nebraska through the Library Innovation Studios grant and subsequent makerspace consultations.[2] Together we will seek answers to unfamiliar topics and use technology to build a better future.

DESIGNING THINKING FOR MAKERS

Design thinking originated at Stanford, and the process has gone through several iterations. Full immersion is recommended to learn the process of empathizing, defining, ideating, prototyping, and testing a technology idea to make sure the product is solving needs as intended. This chapter has adapted Stanford's K–12 "Get Started with Design Thinking" guide to suit the needs of a makerspace designer.[3] It's time to immerse yourself in design. As an example, consider the challenge of choosing an educational robot to include in a makerspace for adults.

Empathize

How well do you know your makers? What are their technology needs and goals for learning? To choose an appropriate robot, we need to know the following:

- What is the makers' current comfort level with technology?
- What is the goal in learning? Do makers want to learn how to use robots but not make them, how to code for robotics, or are they mostly just curious?
- Do adult users have children who want to learn as well?
- How much time do users have to spend in the makerspace on a learning session?
- What types of skills do adult learners need to learn and why?

The answers to these questions will help the makerspace designer choose a tool appropriate to experience level that can expand to a higher skill level.

Define

You will likely gather a lot of conflicting information while empathizing. Now it's time to narrow down focus to what the majority of people want. Choose the most pressing robotics needs in the community and start looking for options. For this example, we will assume most people plan to use robots to learn coding basics and want to know how robots can be functional in everyday life. The hope is to be able to apply these skills in their work and home life.

Ideate

Now you're looking for solutions to the problems. So get online and start searching for robot options. Come up with at least three options, and make a list of pros and cons. You might not be able to hit every criteria on your list, but try to get close. When you have a full list, ask makerspace staff what they are comfortable using. Makers can tell when staff don't like a tool.

Prototype

Eventually you just have to take the plunge and buy the bot. Be brave and try new things. Watch how makers interact with the new robot. It is an amazing experience to provide opportunities to learn new things. Start making a list of factors that go into technology adoption in the makerspace: staff enthusiasm, helpful supporting documents, user-friendliness of the product, maker comfort level, and more. At this stage, observe whether the new robot is being used and how. Try to gather user feedback to find out why the robot is, or is not, being used.

Test

Now is the time to find out if your robot selection is meeting the real-world needs of the makers. So gather more feedback to find out if your makerspace is adding value to makers. Look back at the Define step. Did your selection meet those needs and bring in the right people? Sometimes prototypes work; sometimes they don't. Failure is a fact of life in design thinking.

Whatever you do, keep trying. Do something a little different until you find a combination that works. Keep in mind that design thinking is not linear. At any time during this process, you might find yourself skipping around in the process or going back to the drawing board entirely. Design thinking might require a creative budget, but so does any makerspace. If we want makers to try new things, fail, and try again, we should set a good example.

TECHNOLOGY CONCEPTS

Our design thinking example multitasked and outlined the basics of how to select technology tools for a makerspace. However, we can't learn something if we don't know it exists. This chapter is a broad overview to help you see through the static and pay attention to the details that matter in choosing technology. The 2018 World Economic Forum's Future of Jobs Report has identified artificial intelligence (AI), robotics, the Internet of Things (IoT), cloud technology, drones, virtual reality (VR), augmented reality (AR), and mobile/web technology as the biggest technology concepts that are changing the world now and in the future.[4]

This seems like a lot when listed out separately. Keep in mind that these are all just overarching concepts that can overlap and appear in different technology tools. For example, Fitbit watches that measure your heart rate and movement are actually a combination of IoT and web technologies.[5] Some have a bit of AI and cloud technology thrown in for good measure.

IoT devices connect the sensors in "things" to a smartphone app via an Internet connection. The user can then control the device using the app. The sensor also collects a great deal of data and sends it over the web to the connected device.

AI is great at processing large amounts of data. Machine learning (ML) is one facet of AI. One flavor of ML is designed to identify patterns in large sets of data. This allows both human and machine to look at the data patterns and find different ways to use the data set. All this data can be stored and accessed remotely in the cloud.

Luckily, when you're looking for technology for your makerspace, you will likely only have to buy one or two technology tools to demonstrate all this technology. Robots and AI walk hand in hand, so do drones, web apps, and IoT. We keep these as separate concepts to show people that complex technology is actually made of a combination of different technologies. Providing people with a mix-and-match menu opens up flexibility for making new tech. It also helps to simplify the learning process.

Since all this technology works together to reach a common goal, many of the same concepts are also used to build each technology concept. After sifting through the developer's guide for each technology concept, several commonalities were found.

Robotics, drones, IoT, VR, AR, and web/mobile technology all require skills in circuitry, "coding," "math," varying physics principles, sensors, 3D design, and graphic arts to build the tech from scratch.

In makerspaces, people will often learn from using and manipulating existing technology. The same technology tools used to help people learn skills for one technology concept can also be used to teach skills for other technology concepts. For example, if a maker wants to learn coding for robotics, the obvious choice is to use an educational robot that supports text-based programming. A good beginner language for most of this technology is Python. Programming languages will change and adapt over time, but the concepts of the language will also remain the same.

If a maker recently learned about the Internet of Things and wants to learn coding and sensors, many educational robots can be used to teach these same basic skills. Not everyone wants to make technology from scratch. Making can lead to a deeper understanding of how technology works so makers can join technology teams to design complex technology in the workplace or to solve problems in everyday life. Making technology is a cooperative game.

To get more comfortable with bigger technology concepts, try researching technology. You don't need to know everything. Start by answering these questions for each concept:

1. What is this technology?
2. Find a few examples of how this tech might be used in everyday life.
3. Which industries are using this technology now?
4. What kinds of problems can this technology solve? Use examples.
5. How can this technology help people?

The Institute of Electrical and Electronics Engineers (IEEE), Tech Crunch, Ars Technica, and American Library Association's Library of the Future are great resources to start. Knowing how tech works will help makerspace designers connect makers with a tangible reason to learn.

IDENTIFYING COMMUNITY NEEDS

With a few well-chosen, versatile tools, we can equip our makerspace with the tools to learn just about any major technology. Now communities need to know what exists and how it can help solve immediate problems in the world. Dumping information on people is not a fun way to learn. Instead, try a Community Conversation with a hands-on learning component.

This conversation guide was adapted from the work done by the American Library Association (ALA) and the Harwood Institute for Public Innovation.[6] There is no reason to reinvent the wheel, so look to this guide to learn how to plan and facilitate an event.

This design thinking approach to a Community Conversation means learning through immersion. People retain more information when they learn by doing. To help this process, open with an activity to connect new information from our technology worksheets to identifiable, familiar problems communities want to solve. Adults are more motivated to learn when they know why they're learning and how the new skills can benefit them in the near future.[7]

An easy way to link new technology to existing information is to redesign an app. Depending on the number of people, break the group down into smaller groups of three or four. Have each group pick an app on their phone they use relatively often. Then choose an app that has been gathering dust on their phone. Compare the two apps. Why do we use one app but not the other? Is it user-friendly? What would make you use the other app more? Jot down some notes of what you'd like to change to make the infrequently used app more appealing. Bring the whole group back together and share results with the whole group.

Now what does this say about the design process of technology? Why do we need technology? How can people with different backgrounds and experience levels contribute to the process of making? Everybody is creative and everybody can be a maker. Coding and circuitry is not everything. This is the point where we can start a Community Conversation.

The goal of this conversation is to open doors to new technology and learn about public perception of technology. Find out what people already know and get a feel for comfort levels. Which concepts pique interest and resonate with community issues? Use this as a launching pad to bridge the gap between where people are now and where they would like to be in the future.

Community Conversation Question Template

After the opening activity, provide people with the tech sheets. Ask people to read the sheets and choose a technology that sounds interesting and useful. Then open up a discussion.

Instead of the questions from the ALA Community Conversation guide, use these questions to start framing a conversation about the importance and meaning of technology:

1. Which technology did you choose? How will this technology affect you personally?
2. How is this technology changing the world?
3. What would you like to learn and why?
4. How do you prefer to learn new technology? What works for you?
5. What concerns do you have about emerging technology?
6. What would you like to see change in the world of technology?
7. What do you think is keeping us from learning and using technology that can help?
8. If you could make anything in the world, with any technology, what would you make?
9. How do you see the future of technology?
10. Is technology mostly positive, mostly negative, or somewhere in between? Why?
11. Now that we've talked a bit about emerging technology, what questions do you have?

This discussion about emerging technology has been eye-opening in many communities. Here are some examples of what we have found by doing these discussions with small groups in various communities:

- There is a huge disconnect between the direction the workforce is going with technology and the public's knowledge base and preconceived ideas about technology.
- Dystopian fiction has influenced public thinking about emerging technology.
- People struggle with how to learn technology effectively.
- Overall, many people do not see themselves as being a "technology person," but they also use and implement new technology every day. They just don't design technology.
- Many communities have an interest in technology but do not know where to start.
- Older participants prefer to learn technology from humans they know and trust.
- When communities take part in the planning, they are more likely to use the service.

This is all anecdotal, but that is the point of a conversation. Uncover gaps in knowledge, misinformation, and beliefs of inadequacy in the face of technology. Don't judge or preach; instead use this conversation as a way to *empathize* with your community. Start the process of connecting your community with technology that will change your corner of the world. When you identify a technology concept, start working your way through the design thinking process outlined in the previous section to select an appropriate technology tool for your community. Then repeat the process with a new technology concept.

Design thinking is a continual process. Makerspaces go through many iterations, and not everything works perfectly. Success or failure, design always leads to learning. Empower makers with the tools they need to build a better future.

NOTES

1. Mark Strauss, "Ten Inventions Inspired by Science Fiction," *Smithsonian Magazine*, last modified March 15, 2012, www.smithsonianmag.com/science.

2. Patrick Groves, "Nebraska Makerspaces Ignite Creativity in Libraries Statewide," Government Technology, last modified June 25, 2019, www.govtech.com/products/Nebraska-Makerspaces-Ignite-Creativity-in-Libraries-Statewide.html.

3. "Get Started with Design Thinking," Stanford d.school, accessed June 29, 2019, dschool.stanford.edu/resources/getting-started-with-design-thinking.

4. "The Future of Jobs Report 2018," World Economic Forum, last modified September 17, 2018, www.weforum.org/reports/the-future-of-jobs-report-2018.

5. Molly McLaughlin, "How Does a Fitbit Work?" Lifewire, last modified December 19, 2019, www.lifewire.com/what-is-fitbit-4176010.

6. "New Resources Available: Community Conversations and Theming," American Library Association, last modified July 24, 2017, www.ala.org/tools/librariestransform/blog/new-resources-available-community-conversations-and-theming.

7. John Taylor and Adrian Furnham, *Learning at Work: Excellent Practice from Best Theory* (New York: Palgrave Macmillan, 2005), 16.

Chapter Seventeen

Busting the Doors Open

Makerspace Programs and Services That Engage with the Community

Jennifer Hicks

Makerspaces in libraries have been a hot topic for several years now. Some time ago, our library director decided we should start building our own. The Gardner-Harvey Library at Miami University, Middletown campus, opened the TEC (Tinker, Envision, Create) Lab in the hopes it would be a resource for the campus community as well as the local community. Since then, we have grown not just our physical makerspace but the programs and outreach we do as well.

The TEC Lab started with a 3D printer and some craft supplies. I began running monthly workshops in the fall of 2014. Rather than basing workshops on our bigger equipment, I tried to find inexpensive projects that would get potential makers in the door. Our first workshop involved participants creating terrariums in recycled glass jars, with plants, soil, and rocks provided by the library. In our first semester running, we also offered workshops on 3D printing, green-screen pictures, and an open-house Valentine's Day workshop where participants could make cards and small gifts.

The programs and services in the following chapter were created in an academic library makerspace, but many of the concepts can be translated to a variety of library types. As I am a thrifty person, many of the projects mentioned in this chapter also have a per person cost of less than five dollars. My hope is that the following programs and services can be a springboard for new ideas in your makerspace.

EARLY GROUP PROGRAMS

I wanted to touch on some of the first program collaborations we were able to take part in. While this isn't directly related to the outside community, working with other departments on campus helped us to look at the bigger picture. We realized we could do more than offer basic workshops and assistance to makers who stumbled in the door. The idea of partnering with other departments and groups wasn't at the forefront of our plans, but it ended up shaping many programs and services to come.

For our TEC Lab, we decided to purchase a set of twenty-five 3D pens. Already having 3D printers was an advantage, as we already had an abundance of PLA filament. To go along with our 3D pens, we printed and laminated a variety of letters and pictures that users can trace to create items. We also offer whiteboard markers and blank laminated sheets for users to create their own designs. In terms of items that get regular use, our 3D pens have been some of the most used items in our TEC Lab. Aside from being able to have enough for a class, 3D pens are portable and can be taken to other locations and used.

After the creation of our designated makerspace, the English Language Center (ELC) contacted the library to create a workshop for their students using the TEC Lab. The students participating in the ELC program work as a cohort, so the center tries to plan fun activities for team building. Our library team decided to let the students show off their creativity with our set of 3D pens. The students as well as the faculty had a great time "playing" with the 3D pens, which has led to the ELC requesting this workshop yearly.

For our second partnership on campus, we decided to combine 3D printing and 3D pens. The academic advising department contacted the library for a team-building exercise. They were hoping we could put together an activity for the staff to work on together. This session involved 3D printing business card holders ahead of time. We then gave participants 3D pens to customize their card holders. Due to the filament being the same material for the printer and pens, the pen filament easily adheres to the printed object.

Getting to work with groups such as the ELC and the academic advising department gives way to working with other groups. One way I hope to reach out is to offer closed workshops. An example that you may be familiar with is businesses that offer group painting. A similar concept could work with the makerspace. These sessions could also be used to generate income for the library if a fee is charged.

STEAM PROGRAMS

Our first venture with STEM/STEAM programming came by chance. Our campus worked with local K–12 schools to create a STEM day camp. This program brings local eighth-grade students to campus for a day of STEM projects taught by different departments. The library's participation in the camp revolved around our TEC Lab. Our goal was to create stations based on the STEM fields. Over the past several years, we have included projects that used both large and small tools within the TEC Lab, including paper-clip circuits, green-screen photos, and 3D pen bridge-building competitions.

The second opportunity to work with K–12 students came from our work with the day camp. The regional campuses of Miami University put together multiple week-long STEAM camps for local students in sixth to eighth grades. There were three weeks of camp on our campus with different themes for each week. Camp themes included movie making, video game design, and roller-coaster physics. During movie week, participants worked in the TEC Lab to create props as well as at One Button Studio located in the library for filming. During video game week, students worked in the TEC Lab to create physical representations of the video game characters they created using perler beads and 3D pens.

Working with K–12 students has been a great step out into the community, that is, metaphorically speaking. While the students came to us, it expanded our visibility. It is definitely a symbiotic relationship. We enjoy having younger students visit to experience what we have to offer, and hopefully this in turn will bring future students to our university. No matter what type of library you work in, partnering with local K–12 schools for STEAM programs in your makerspace can be beneficial all around.

VOLUNTEC LAB

While our initial programming brought new faces into the TEC Lab, I wanted to break out of the box. I wanted to create programming that had more purpose than just getting people in the door. And though I am grateful I have had the opportunity to present at several conferences on makerspaces, I think I had reached a point where I was blue in the face talking about how to start a makerspace. Despite running a variety of workshops on different makerspace technology, the process still started to feel monotonous. I have yet to get tired of makerspaces, but I needed something new to find my spark. Thankfully, I work in a library that embraces new ideas and the evolution of older practices. This flexibility allowed me to eventually start planning workshops that have a volunteer element to them. In the fall of 2016, I started the VolunTEC Lab workshop series.

The purpose of the workshops was to create an item to give, an item to take, or both. The "Make One, Take One" policy has worked well, as most participants make at least one item to give. Past workshops included decorating holiday wreaths for the local nursing home (figure 17.1), creating cat tents and dog toys for a no-kill animal shelter, and chemo socks for cancer patients. Overall, the VolunTEC Lab workshops have been some of our most attended sessions.

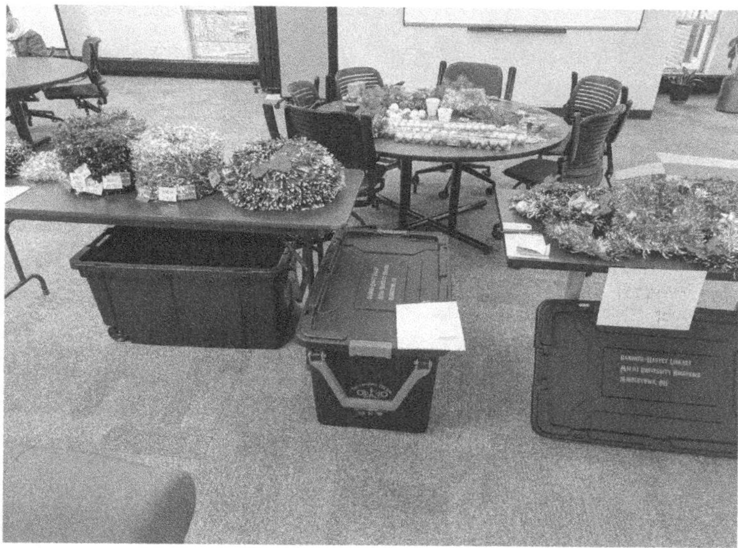

Figure 17.1. Wreath supplies for VolunTEC Lab Workshop. ***Jennifer Hicks***

Traveling TEC Lab

There have been many makerspaces that started mobile and moved into a permanent space. We ended up doing things a little backward. The thought of a movable makerspace wasn't one of our original goals; however, the need for something more mobile came from our work with other departments and community partners. I created the Traveling TEC Lab for use in classrooms and community spaces. The VolunTEC workshops had such great turnout that we wanted to move them to a larger location. Access to larger spaces on campus is not a problem, but moving all of our supplies was a mess. With a few cheap storage containers and a Silhouette machine, I was able to brand our new Traveling TEC Lab.

Our Traveling TEC Lab consists of two large totes with wheels and handles, a folding utility cart, a collapsible clothes rack, and some shoe organizers that hang from the clothes rack. In total, we spent around $50 on the storage; then we were able to brand the items with our Silhouette vinyl cutter. While it wasn't a large investment, it enabled us to easily move most of our TEC Lab equipment out of the library for different events. Students and community members have also come to recognize the Traveling TEC Lab logo, stopping in when we are set up on different parts of campus or out in the community.

Due to staffing constraints, I haven't been able to take the Traveling TEC Lab station to as many locations as I would like. I have done networking with the local K–12 school and the public library and would like to start offering programming at these remote locations. Having the ability to move tools and supplies from your makerspace can help build connections with future users (figure 17.2). There are several future collaborations I would like to look into, such as nursing homes, community centers, and even coffee shops.

Figure 17.2. Traveling TEC Lab supplies. ***Jennifer Hicks***

GUEST TEACHERS

While I enjoy running a variety of workshops, I am only one person, with only so many class ideas. Our library is constantly on the lookout for guest presenters with skills they would like to share. We do not offer compensation, but we do provide supplies for the workshops taught by guest teachers. As of yet, this has not been a problem. Many patrons that come in are happy to have a place to teach others their craft. Past guest presenter workshops have included stained glass, sewing, and laser engraving.

These fresh perspectives are important, especially in an area where innovation is key. From students to professors to community patrons, there are plenty of people in your area with skill sets they would like to share. Our stained glass workshop was taught by a retired veterinarian. We have offered multiple sewing and clothing repair workshops that are taught by a geology professor on campus. Finding guest teachers doesn't mean waiting until someone walks in the library either. Keeping an eye open while you are out and about could lead you to your next guest workshop teacher. There could be hidden gem instructors lurking at local colleges, art museums, or even next door.

In the scheme of things, makerspaces are relatively new. We find ourselves still navigating within this experiment in creativity. This means there are still so many ways to stretch and grow what we can offer our users. I am excited to see what innovative ideas come out of makerspaces in the next several years. I hope this chapter has provided at least some brainstorming material for new and seasoned makerspace leaders alike.

Chapter Eighteen

Maker Programming for Adults with Disabilities

"Library for All" Best Programs and Best Practices

Sarah Coleman and Stephanie Douglas

Library for All is a maker program serving adults with disabilities, a vulnerable population that has a long-standing presence in libraries. According to the American Library Association, libraries play a catalytic role in the lives of people with disabilities by facilitating their full participation in society.[1] Adult day groups such as Easter Seals and other similar organizations frequent our library to use computers and check out materials. While collection use is important, programming that would satisfy the unique needs of this population was lacking. This led to the creation of Library for All, programming that offers adults with disabilities the opportunity to engage with emerging technologies and trends.

The library in which we work has been a focal point for makerspaces in our library system. A variety of maker tools are available for public use. Thus, it was a natural extension of our library's culture to create a maker experience for adults with disabilities. Our goal was to remove barriers from the makerspace through careful project selection and leveraging our patrons' abilities to allow them to experiment with STEAM (science, technology, engineering, art, and math). A conversation with the program coordinator at the local Easter Seals chapter confirmed that a maker program would be a good fit for their clients. As such, attendance increased rapidly during its first year. The inaugural program hosted fifteen patrons. By the end of its first year, thirty to forty patrons attended the program monthly. Participant response has been so positive that Library for All has been expanded to a system-wide program and is now offered at five locations in our library system, reaching hundreds of adults with disabilities each year.

It is hoped that the programming success described here will inspire you to start a Library for All program at your library and provide an engaging offering for this underserved population. The following suggestions for supplies, activities, and best practices are presented with the objective of quickly establishing a Library for All program at your library location. With a very modest set of supplies and staff training, you will be ready to start making a difference in the lives of patrons with disabilities in your community.

SUPPLY AND ACTIVITY SUGGESTIONS FOR ALL BUDGETS

Maker programming for adults with disabilities can be low-cost, low-investment programming with high rewards in terms of patron satisfaction. More sophisticated STEAM equipment can be purchased for libraries with ample budgets. Though the Library for All program at our library is well-funded, activities from the low- and small-budget suggestions listed below are offered regularly to increase the breadth of activities that patrons experience on a monthly basis.

General Supply Suggestions

The supplies listed here are frequently used most months. It is recommended that these supplies be kept on hand due to frequent use. As you develop this program and target it toward your particular patron profile, your general supply needs may differ from ours. Supply suggestions given here will get you started.

- baking soda
- beads
- bubble solution (homemade or store bought)
- chenille stems
- construction paper
- colored pencils
- coloring sheets
- food coloring
- glue
- markers
- scissors
- vinegar

Very Low-/No-Budget Activity Suggestions

The following suggestions for very low-budget libraries assume that your library has some basic office supplies available. Other materials can be collected outdoors for art programs. The dollar store is a fantastic retail resource for very low budgets.

- bubble blowing
- bookmark making
- baking soda and vinegar science experiments
- beading
- cardboard construction project
- coloring pages
- DIY cornhole game
- food coloring science experiments
- nature art
- origami

- popsicle stick bridge building
- shadow animals

Smaller-Budget Activity Suggestions

Libraries with a small budget will also benefit from dollar store purchases. With increased budget there is more opportunity for make-and-take projects. Our program includes at least one make-and-take item per session.

- button making
- clay sculptures
- decorating coasters
- kinetic sand sculptures
- LED project
- LEGO
- painting
- Play-Doh
- print making
- Mod Podge
- seed planting
- sensory bags
- wreath making

Ample Budget Activity Suggestions

For well-funded libraries, a great deal of fantastic STEM equipment is available for purchase, including robotics, 3D pens, KEVA planks, and more. Many equipment purchases present additional cost if consumables are required on an ongoing basis (such as rolls of PLA for the 3D pens), and this future cost should be taken into consideration when making the initial equipment purchase. The possibility of booking paid presenters is another option with an ample budget.

- 3D pens
- board games (preferably giant size)
- Cubelets
- Dash and Dot robots
- instrument petting zoo (paid presenter)
- karaoke
- KEVA planks
- screen printing
- sewing machine projects
- storyteller (paid presenter)

As it is imperative that the program is fun and rewarding while being geared to the special needs of our adult population, our program consists of four distinct activities per month, with one activity being from the ample-budget category, two activities from the small-budget category, and one from the low-budget category. This particular mix of activities allows for presentation of tried-and-true favorite activities, which patrons request be repeated frequently, along with high-impact activities that may be novel and involve new skill acquisition. Our patrons have indicated that they can be overwhelmed by too many unfamiliar activities presented in a single program. Responding to and incorporating patron and caregiver feedback is important and will be illustrated in greater depth in the following sections.

BEST PROGRAMS

Programs referred to in this section are the most popular and successful run to date at our library. This collection discusses the main activities of the programs, which can be paired with several others from the lists of suggestions previously given to form a complete Library for All experience for patrons.

Messy Science

Of all the scientific activities presented, the explosive power of baking soda and vinegar volcanoes[2] has captured the hearts of participants. Witnessing repeated patron-created volcano eruptions, the delight it evokes in our guests is palpable. The chemical reaction is safe, reliable, and forgiving, so a great deal of fine motor control or measuring ability is not required. Similar fun is had through inflating balloons[3] with the same chemical reaction, as the foaming action and gas are observable by touch alone, perfect for patrons with sight impairments.

Fandom Event

As familiarity has grown with our regular attendees at the Library for All program, fandom has emerged as a huge interest. Participants love to celebrate their fandoms, specifically their love of local sports teams.

Broncos Tailgate Party (self-contained themed program)

- DIY foam fingers[4]
- DIY pom-poms[5]
- tailgate snacks (pre-plan for allergies, food restrictions with caregivers)
- Broncos-themed cornhole game (owned by staff)
- Broncos button making
- beading blue and orange Broncos bracelets

LEDs and Robotics

Participants are able to work with Dash and Dot Robots[6] easily due to their familiarity with cell phone and iPad technology. Discovering this avenue of technical knowledge our patrons possess allowed for an easy transition into robotics. While LED light-up cuffs[7] are a more detailed project requiring manual dexterity, this project was adapted to our group by pre-sewing the conductive thread and having patrons attach and wire the LEDs.

Service Project

Care for others has emerged as a recurring theme in the lives of our Library for All patrons, and they frequently make an item to take home for a relative, friend, or loved one before creating another item for themselves to take home. Patrons are community-minded and care deeply about creating happiness in others' lives. To create community impact through a caring disposition, Library for All patrons participated in a community service project as part of the 2018 Summer Reading Program, themed "Build a Better World," making bookmarks for homebound library patrons. Additionally, a Mother's Day sugar scrub and cards[8] program was the perfect opportunity to thank Mom for her love and support.

Music Programs

A love of music is closely related to fandom, and Library for All patrons at our library love to listen to music. Many patrons are natural performers and love singing for others! Creating a functional piano from a bunch of bananas really appealed to our patrons' fun-loving nature.

- instrument petting zoo (paid performer)
- karaoke
- DIY instruments[9]
- Makey Makey banana piano[10]

Program planning is typically done well in advance of program dates, usually encompassing six months' worth of programs. Individual programs are mapped out for six months to ensure that equipment and supplies are ordered and on hand well before the items are needed. This practice also builds in time for mastering any new STEAM equipment before the program date. Of equal importance to supplies and good planning is how the program is presented to patrons by staff, volunteers, and presenters, and this will be expanded upon next, with Library for All best practices.

BEST PRACTICES

In an effort to ensure the Library for All experience is a positive one for participants, caregivers, volunteers, and staff, best practices should be implemented. While baseline best practices should be in place before you begin, they should also allow for flexibility in order to be reflective of the needs of the participants and caregivers attending the program. Periodically reviewing and revising best practices is recommended. The following eight areas of best practice form the basis of our Library for All program delivery.

1. Provide training for library staff and volunteers. Introducing staff and volunteers to People First Language (PFL) is a good place to start. PFL is language that refers to the person first and the ability second. It is important to share this information with your staff as well as model this language behavior. Library for All is about what people can do, rather than what they can't do.

   Prepare staff to be open to a variety of interactions with patrons during the program (hugging/touching, lack of personal space, personal conversations, open displays of emotion, etc.). Be sure that staff and volunteers not only share your passion for working with this population but are equipped with the tools they need. While volunteers may not be a necessity when you first begin offering these types of programs, be conscientious that it may become a need if your program grows in popularity.

   A quick note about hiring presenters: it is imperative that you hire and work with presenters who are comfortable working with this population. Explain to them in advance that there may be distractions or lack of participation, and they need to be able to present their material regardless.
2. Have caregivers remain in the room while you are doing the program. You will need special training to offer a respite program where caregivers are absent. Be sure to emphasize this in your marketing materials. Caregivers will respond to personal and medical needs of their clients as well as address behavioral issues. At Library for All sessions, caregivers present give some assistance to patrons who are working on their projects; however, this assistance is not relied upon when calculating staffing levels for a program.
3. Cap your attendance based on staffing and room size. Opting for quality over quantity for this program will result in a success for the participants. When considering attendance, reflect on the size of the room and the ability of patrons in wheelchairs and with walkers to move about. Other patrons may have impairments in gross motor skills and may need extra room to safely maneuver. Check in with caregivers to determine if their clients are comfortable in large groups. Provide seating in a quiet corner of the room for those who do not wish to interact with others. However, the majority of Library for All patrons attending love meeting others and making new friends.
4. Make sure you have enough staff and volunteers for your program. In this setting, minimizing frustrations is important. Having enough helpers on hand can alleviate activity wait times and other potential stressors. This is particularly important when working with a STEAM activity that is new to the group. It may take multiple tries for patrons to master a new process or piece of equipment, and extended attention from a staff member or volunteer is needed during that time. Ample staffing also allows for personalized one-on-one time with participants, fostering important social interaction.
5. Allow for flexibility. Change your program up on the fly if something is not working for patrons. One way to do this is to keep a simple alternate activity on hand.

Whether patrons attempt an activity and do not like it or whether a piece of maker equipment malfunctions, having an easily accessible backup can prevent frustration, as well as overcrowding at the other remaining activity centers. Be ready for all possibilities and have standby alternatives easily available.

6. Respond to patron needs. Turn off background music if it's a sensory issue. Accommodate patrons by helping them get what they need to feel comfortable; assist when needed but allow for the experts in the room, the caregivers, to take over.
7. Refine your program based on observation. What worked? What didn't work and why? This is vital to the success of your program. Paying close attention to participants' reactions to projects, the atmosphere in the room, and what patrons ask for regularly will also help you have a complete idea of what is working and what is not.
8. Solicit feedback and program ideas from caregivers. What did they feel worked or didn't work? What do their clients like and want to see more of? Asking patrons alone may not yield a complete picture with the feedback you are looking for. Incorporate caregiver feedback into future program offerings.

Best practices and staff training allow for a positive experience for staff, patrons, and caregivers alike. The practices discussed here provide a flexible framework for ensuring a quality patron experience and allow for valuable feedback from caregivers and program attendees that will inform future Library for All programming.

In conclusion, making is an excellent way to offer meaningful experiences for adults with disabilities at your library. No matter your budget, this programming can have an impact. Best practices presented constitute eight areas of consideration that will result in a fun, inclusive experience for your patrons. Feedback from patrons and caregivers is taken into account and is incorporated into new program planning. Tried-and-true programs have been presented that will allow for a quick start for a new Library for All endeavor at your library. It is hoped that you have been inspired to present a Library for All program at your library.

NOTES

1. "Outreach Resources for Services to People with Disabilities," American Library Association, last updated October 16, 2018, www.ala.org/advocacy/diversity/outreachtounderservedpopulations/servicespeopledisabilities.

2. Abdul Wahab, "How to Make a Vinegar Volcano," Science4Fun, accessed May 26, 2019, science4fun.info/how-to-make-vinegar-volcano/.

3. Brooke Greco, "How to Inflate a Balloon Using Baking Soda and Vinegar," Education.com, accessed July 26, 2019, www.education.com/science-fair/article/balloon-gas-chemical-reaction/.

4. Bunnings Warehouse, "How to Make a Giant Sports Foam Finger and Hand," Bunnings Warehouse, accessed July 26, 2019, www.bunnings.com.au/diy-advice/kids/craft/how-to-make-a-giant-sports-foam-finger-and-hand.

5. Emma, "How to Make Cheerleader Pom Poms," Kids Craft Room, accessed July 26, 2019, kidscraftroom.com/how-to-make-pom-poms/.

6. Make Wonder, "Dash The Original STEM Learning Robot," MakeWonder.com, accessed July 26, 2019, www.makewonder.com/robots/.
7. Heidi Gustad, "DIY Light-Up Cuff Bracelet," Hands Occupied, last updated February 4, 2014, www.handsoccupied.com/diy-light-up-cuff-bracelet/.
8. Debbie, "Homemade Sugar Scrub Lavender and Lemon Sugar Scrub," One Little Project at a Time, last updated August 1, 2016, onelittleproject.com/homemade-sugar-scrub/.
9. Lorraine Brummer, "52 Homemade Musical Instruments to Make," Felt Magnet, last updated September 18, 2018, feltmagnet.com/crafts/Music-Instruments-for-Kids-to-Make.
10. Maker Camp, "Way Out Sound Fruit Piano," MakerCamp.com, accessed July 26, 2019, makercamp.com/projects/fruit-piano.

Part IV

PROJECTS IN ACTION

Chapter Nineteen

Multimedia Dickens

Teaching Language and Illustration through the Makerspace

Elizabeth M. Henley and Susan E. Cook

BACKGROUND

This project was developed for Susan's college-level senior seminar on British Literature and Visual Culture and asked students to create their own visual representations of scenes in a Charles Dickens novel using technologies housed in our university's makerspace. Dickens is famous for his lively and capacious language, but the illustrations that accompanied his works are also central to his fiction. Students were assigned to create a visual representation of *Great Expectations*, one of only two novels Dickens did not initially publish with illustrations. The assignment asked students to think about Dickens's language deeply in order to craft a successful visualization, to apply what they learned about the illustrated novel to more contemporary technologies, and to practice using technologies that are typically reserved for STEM disciplines in order to trace similarities and differences between humanities and science applications. The project's goals, in other words, were to break down barriers: barriers between critical discussions of Dickens's language and the illustrations, barriers many twenty-first-century college students encounter when faced with centuries-old literature, and barriers between disciplines within the academy.

The class spent four weeks reading and discussing works by Victorian author Charles Dickens, alongside accompanying illustrations and critical articles. The class read *Great Expectations* and discussed ways the novel negotiates visual culture. After these discussions, Liz came to the class and introduced the makerspace project. This project asked students to use the makerspace on campus to create a twenty-first-century visual representation based on *Great Expectations*—an illustration, of sorts. Students had part of two class periods—amounting to around two hours—to start their work at the makerspace, with the understanding that they would then need to schedule a time to return and complete their projects. In addition to creating an object, the project asked students to generate a three-page paper describing their project, their thought process while generating the project, and a defense of its relevance to the course. Students were asked to address pointed questions in their papers about their plan: their choice of technology; the way they saw their project as relevant to Dickens,

Great Expectations, and illustration; and how they understood their project as an adaptation of Dickens's language.

Students used the 3D printers, laser engraver and cutter, embroidery machine, and graphic tables in our college campus's makerspace. Due to the range of technologies available at the makerspace and the large degree of creative latitude afforded to them by this project, students produced a wide range of projects (see figure 19.1), some illustrating a specific scene in the novel and others more expansively "illustrating" broader motifs, objects, or characters.

Figure 19.1. Projects created by students. *Elizabeth Henley*

SUPPLIES

- technologies in the makerspace, including 3D printers, laser engraver/cutter, embroidery machine, graphic tables (project was open-ended, so students could pick what they wanted to work with)
- materials for their chosen technology. Some materials, such as the filament for the 3D printers and thread for the embroidery machine, were supplied by the makerspace and available to any student using the space. Other materials, such as a chalkboard to engrave or fabric to embroider, were provided by the student.

INSTRUCTIONS

1. Guide students through an analysis of *Great Expectations* and ask them to decide how they would create a visual accompaniment to the text using the makerspace.
2. Have students double-check with the faculty member partnering on the project and the makerspace staff to make sure their idea can be accomplished given technological and time constraints.
3. Show students how to use their selected makerspace technology, providing safety information for the specific technology as well as information about types of materials.

4. Work with students as they create their visual object.
5. Ask students to write a thoughtful paper in which they address the following:
   - What was your plan from the start, and how did it go? What went well and what was more difficult?
   - Why did you pick the technology you picked, and how does it relate to *Great Expectations*?
   - How does your project connect to Dickens's language?
   - Why did you pick this portion of the text to render in visual form?
   - Does your project relate to illustration—and why/why not?
   - How is your object distinct from an illustration—how does this do something an illustration cannot do?

TIPS/SUGGESTIONS/CAUTIONS

- Provide several examples of items that can be made in the makerspace to spark ideas for students who have never seen these technologies before.
- Request staff be on hand to assist students with their projects.
- Push students out of their comfort zones. Some of them initially generated very basic ideas and needed encouragement to go further.
- Make sure to allot time for students to start their projects during class time and then enough time outside of class for them to complete the projects. This is particularly important if multiple students want to use a limited technology.

FEEDBACK/REFLECTIONS

Most students found themselves thinking intently about the nature of Victorian illustration as they worked on their own twenty-first-century multimedia illustrative pieces. Students carefully considered which type of makerspace technology to use. As one wrote, "I specifically wanted to use the engraver . . . because . . . a novel is engraved to an extent. For example, the ink is 'engraved' onto the page." Students also found value in the "physical interaction" element of this assignment, one writing that this "allows one to better appreciate the world of the text."

The majority of the students in this class had never visited the makerspace before nor had even thought about using it. As one individual noted with surprise, "A student doesn't necessarily need to know a ton about computers or technology to make an awesome project in the makerspace." Students reportedly felt that the assignment helped demystify technology—thus helping to break down some of the barriers that exist between fields of study.

Making material matter—in this case, by materializing it visually—is a powerful methodological strategy for approaching Dickens's language. Dickens's fondness for technological innovation makes his writing a particularly appropriate test case for techniques of reading and seeing anew.

Chapter Twenty

Sharing a Common Thread

Quilting Projects in the Makerspace

Christine Keenan

BACKGROUND

Don't be intimidated to take on quilting even if you have never done it. It does not need to be complicated; it only needs to be finished! This project requires basic straight-stitch sewing skills. Start simple. Each quilt you make will bring new learning opportunities. Women have worked alongside each other hand stitching and sharing stories for hundreds of years without technology. We now have electronic sewing machines parked beside laser engravers and 3D printers that speed up the assembly. You've got this.

This project was developed when a group from the Women's Center came to the makerspace looking for a project that was fun and collaborative and had a feminist theme. We decided to create quilt blocks to be embellished to reflect messages of community, inclusiveness, and empowerment. The project was broken into three distinct pieces: creating the blocks, making blocks available to embellish using fabric markers, and then finally putting it all together.

There are infinite ways to go about making a quilt; this is one simple way. One consideration in the planning stage is to decide how many people will be involved in the project. This will play a factor in how tasks can be broken down. Will one or two people be constructing blocks with fifty people just signing them? Will another group put it together? How big would you like your quilt to be? For the purpose of walking you through this project, the directions here will provide the steps to complete a wall size quilt with twenty-five blocks with a finished size of approximately 38 inches × 38 inches. If you desire a larger quilt, you can either make more blocks or make each block larger.

SUPPLIES/EQUIPMENT

- 2.5 yards of muslin for the center of blocks and back of quilt
- 1 yard of contrasting fabric (recommend 100 percent cotton)
- packaged crib-sized batting (will be approximately 45 feet × 60 feet)
- thread

- rotary cutter and acrylic ruler and mat—if you are not familiar with how to use these tools, YouTube will be quite helpful. Cutting will be easier and more accurate.
- fabric markers
- sewing machine
- iron

A quilt is made of a series of individual blocks arranged into a particular pattern. The quilt "top" is then layered with batting and a backing fabric and stitched together. We will start by making the blocks.

INSTRUCTIONS

Creating blocks

1. Cut five (6-inch) strips from the muslin; then cut each of these strips perpendicular to create twenty-five (6-inch) squares—it doesn't hurt to have extras!
2. Cut seven (3.5-inch) strips from the contrast fabric; set aside four strips to be used for the border.
3. Using the remaining strips, cut fifty (3.5-inch) squares
4. With a straight edge, draw a diagonal line across each 3.5 square, as seen in figure 20.1, step A.
5. With the right sides of the fabric facing each other, line up the small square on top of the larger square as shown in figure 20.1, step B.

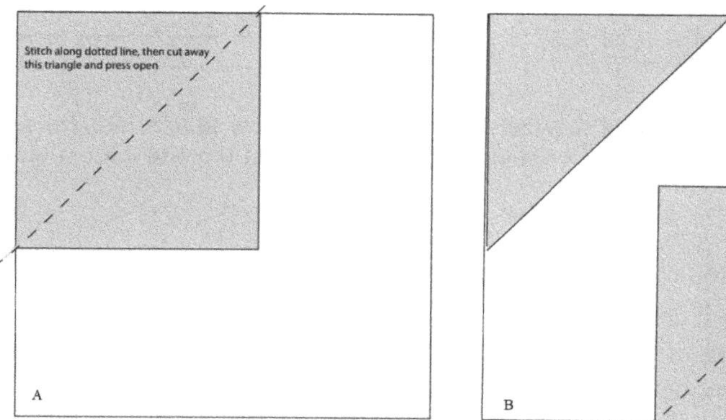

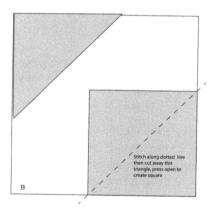

Figure 20.1. Steps of making quilt squares: (A) Stich along dotted line, then cut away this triangle and press open. (B) Stich along dotted line, then cut away this triangle, press open to create square. *Christine Keenan*

6. Sew along the drawn line; then cut away the top triangle.
7. Press open.
8. Line up another small square on the opposite corner; sew, trim, and press.
9. You made your first block!
10. Now repeat to make the remaining blocks.

Decorating Blocks

You are now ready to embellish your blocks! Instruct people not to write to the edge. Allow a half-inch so their sentiment will not be cut off when sewing them together. If someone has difficulty writing on the fabric, you can iron a piece of freezer paper on the back of the block to give it stability. It will peel right off and can be reused.

Putting It All Together

1. Arrange the blocks in a pleasing manner with contrasting triangles meeting in the center.
2. With the right sides facing each other, sew blocks together into rows and then sew the rows together. See figure 20.2, step D.

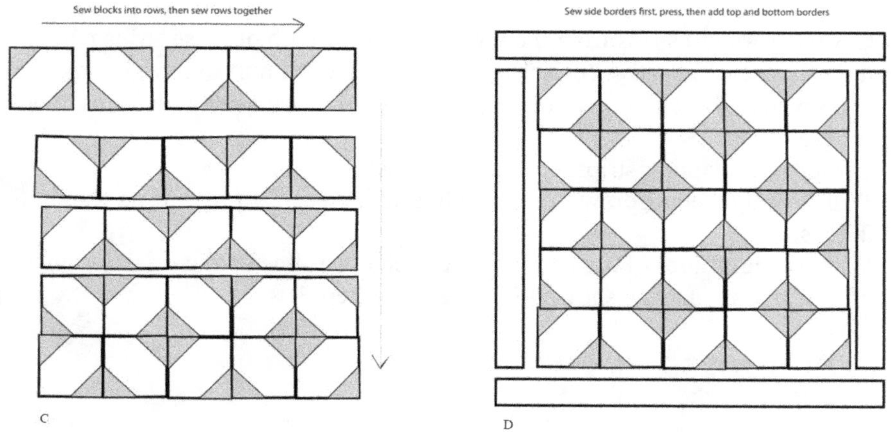

Figure 20.2. Steps of putting together quilt squares: (C) Sew blocks into rows, then sew rows together. (D) Sew side borders first, press, then add top and bottom borders. *Christine Keenan*

3. Measure the length of your quilt; then cut two of the 5-inch strips the same size.
4. Sew a strip to each side of the quilt; then press open.
5. Measure the width of the quilt and cut the remaining two 5-inch strips to size.
6. Sew to the top and bottom of the quilt and press the entire quilt well.
7. Spread the batting out and lay the backing fabric on top.
8. Lay the completed quilt top face down on the backing fabric and pin around the edge of the quilt.
9. Sew around the entire edge of the quilt, being careful to sew through all three layers and leave a 12-inch opening.
10. Trim away excess fabric and batting.
11. Now the fun part, reach your hand in between the backing and quilt top, grab the opposite side of the quilt and then gently turn it right side facing out, just like a pillowcase.

12. Finishing: there are many methods to finish a quilt, but again, we are keeping it simple. Hand stitch the opening; then tack the quilt together either by hand using a curved needle or by sewing machine.
13. Ta-da! You did it!

Figure 20.3. Finished quilt project. ***Christine Keenan***

FEEDBACK/REFLECTIONS

This very versatile project can be adapted to make a pillow with as few as four blocks or expanded into a king-size quilt by adding blocks. As an individual project, I created a stack of quilt squares to bring to Japan. During my month-long visit as a cultural exchange chaperone, I asked people to sign my blocks and then sewed them together when I returned home to create a memorable souvenir! (See figure 20.3.)

Contacting a local quilting guild might be helpful if you are interested in expanding your knowledge or looking to kick things up a notch. May the common threads that bring you together be threads of joy and laughter.

Chapter Twenty-One

Building a Simple Oscillator and Engaging Makers through the Building of Lunetta Electronic Music Instruments

David Luftig

BACKGROUND

This chapter provides instruction regarding (1) how to build a very simple tactile noise machine and (2) how to use that simple noise machine as a catalyst to engage makers to further create a complex and highly personalized electronic musical instrument.

This project details a very simple two-voice oscillator that is controlled by light-dependent resistors, which means that the device will squeak and warble as it is exposed to varying degrees of light (such as waving your hand over the sensor). Although many tinkerers have experimented with using the CD40106 integrated circuit as a noise source, this particular project was designed, in large part, based on the open-source materials provided by "Bbob" Drake[1] and the Electro-Music.com[2] Lunetta forums.

While this particular project is simple in its design, the appeal of this project is that (1) it's an easy build, (2) it utilizes cheap and plentiful components, (3) it allows skills to be scaffolded in an engaging way, and (4) it provides some insight into the history of electronic music.

Although this noise machine can be used as a stand-alone device, the true intention is to introduce makers to building modular music circuits. This simple oscillator can serve as the first building block in creating a more complex, customizable electronic instrument. By focusing on creating small music circuits that can be easily chained together, the makerspace can provide a unique programming opportunity that draws makers back to the space.

Instruments like the one described may be called CMOS synthesizers or simply noise boxes, but those familiar with the history of DIY musical electronics call them Lunettas. Today, Lunettas have become synonymous with low-cost logic ICs and improvisational beeps, squeals, drones, and glitches.

Lunettas date back to the late 1960s when integrated circuits (IC) began to be manufactured cheaply and abundantly. Although many artists and tinkerers utilized these cheap processors to make sound machines, it was Stanley Lunetta who really made his mark with such devices. Stanley Lunetta was a professional jazz and classical percussionist, an audio and visual artist, and a stalwart of the West Coast United States Avant Garde scene for nearly fifty years.[3]

Stanley observed that if a musician was more interested in creating spontaneous soundscapes instead of playing musical scales, musical instruments could be built cheaply and easily. Stanley called these early machines "Moosack Machines 4," and he taught building skills to others.[4] To Stanley's objections, those other builders started calling their machines Lunettas, and the name has stuck.

Although Stanley Lunetta focused much of his design on unique tactile inputs (like dependent resistors and potentiometers), some of these machines were voltage controlled, which meant functions, such as pitch, could be automated. Although the oscillator that we are building in this chapter is not voltage controlled (see figure 21.1), it can be implemented into a Lunetta instrument as a stand-alone oscillator or patched into a more complex voltage-controlled oscillator to create frequency modulation effects.

The rest of this chapter will detail how to build a noise source with two separate sounds that can be controlled by adjusting the amount of light received by the input sensors.

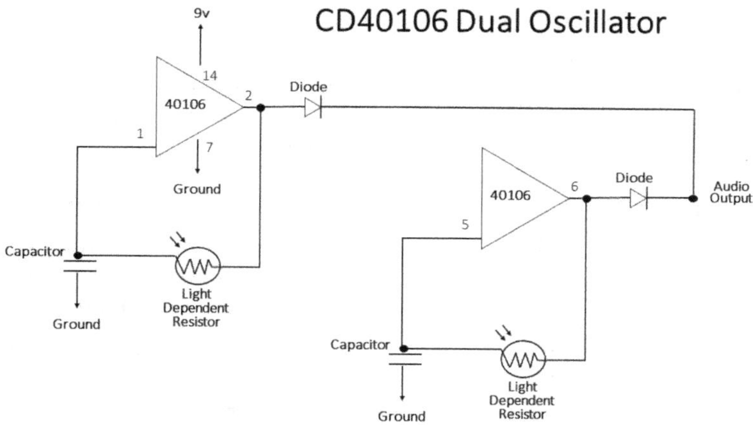

Figure 21.1. CD40106 Dual Oscillator diagram of layout. ***David Luftig***

For a picture of the completed project with the parts labeled, see figure 21.2.

SUPPLIES

- 1 × CD 40106 DIP integrated circuit (IC)
- 1 × 14 pin DIP IC Socket
- 1 × .1uf electrolytic capacitors*
- 1 × .01 capacitor (any type)*

  *The different size capacitors will give you different base pitches. A .1uf capacitor will provide more percussive and bass sounds while a .01 capacitor will provide higher pitches.

- 2 × diodes (any diode should do; 1N4148 are typically easy to find and cheap)
- 2 × light-dependent resistors
- 1 × audio/output jack
- small amount of wire (I use 22–24 AWG stranded wire)
- 1 × 9v battery and 9v battery clips (if powering by battery)
- 1 × circuit or breadboard if the maker chooses to build using a circuit board

INSTRUCTIONS

1. On your circuit board, place the 14 pin IC socket so it straddles the middle area (sometimes called the "gutter") of your breadboard. The indent of the chip/socket needs to be facing left. On the circuit board, in this configuration, the very top row will be the 9v power source and the very bottom row will be the ground.
2. Connect a .01uf capacitor between pin 1 of the IC and the ground row. Connect a .1uf capacitor between pin 5 of the IC and the ground row. If you are using an electrolytic capacitor for your .1uf capacitor, make sure that the "–" or striped side faces the ground. Go ahead and experiment with capacitor sizes to get different pitches.
3. Connect a diode from pin 2 and pin 6 of the IC to a vacant row on the circuit or breadboard. Make sure the stripe on the diode is on the side that faces that blank row. These diodes serve as a kind of one-way street so the two audio outputs generated by our IC will be mixed together. Make sure the two ends of the diodes touch. This will be your audio output connection.
4. Attach a light-dependent resistor (LDR) so it connects to the IC's pin 1 and pin 2. Attach the other LDR to one end so it connects to pin 5 and pin 6. If you are connecting the photo resistors to a metal panel, make sure that the metal on the resistors legs and the panel are not touching the panel (or each other). If you don't want to use LDR, you can use 100K potentiometers or any other tactile input you can think of. Experiment!
5. Connect pin 14 of the IC to the positive end of the power source (on top of our breadboard). Connect Pin 7 of our IC to the ground section.

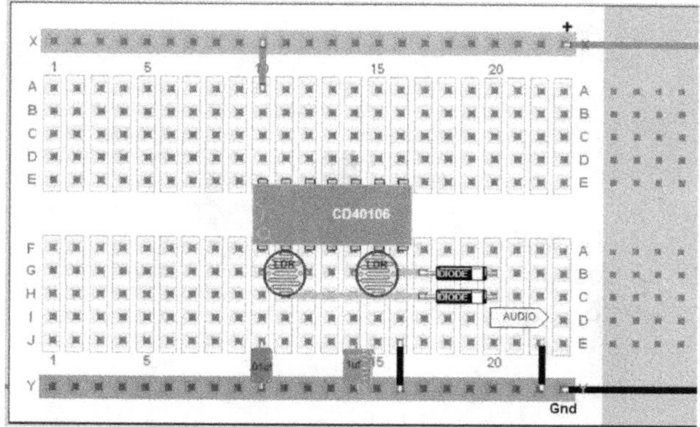

Figure 21.2. Completed circuit on a virtual broadboard. ***David Luftig***

6. There are multiple connections for this step.
   a. Connect your audio jack or output jack to the junction of the two diodes (see row 20 on the breadboard of Step 6). If you are using an audio output jack, you can connect the ground of that jack to the ground section of the breadboard.
   b. Connect your power or battery clips so the + end goes to the top of the breadboard and the ground goes to the bottom section of the breadboard.
   c. Plug the battery in and patch the audio output to your amp. Be careful: the circuit can be loud!

Note: the CD40106 can actually be used to build six separate oscillators! We're just using pins 1 and 2 and 5 and 6 for simplicity. That said, you can add capacitors and resistors to pins 3 and 4, 8 and 9, 10 and 11, and 12 and 13 in the way we described to get more oscillators.

REFLECTIONS

This project has the ability to be the first block of a larger electronic music system and can be powered either by batteries or through a power adapter. The builder can start off using batteries and utilize a more sustainable power supply as they add more modules to their instrument. If the builder wants to chain a lot of projects together, it might be best to use a power source that doesn't have to be periodically replaced like a battery. That said, the project detailed in this chapter can easily run off a single 9v battery. If the maker is a novice, it is important that they get assistance with utilizing any power supply that plugs into an electrical outlet.

NOTES

1. Bbob Drake, "40106 Hex Oscillator Workshop Instructions," accessed July 29, 1019, www.fluxmonkey.com/pcbDocs/40106_files/Flxmnky_40106HexOscillator.pdf.
2. Electro-Music, "Lunettas - circuits inspired by Stanley Lunetta," last modified October 1, 2019, electro-music.com/forum/forum-160.html.
3. Marcus Crowder, "Stanley Lunetta was a legendary Sacramento Percussionist," *The Sacramento Bee*, March 10, 2016, www.sacbee.com/entertainment/arts-culture/article65297502.html.
4. Stanley Lunetta, "Moosack machine," in *Music of the Avant-Garde, 1963–1973*, eds. Larry Austin and Douglas Kahn (Los Angeles: University of California Press, 2011), 279–81.

Chapter Twenty-Two

Design, Cut, Etch

Using Vinyl Cutters to Create Custom Etched Glass

Jessica Martinez and Courtney Pace

BACKGROUND

The University of Idaho is the state's land-grant institution, focusing on outreach and education for all Idaho residents. Located in Moscow, Idaho, the residential campus is home to the UI Library, the largest in the state, serving students, staff, faculty, and the surrounding community. Founded in 2016, the Making, Innovating, and Learning Laboratory (MILL) is the UI Library's premier makerspace, dedicated to collaborative learning and featuring many maker tools that are available for both student and community use.

One of these maker tools is the Silhouette Cameo vinyl cutter, which acts as a versatile piece of machinery. It can cut vinyl, cardstock, and a variety of other materials. The most frequent use of this machine is cutting vinyl; this creates custom stickers that are very popular with all visitors to the MILL. Vinyl decals can be affixed to laptops, water bottles, cars, and most smooth surfaces. Once a vinyl decal is created, this can serve as a launchpad for many other different projects. For example, with a vinyl decal and a little glass-etching cream, patrons can create beautiful, custom-designed glassware.

The MILL takes a scaffolded approach to teaching glass-etching workshops: first teaching how to use the vinyl cutter and software and then how to apply those skills to the glass-etching process. Because this is a hands-on activity that requires learning different softwares and skills as well as sharing resources, glass-etching workshops in the MILL are limited to ten people per instructor. Patrons leave having familiarized themselves with the makerspace and also having learned two skills that boost their confidence in their creativity and technical proficiency. To see a finished product and all the supplies needed for this project, see figure 22.1.

SUPPLIES

- vinyl cutter and appropriate blades (e.g., Silhouette Cameo)
- computer and appropriate software (www.silhouetteamerica.com/software)
- adhesive-backed vinyl (e.g., EZ Craft USA)

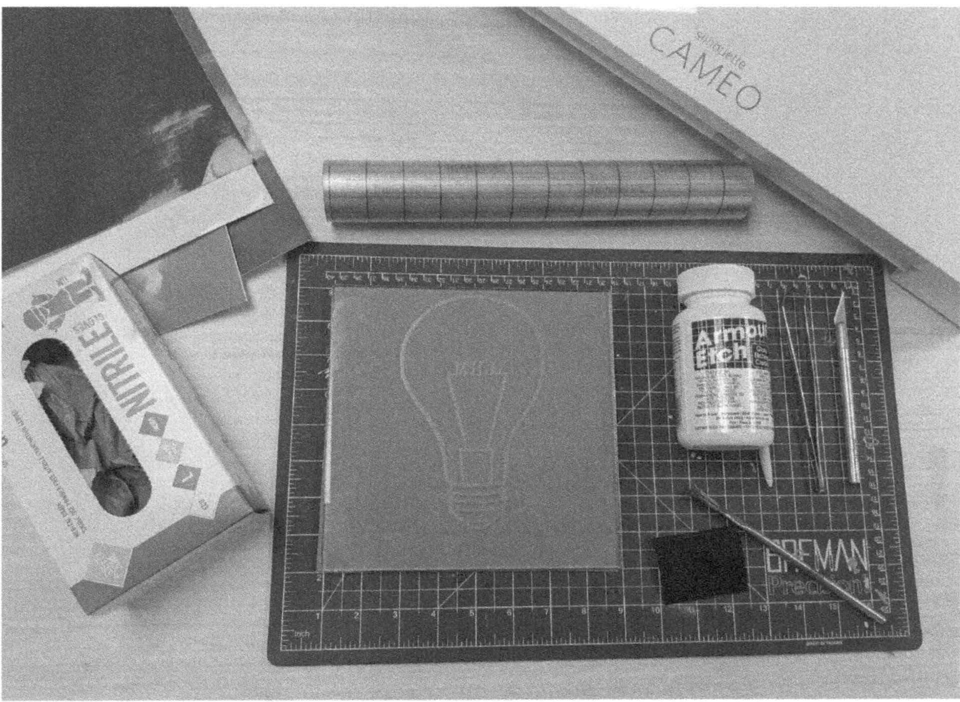

Figure 22.1. Finished project and supplies. ***Jessica Martinez***

- transfer paper (e.g., TransferRite)
- weeding tools (tweezers, craft blade, scraping tool)
- glass-etching cream (e.g., Armour Etch)
- nitrile/safety gloves
- acid brushes
- paper towels
- water access

Note: Various brands of vinyl cutters, transfer paper, and glass-etching cream exist.

INSTRUCTIONS

1. To start designing, download Silhouette Studio (see supplies list for link).
2. Design the etching using Silhouette Studio. Silhouette Studio uses a trace function, allowing users to import and replicate a variety of images and designs. The Silhouette Studio tutorial video is a great resource for design assistance: www.youtube.com/watch?v=zJZTW0E_dqQ.
3. Once the design is complete (see figure 22.2), load a piece of vinyl onto the Silhouette Cameo cut mat. Ensure the blade and cut settings are on the recommended

setting for the respective vinyl. For assistance, visit www.youtube.com/watch?v=SNZ1MvT0zUc.

Figure 22.2. Silhouette Studio design software screen. ***Jessica Martinez***

4. After the design has been cut into the vinyl, use weeding tools (such as tweezers and craft blades) to peel out the design. This will leave behind a stencil (see figure 22.3).

Figure 22.3. Participant removing excess vinyl from image. ***Jessica Martinez***

5. Cut a piece of transfer paper large enough to cover the stencil. Use a scraping tool to ensure the transfer paper sticks to the stencil.
6. Peel the transfer paper from the wax paper backing; the stencil should adhere to the transfer paper, adhesive side facing out. Apply the transfer paper and stencil to a clean glass.
7. Use the scraping tool to remove any air bubbles or wrinkles, and remove the transfer paper. The stencil will be left behind on the glass.
8. Use an acid brush to apply a thick layer of glass-etching cream over the stencil; take care to stay within the edges of the stencil as the cream will immediately start to etch the glass (see figure 22.4).

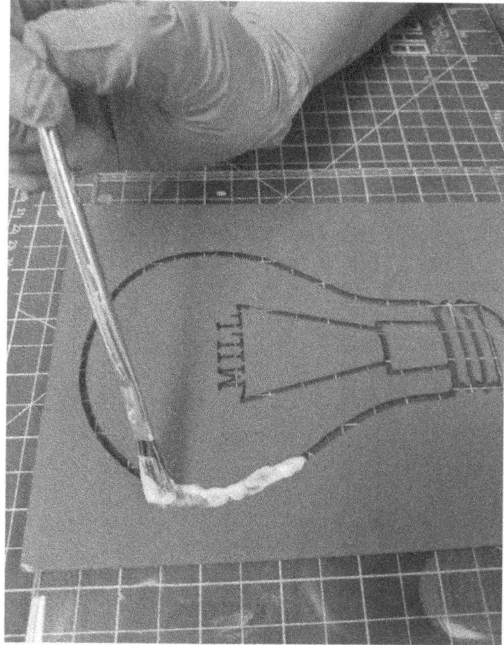

Figure 22.4. Participant applying glass etching cream to stencil. ***Jessica Martinez***

9. Let the project sit for ten minutes. Use an acid brush to scrape excess cream back into the armor etch jar.
10. Rinse the project with water and dry thoroughly; remove stencil.

TIPS/SUGGESTIONS/CAUTIONS

- This workshop is most appropriate for those ages ten and up.
- Typically, both skills can be learned and applied in less than one hour.
- Have patrons bring in their own glass, but provide the vinyl, transfer paper, and glass-etching cream.

- When designing the stencil, create the design within a larger box in Silhouette Studio. This will make applying the stencil easier.
- Don't make your design too intricate (such as script- or calligraphy-based designs).
- Measure twice; cut once!
- Rubbing alcohol acts as a quick and effective glass cleaner.
- Teach this activity in a well-ventilated area and wear safety gloves while applying the glass-etching cream to ensure safety.

FEEDBACK/REFLECTIONS

Participant feedback has been consistently positive; specifically, participants felt the project acts as an introduction to makerspaces. The scaffolded organization of the project allows users to build skills that apply to multiple projects, building confidence in users' ability to create. This project has been used for glass ornament etching workshops, Valentine's workshops, and other gift-giving themed workshops. Vinyl cutting and glass etching are also popular for de-stressing sessions during stressful times of the semester on campus at the University of Idaho. The visualization skills required for this project allow users to better develop an understanding of how 2D concepts can translate into 3D designs. This understanding gives patrons a foundation, which makes learning easier, leading to an overall increase in patronage and interest in projects.

Chapter Twenty-Three

Laser-Cut Snowflake Workshop

Introducing Design and Fabrication to Makerspace Beginners

Kelsey Sheaffer

BACKGROUND

The Laser-Cut Snowflake Workshop introduces makerspace beginners to design software and fabrication using a laser machine. Designed in part as outreach to meet and integrate new members of the community, the workshop has become a popular activity around the winter holidays. This workshop is accessible even for makerspaces without extensive funding for programming, as a workshop for ten to fifteen participants can cost as little as $30 for a single sheet of acrylic.

The project was originally developed as a collaboration between a university makerspace and a library-based digital media design center. The activity is intentionally short and extremely specific to alleviate anxiety stemming from the perception of makerspace and design technology as difficult or inaccessible. Many groups within the university have attended or expressed interest in the activity, including students, faculty, and staff.

SUPPLIES

- laserable acrylic, thickness dependent on machine capabilities but generally between $^1/_8$ inch and $^1/_4$ inch, 4 inches × 4 inches for each participant you anticipate
- string to hang ornament
- computers with Adobe Illustrator or Inkscape

INSTRUCTIONS

Introducing the Software

1. Each participant should bring or be provided a laptop with the vector software installed. Open the vector software (recommended: Adobe Illustrator or Inkscape). Introduce vector and raster graphic types. Raster images, like digital photographs,

consist of small dots called pixels and can be engraved by the laser machine like a printer. Vector lines are composed of mathematical formulas and are generally used to cut lines using the laser. This project will create a shape using vector lines, which the laser will then cut.

2. Create a new 4-inch × 4-inch workspace.
3. Introduce the software workstation and tools.

Designing the Snowflake

1. Create an approximately 1-inch diameter circle in the middle of the workspace, which will be the center of the snowflake. Introduce the concepts of stroke and fill and show how the vector lines constitute the shapes. Explain that the laser will cut any line (stroke) of a particular width. At the end of the project, we will have a series of lines that we will join together, which the laser will cut.
2. Use the rounded rectangle tool to create a long, skinny rectangle radiating from the top of the circle, which will be the first rib.
3. Use the rounded rectangle tool to create a small, skinny rectangle, which will be a feather on the first rib. Rotate the feather to be at a 45-degree angle from the rib and place radiating out from the rib.
4. Select the small rectangle and then copy and paste to create additional feathers.
5. To create the symmetry of the rib, holding down the shift key, select all of the feathers and then copy and paste. Reflect the feathers across the vertical axis (in Illustrator: Object > Transform > Reflect > Vertical). See figure 23.1.

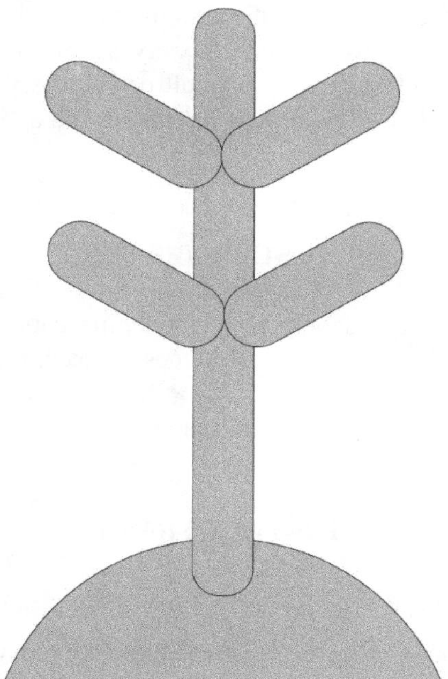

Figure 23.1. Computer design of snowflake creation. ***Kelsey Sheaffer***

6. Pause to allow participants to design their first rib. Remind them that they can use any shapes or lines but to maintain symmetry. It can be helpful to display images of snowflakes on the screen. Also remind them to not make any of the elements too narrow or small.
7. Explain how to cut shapes out of shapes. Place a smaller circle within the larger center circle; select both shapes and then subtract (in Illustrator: Window > Pathfinder > Shape Modes > Remove Front).
8. When the rib is completed, select all of the shapes of the rib (excluding the center circle) and merge the paths (in Illustrator: Window > Pathfinder > Pathfinders > Merge).
9. Select the rib; then copy and paste. Rotate the rib 90 degrees. Repeat; rotate the rib 180 degrees and 270 degrees. Repeat at 45-degree angles or create a new minor rib.
10. To create the ornament holder, add a new ring (a circle within a circle) at the top of one rib. Be particularly careful here to not make the ring too small.
11. Select all of the shapes and join all of the paths (In Illustrator: Window > Pathfinder > Pathfinders > Merge).
12. For ease with the laser cutter, all of the snowflakes should be shared with the instructor to compile into one file. Have the participants add their snowflake to a Google Drive folder or e-mail the file.

Introducing the Laser Cutter/Engraver

1. While one instructor introduces the laser cutter, another instructor puts all of the snowflakes into one workspace.
2. Explain the safety precautions for the laser cutter.
3. Explain the workflow of the laser cutter: how to focus; introduce speed, power, and frequency; and select laser material preferences.
4. After the orientation to the machine, the instructor starts laser cutting the snowflake ornaments.
5. While the laser runs, the participants are given a tour of the makerspace. See figure 23.2.

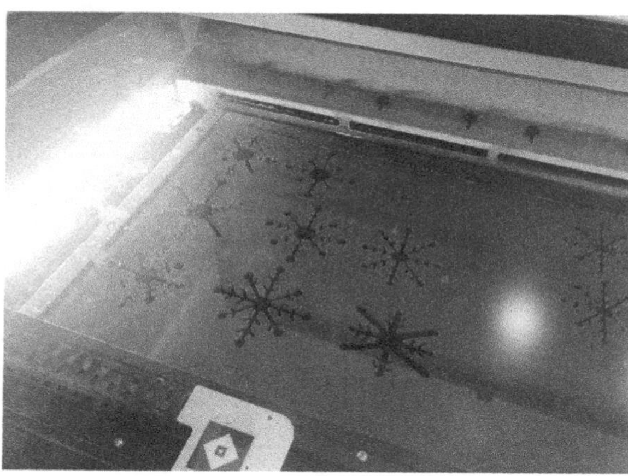

Figure 23.2. Laser cutting snowflakes. ***Kelsey Shaeffer***

TIPS/SUGGESTIONS/CAUTIONS

The workshop can be taught using any vector-based software. The most common paid program is Adobe Illustrator and the most common free program is Inkscape. E-mail the participants before the workshop with instructions to download the software on their computer before the workshop.

Makerspaces generally have training procedures specific to their laser cutter/engraver. Decide whether you want to conduct a full training session on the machine, so that each participant will be authorized to use the machine after the workshop, or whether you are going to provide a quicker introduction to the machine. This will make a difference in timing. For a brief introduction and fewer than ten participants, the workshop can take 1.5 hours, with 45 minutes for each part (designing and fabricating).

FEEDBACK/REFLECTIONS

Response to the activity has been overwhelmingly positive. Participants liked having a specific project that allowed them to be creative but also generated a tangible object. We've found that people new to the makerspace have a hard time conceptualizing possible projects, but this workshop lets new participants imagine the possibilities of the space. The workshop works well to form an understanding of multileveled design and fabrication, on a beginner scale. See figure 23.3.

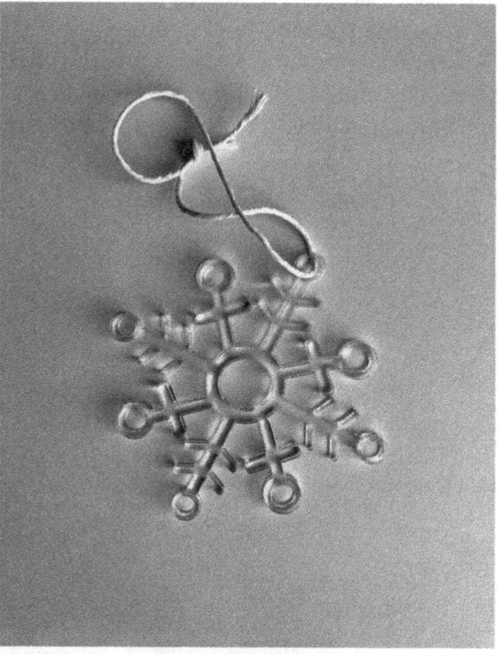

Figure 23.3. Finished snowflake project. *Kelsey Shaeffer*

Chapter Twenty-Four

Why Don't You Make Me?

Laser Cutting a Statue/Bust

Michael Price

BACKGROUND

As a librarian at the University of Montevallo, working alongside students, I developed a makerspace project in a Digital Fabrication art class, which included the use of a 3D scanner, manipulation of a 3D file, and a laser cutter. First, the students used the 3D scanner to capture the bust of an individual. Once an individual is scanned, an OBJ (object file) is created. Next, students learned how to manipulate their file using Rhino, a commercial 3D computer graphics software. This enabled the students to see their scan in four dimensions: left, right, top, and perspective. The software enables them to add or subtract components of their scan and allows the scanned image to be sliced into layers. Once the file had been manipulated to their satisfaction, the students created the object with a Glowforge laser cutter.

This project was possible due to a collaborative purchase of the Glowforge. I wrote a grant for the library's portion, and we received additional funds from the art department. The Glowforge was implemented during the spring and May terms of 2019. The design being discussed in the instructions below was an abstract interpretation of a sculpture project created by a student in this class. Other students in the class used 3D printing or the CNC machine for their projects. This collaboration between the library and Digital Fabrication class was a successful use of our makerspace.

SUPPLIES

- iPad Mini 4
- Structure Sensor 3D scanner
- Glowforge laser cutter
- Rhino design software
- Adobe Illustrator
- scissors or fabric cutter
- fabric cutting mat (optional)
- ¼-inch felted fabric (any color)

- painters tape
- spray glue or super glue

INSTRUCTIONS

1. Scan the individual with the Structure iPad and Scan Software. See figure 24.1.

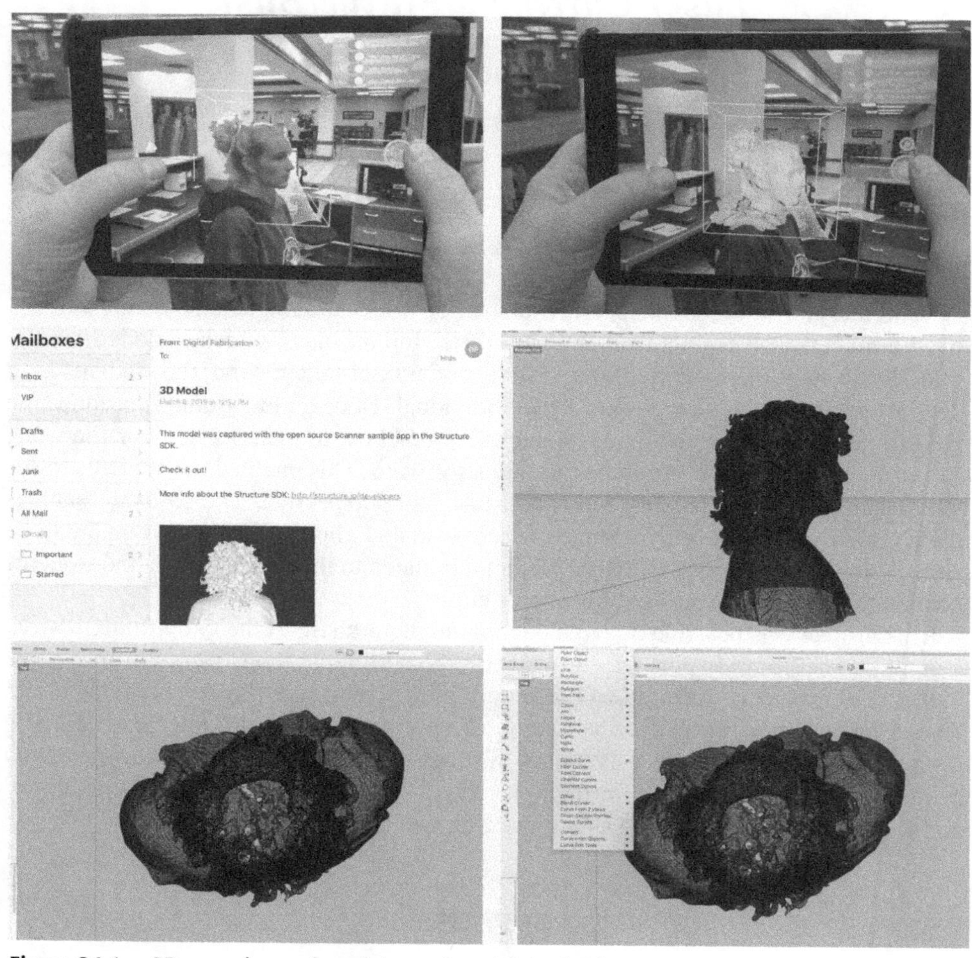

Figure 24.1. 3D scanning and model creation. ***Michael Price***

2. E-mail the scan to the student.
3. Launch Rhino CAD software and import the file. Switch to Top.
4. Using the Curve Tools in Rhino, select Contour and then the image can be sliced in any direction and in multiple layers. The scan of the student project was sliced into 236 layers. See figure 24.2.

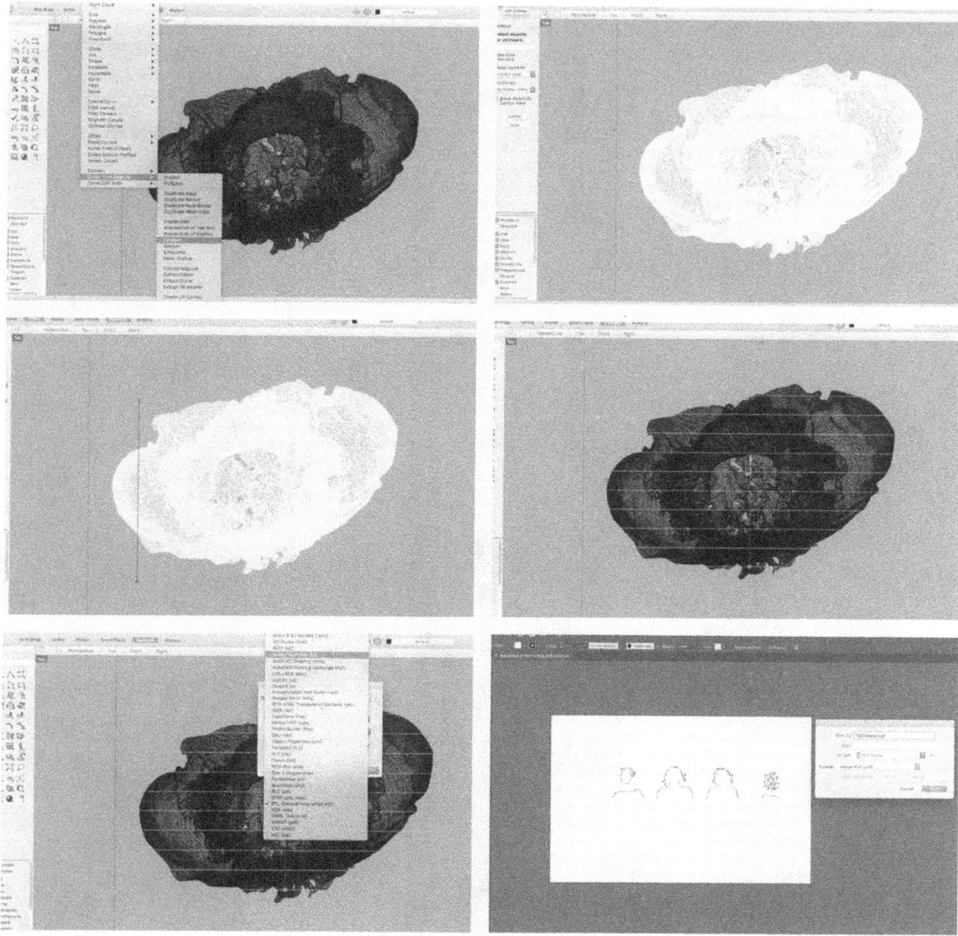

Figure 24.2. Rhino CAD software used to slice 3D model. ***Michael Price***

5. Resize your object. When imported, it shows up as a 0.01mm OBJ file. Scale up to larger size (e.g., 3mm) so that when it is exported you are able to see the file.
6. Start by creating a line with two points in the Contour setting.
7. Rhino then generates a corresponding calculation that tells you how large the segments will be in each layer and reveals the slices.
8. Export layer(s) as Adobe Illustrator file.
9. Launch Illustrator and convert to a PDF.
10. The PDF file is uploaded to the cloud server of the Glowforge laser cutter.
11. Input the settings for power and speed of the laser. These will vary depending on the material used.
12. Tape a piece of pre-cut felt on the inside of the laser cutter. Once the felt is in place, tap the Print button on the Glowforge and the laser begins the cutting process.
13. After printing, the pieces can be removed and glued to one another. See figure 24.3.

Figure 24.3. Use of Glowforge machine and finished project. ***Michael Price***

TIPS/SUGGESTIONS/CAUTIONS

- Make sure your measurements of your design are the same across the software you are using. Rhino can be saved in mm or inches. That can affect how you save your file in Illustrator and, in turn, change the cut on the Glowforge.
- Tape down your felted material. Most of the time materials used in the laser cutter are woods and plastics, and they will adhere correctly on the print bed. Felt (or any soft material) will move around and affect the cut due to the blower that ventilates the burning smell of materials being etched or cut.
- On average each layer would take ten to twenty-five seconds depending on the surface size of the slice being cut at the time. The nose area took eight seconds compared to one of the pieces located near the center of the head taking eighteen seconds to cut. Using the average time multiplied by the number of pieces, the time

to make this entire structure was about fifty-nine hours in the lab. The student came in at different times to complete the cuts.

- If a laser cutter is not available, the templates created could be printed and cut by hand. Or if using a different material, a saw or Dremel cutting tool could also be used.

FEEDBACK/REFLECTIONS

The student that chose to use the felt material for their sculpture enjoyed the project but admitted that it took a very long time and wasted some material due to different types of felt used in the process. Materials are usually provided by the library or the class instruction lab fee, but something outside of the normal supply budget is purchased by each student and this became an expensive project. There was also a bit of trial and error. The laser cutter is a new device, and experimentation was taking place with speed settings and power settings of the device.

A student or patron would not necessarily need to have as many layers. This specific piece was created by a sculpture student that was experimenting with layer design within the Rhino software and the new laser cutter.

Chapter Twenty-Five

A Tale of Two Tortoises

How the Cline Library MakerLab Is Building Curriculum, Community, and Cohesive Service Design

Kathleen L. Schmand, Andrew See, and Bridget Rowan Wipf

BACKGROUND

Today's academic libraries are driven by innovation, technology, experiential learning, exploration, and collaboration. Serving as the center of college and university campuses, they strive to meet the multidisciplinary needs of students and faculty and lead new initiatives that drive research and student success. Northern Arizona University's Cline Library serves more than twenty-three thousand students on the Flagstaff campus and more than thirty-one thousand total enrollment statewide.

In 2016, Cline Library was awarded a Library Services and Technology Act (LSTA) grant by the Arizona State Library, administered by the Institute of Museum and Library Services. As a result, the MakerLab became the largest 3D-printing environment in northern Arizona also serving the regional community.

Our story of two tortoises begins with a local veterinarian inquiring about the MakerLab and 3D-printing capabilities. Daisy, a seventy-five-pound desert tortoise, was injured and needed assistance with her damaged shell. We confirmed that PLA (polylactic acid) filament was suitable for replicating tortoise shell pieces. A small team including Schmand, See, and David Van Ness, an NAU faculty member who is a 3D design expert, quickly traveled to the vet to see how the library could help. The team brought a 3D scanner (Skanect Pro mounted to an iPad Mini) to capture initial scans (see figure 25.1). Taking the damaged shell pieces with them, the team began the scanning process with a higher-resolution NextEngine 3D scanner.

Two weeks later, with final scans in hand, the prototyping process began. In July of 2018, Cline Library received another call from a tortoise owner about a damaged shell. The team gathered and met with Tim and his owner in the MakerLab. Tim was a 1.5-pound Mojave Desert tortoise whose shell had been chewed on by a puppy (see figure 25.2).

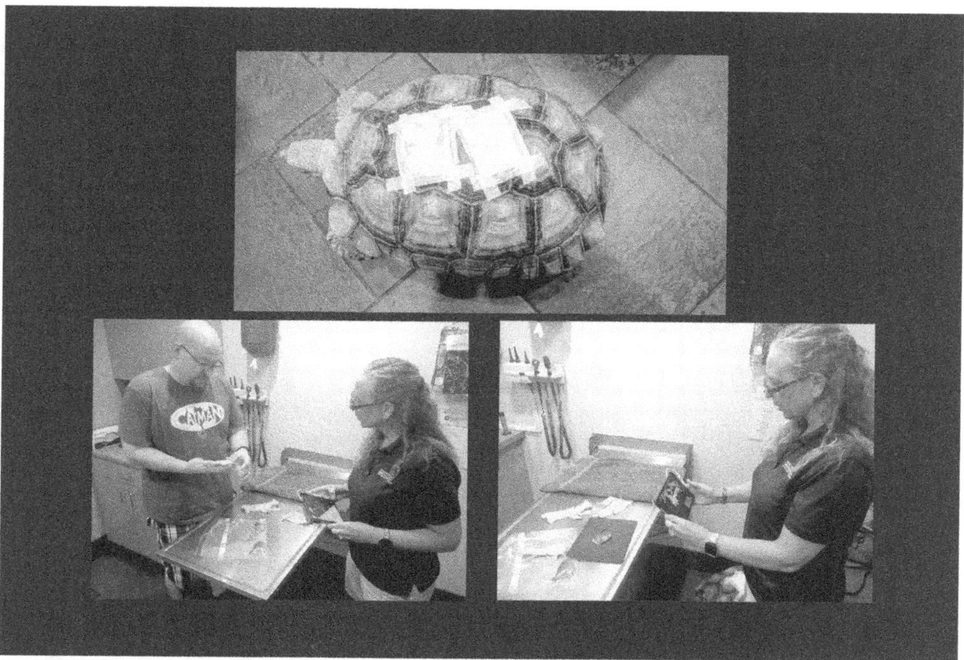

Figure 25.1. 3D scanning of damaged tortoise shell pieces. *Kathleen L. Schmand*

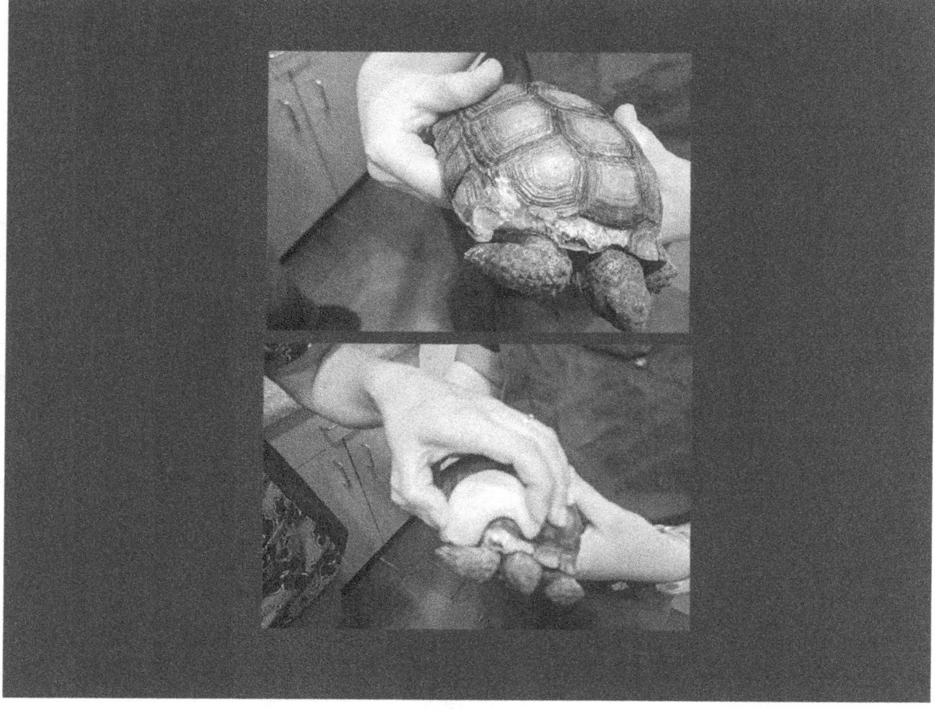

Figure 25.2. Tortoise shell with damage. *Kathleen L. Schmand*

Although we had two tortoises, both with shell damage, the approaches required were quite different. Daisy's injuries required a long-term solution, and there was a waiting period for the initial injuries to heal. Subsequently, significant design and prototyping of the shell pieces were involved. Tim's injuries required a more agile and creative response as his liver was exposed. Consequently, we had one shot at designing and printing a piece that might help Tim protect his liver and provide the time to recover.

SUPPLIES

- 3D printer compatible with PLA filament
- PLA filament
- high-resolution 3D scanners
- cardboard
- modeling clay
- Dremel
- sandpaper
- sterilization solution*
- surgical adhesive*
- UV protectant spray

*Administered by a veterinarian.

INSTRUCTIONS

1. Assess the case in consultation with a veterinarian; determine if the problem requires an immediate solution or if you have time to apply iterative design to the project.
2. 3D scan broken shell pieces if available. This is complicated with animals that are very mobile or with injuries in difficult-to-reach areas. Photographs and measurements of the injured area can help.
3. If immediate solutions are needed and you do not have access to the broken shell pieces, we recommend a simple molding of the shell using low-tech materials such as cardboard or modeling clay. Consult with the veterinarian to ensure that the materials used are non-toxic.
   a. Create a 3D model of the clay mold using the high-resolution 3D scanner.
4. Use 3D modeling software such as Meshmixer to modify the scan of the broken piece.
5. Print shell piece models with 20 to 30 percent infill and two to four shells. Make the model strong but not so rigid that it will crack.
6. Once printed, ensure sides and edges are smooth.
7. Return pieces to veterinarian for fitting and sterilization. Bring cardboard and molding clay as well as subtractive tools such as files and sandpaper for fine tuning and repeat steps 2 to 7 as needed (see figure 25.3).

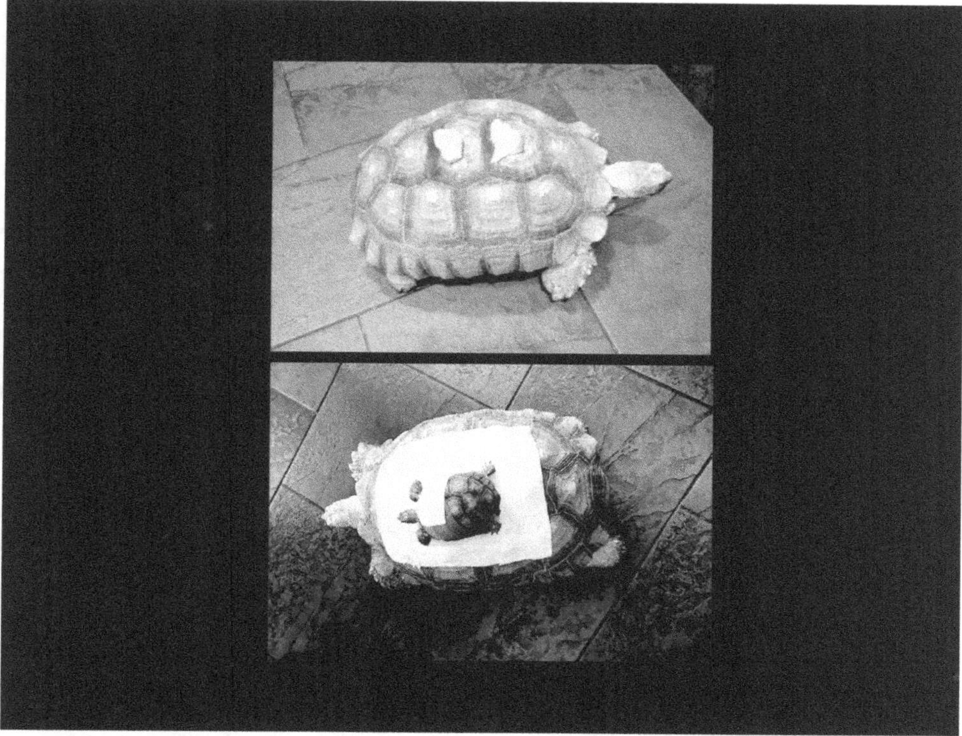

Figure 25.3. Tortoises with 3D-printed shell patches. *Kathleen L. Schmand*

TIPS/SUGGESTIONS/CAUTIONS

Annually, the MakerLab handles more than three thousand 3D prints, half of which are original designs. However, working with live animals of various sizes presented some new challenges. With Tim, we had no shell to scan, so it became a design guessing game using a series of photographs we took of the injured area. Additionally, we printed two possible sizes of the initial prototype for the veterinarian to choose from based on size and fit. We learned a week later from the owner that Tim was recovering at an unexpected pace and wouldn't need a shell replacement long term.

Be flexible and understand this won't be a one-size-fits-all fix. It is a learning experience for everyone involved. After creating a working prototype, it still needed to go to the veterinarian for sterilizing. We also recognized that PLA is susceptible to UV damage and needed to find a protectant spray that was also non-toxic. We continue to work with Daisy's family, and it is entirely up to them on how they wish to proceed. We didn't have all of the expertise or technology needed for the project in-house. Gratefully, we had a faculty partner that was interested and available to provide some of those missing pieces.

The prototyping process may involve a variety of strategies and approaches. We started with 3D scanning, moved to using a cardboard cut-out for initial measurement, and returned to the design phase. The next prototype involved modeling clay. The results were all close, but as Daisy continues to grow and the wounds heal, new prototypes are necessary.

Not all tortoises will react the same to their new shell pieces. Consult with your local veterinarian to determine the type of prosthetic piece needed and whether it requires continual modification (as a more permanent piece) or if the tortoise will only need it temporarily while its shell repairs.

Moving a seventy-five-pound tortoise presents its own challenges, so be flexible with them. It is difficult for the owners to simply bring her in for a new measurement. Rather than the library making the clay mold, the owners purchased the clay, made the mold, and delivered it to the library.

Prototyping involves a variety of resources and expertise. Be thoughtful about how those resources are deployed and who has the necessary expertise. Can you grow it within the department or not, and how much time can be allocated to the project?

FEEDBACK/REFLECTIONS

Given the opportunity again, the Cline Library MakerLab would gladly partner with a local vet to help fix a damaged animal with 3D design and printing. The entire project was a tremendous learning experience and allowed us to explore 3D-printing solutions in a collaborative way. Both tortoise owners started with their veterinarian, who referred them to the MakerLab. The veterinarians' creative thinking made this project a reality.

Since the creation of the MakerLab, the library has driven a collective and cross-functional effort to engage the academic and regional community through programming, curriculum design, and multidisciplinary collaboration. The tortoise project, while unique, exemplifies the opportunities to think creatively and respond innovatively, no matter the project.

Chapter Twenty-Six

Bringing the Field to the Classroom using 3D-Printed Fossils

Tammie L. Gerke and John J. Burke

BACKGROUND

Students that have a combination of classroom and "field learning" experiences are better able to develop a connection between theory and practical concepts; however, it is not always possible to combine the two. The development of inexpensive 3D scanners and printers has begun to change that, thus bringing the "field to the classroom."

Students better connect to their geologic surroundings if they have some understanding of how they formed and why they are interesting. Even the least interested students become totally engaged and involved in their own learning and "backyard" when classroom and field-based activities are included in a course. However, it is usually not possible to get students into a field-based setting. Thus this activity is designed to introduce students to the regional geology and fossils in southwestern Ohio, southeastern Indiana, and northern Kentucky (tri-state region) with the use of 3D-printed fossils. The activity, however, can be adapted for different regions that contain fossils in the local rocks.

In addition, this activity can be used as outreach events for the local community by faculty and students. Students interested in pursuing outreach-based science careers can present this activity as part of an outreach event, which will help develop skills in explaining complex scientific ideas to the general public in a manner that is understandable.

SUPPLIES

Making the fossils required two distinct operations: (1) creating a 3D model of the original fossils, and (2) 3D printing copies of the fossils. Two different methods were used for creating 3D images of fossils.

Method 1 required the following supplies:

- digital camera and tripod (a digital single-lens reflex [DSLR] camera and Canon EOS Rebel tripod)
- small turntable such as a lazy Susan
- variety of small plastic risers, modeling clay, and other items (including a large bolt)
- software (such as Agisoft PhotoScan, now called Agisoft Metashape)

Method 2 required the following supplies:

- HP 3D Structured Light Scanner S3 Pro
- variety of small plastic risers, modeling clay, and other items (including a large bolt)

Once an image is created using Method 1 or 2, the following items are needed to print a 3D replica of the original fossil:

- 3D printer (all four of the following were used: MakerBot Replicator 2, MakerBot Replicator [Fifth Generation], MakerGear M2, and Prusa i3 MK3)
- 3D printing software (MakerBot's software was utilized for first two printers and Simplify 3D for final two)
- 3D printer filament in desired colors (PLA gray and purple filament were used)

INSTRUCTIONS

Scanning Fossils

Method 1:

1. Place digital camera on tripod.
2. Place fossil on turntable or other raised surface so when the camera is raised or lowered, images can be taken from perspectives above, below, and even with the fossil. Modeling clay, risers, and other items can be used to lift the fossil off of the surface.
3. Using tape, make marks on the turntable to make sure images are taken from every angle.
4. Move the tripod and camera into position above fossil, and then rotate the turntable, taking an image at every mark.
5. Lower the tripod so the camera is even with the fossil and rotate the turntable, taking an image at every mark.
6. Lower the tripod so the camera is below the fossil and rotate the turntable, taking an image at every mark.
7. Upload all images into PhotoScan/Metashape, and run through sequence of adjustments, following preset workflow in the software. Merge all the images into a single 3D model file.

Method 2:

1. Place the fossil with any necessary risers on the turntable of scanner.
2. Zoom and focus scanner cameras on the fossil and follow scanning process.
3. Review scanned images and make any necessary adjustments.
4. Create a merged 3D model file.

Printing 3D Fossil Replicas

1. Open 3D model file in 3D-printing software.
2. Make adjustments in print settings and rotation of image as needed.
3. Start printing.
4. Monitor printing.
5. Once printing is completed, remove printed fossil.

Classroom/Outreach

1. Determine if fossils are present in the region of your institution.
2. Determine the main category(ies) of fossils (brachiopod, crinoid, gastropod, etc.) in the local rocks.
3. Obtain high-quality examples of each category of fossils.
4. Develop a handout that provides definitions and information on the following: fossils, index fossils, index locations, how index fossils are utilized by geologists, a general summary of paleogeography for your region, and images of actual fossils for each category excluding the samples used to make the 3D fossils.
5. Make a general presentation to the class or organization reviewing all the information in step 4.
6. Divide the class or organization into small groups, provide each with a bag of fossils, and ask them to sketch each and identify. For underaged groups, fossils could be buried in sand and "dug up."

TIPS/SUGGESTIONS/CAUTIONS

3D Fossils

Early scanning attempts resulted in images of varying quality; many had shadows or captured the background, which caused distorted and inaccurate merged 3D models. Even lighting across the fossil and the placement of a three-sided cardboard enclosure behind the fossil aided in improving the quality of the scans. During the processing of images, a computer with sufficient RAM and a faster-than-standard processor was needed to efficiently generate the 3D models when using PhotoScan and Metashape or when using 3D scanner equipment and software.

Smaller fossils, approximately one inch or less, regardless of scanning method, were difficult to place on the turntable and ensure image capture from all needed perspectives, resulting in loss of detail in the merged model. Some of the smaller fossils ended up being too small for successful scanning with either method, which may indicate that with the use of either method, there is a definitive minimum fossil size that can be scanned.

Classroom/Outreach

The following are tips for classroom success. Develop ways to assess students' understanding of differences between fossils, index fossils, and an index fossil location. Provide enough information that the students are able to grasp the basics, however not too much information so students are challenged to make connections between types of fossil, their ecosystem, and the paleogeography for the region of interest. One wants to have real example(s) of each 3D fossil and do not expect students to provide genus and species names; rather they should be able to identify larger category names such as brachiopod, gastropod, bryozoan, crinoid, trilobite, and so on. Relate the different categories to things students can relate to, for example horn coral looks like Bugle snacks, bryozoan look like branches, individual pieces of a crinoid stalk look like Cheerios, and make the activity fun.

Tips for using this as an outreach activity include presenting the same material as you would in classroom setting but make sure you take more time to explain concepts so all get something from the activity. Do not "dumb down" the activity as participants will pick up on that and it will only enhance their negative view of science. When working with younger students (scouts groups etc.), the food analogies work very well as does having them "dig" the 3D fossils out of sand and then having the participants identify each fossil "found." If you live in a region that has fossils in the rocks, make sure to describe the types of rocks and how to identify them, and provide participants with location(s) of where they could go to collect their own fossil samples.

FEEDBACK/REFLECTIONS

3D Fossils

Overall, 3D printing of fossils has worked very well and allowed for reliable facsimiles of actual Ordovician-aged fossils. The process initially started with Method 1 and evolved into Method 2 based on the acquisition of a scanner. Fossil images produced using the 3D scanner resulted in more detailed printed fossils. However, that level of detail was not able to be replicated with all fossils. Updated Metashape software was purchased to attempt to address this issue, though it has not yet been attempted and will be used in conjunction with Method 1. Though Method 1 requires more hands-on time than Method 2, it allows for more fine adjustments to be made during the imaging process and end results may be superior.

Classroom/Outreach

The success of this project has exceeded expectations. It has been used in an introductory geology laboratory setting twice a year for the past three and a half years and improved students interest in the local geology and, when in the field, their ability to identify fossils they find. In addition, students seem to be less stressed about the activity in the field when they have had this pre-trip exposure to the material (i.e., it is not as scary to them as they have some idea of what they are trying to find). Outreach events that have utilized the 3D printed-fossils have also been successful. For example, an activity was presented to a local scouting troop, and it was difficult to determine who was more excited, the parents or the scouts, about the fossils and learning about them. One thing that would be ideal would be to have 3D-printed fossils of some of the smaller local fossils and a broader range of "specimens." Both of these issues are currently being addressed.

Copies of the 3D print files developed for this activity can be found at www.mid.miamioh.edu/library/3Dfossils.htm.

Chapter Twenty-Seven

3D-Printed Selfie

Stew Wilson

BACKGROUND

This project was developed as part of a 3D-printing demonstration at the Community Library of Dewitt and Jamesville in Syracuse, New York. In this project, librarians demonstrate the "hacking" ethos of makerspaces by connecting an Xbox Kinect to a Windows 10 PC as a 3D scanner. Users are scanned with ReconstructMe software to create a head and shoulders "selfie"; this image is processed in Autodesk Meshmixer and exported to a slicer for 3D printing.

This process is a streamlined version of other guides found online and is designed to be easy to set up and implement in a public library setting. The process should take less than ten minutes to demonstrate and approximately one hour to print.

SUPPLIES

Hardware

- Xbox Kinect (360, Xbox One, or Kinect for Windows): While you can use any Kinect, this process is designed for an Xbox 360 (or generation 1) Kinect.
- Xbox Kinect to USB adapter: You'll need this to connect your Kinect to your PC.
- 3D printer: For this guide I used a Lulzbot Mini. In step 14, make sure you export your image from Meshmixer in the correct file type for your slicer (3D-printing software).
- Windows 10 PC: You'll need a Windows 10 PC with a good (6GB and up) graphics card. Setting up a Kinect with a Mac is possible but has a more complicated setup process, and ReconstructMe is not available for Mac.

Software

- OpenNI2: The defunct OpenNI SDK (Software Development Kit) is now hosted by Occipital, makers of the Structure iPad camera. This program allows the Kinect to communicate with the PC.
- Kinect for Windows SDK and Developer Toolkit: Extra functionality for the Kinect on Windows.
- ReconstructMe: Free 3D-scanning software.
- Autodesk Meshmixer: A free 3D image editor, for cleaning up our image before printing.
- 3D Slicer: The "slicer" is your 3D-printing software. For this guide, I used Cura, the default slicer for the Lulzbot Mini 3D printer.

INSTRUCTIONS

Setup

1. *Before connecting the Kinect to the PC,* download the OpenNi driver, and follow the installation steps. If you don't know whether you need x64 or x86, navigate to Windows settings > System > About, and check your chip architecture under the Device Specifications heading, next to System type.
2. After installing OpenNi, download and install the Kinect 1.8 SDK. You may notice that this isn't the latest version of the SDK, but 1.8 works with the Kinect v1, or Xbox 360 Kinect. If you have a later Kinect, download Kinect 2.0 SDK.
3. Next, download and install the Kinect for Windows Developer Toolkit v1.8. This step may not be completely necessary but has a lot of features you may want to experiment with.
4. Download and install ReconstructMe. This free 3D scanning software works with other scanners too.
5. Connect the Kinect to your PC and open ReconstructMe. Click on the pop-up asking you to configure your sensor; select Microsoft Kinect (1st gen). Place the Kinect next to your monitor, at or slightly above eye level.

Scanning, Editing, and Printing

1. Open ReconstructMe: Make sure you're situated within the blue box in the ReconstructMe window. Position yourself in a chair that can spin 360 degrees. Click Start.
2. Turn very slowly in a circle, keeping as still as possible. ReconstructMe will let you know if you're moving too fast.
3. When the scan completes, save your file as a PLY.
4. Download and install Autodesk Meshmixer (or your preferred 3D image editor).
5. Import your PLY file in Meshmixer.

6. Use the “inspector” tool (Analysis > Inspector) to clean up your file, and use the “plane cut” feature (Edit > Plane Cut) to remove extraneous print and create a head and shoulders “bust.”
7. Click on File > Export > Save as OBJ (or the file type for your slicer).
8. Open your file in your slicer. Reduce the size of the print until the estimated print time is approximately one hour. In Cura, this generates prints of the size and quality in figure 27.1.

Figure 27.1. Finished 3D-printed busts. ***Stew Wilson***

TIPS/SUGGESTIONS/CAUTIONS

You may notice imperfections in your image when you import to Meshmixer. Keep in mind that when you open your image in your 3D print slicer, you’ll likely reduce the image size to print within one hour. Reducing the image size usually hides these imperfections. If it still looks wrong after you’ve reduced the size in Meshmixer, consider scanning again. After scanning a few times in ReconstructMe, you’ll learn how to recognize a scan that will translate well to a 3D print.

FEEDBACK/REFLECTIONS

This project is very popular with staff and patrons. Filament cost is negligible, so it can be a fun giveaway to your scanned volunteer. Print quality and facial definition (see figure 27.1) will depend on the settings in the slicer and on the amount of time you spend cleaning up your image in Meshmixer.

Chapter Twenty-Eight

Chemical Education in the Digital Makerspace

Soon Goo Lee, Jason Fleming, and Peter Fritzler

BACKGROUND

Students currently attending University of North Carolina Wilmington (UNCW) are considered to be Generation Z (Gen Z).[1] They are the first generation to be born and raised in a tech-savvy, Internet-connected environment. Gen Zs are familiar with visual media and have a higher percentage of visual learners in the classroom. Since they are very different learners from previous generations, the traditional teaching methodology may not be effective in conveying complex scientific knowledge. For Gen Z students, the use of visual tools can attract students' attention in the classroom and enhance their academic performance, especially for chemistry.

Randall Library is committed to meeting the challenge of developing new teaching methodologies and has created a technology-rich space within the library to lay the foundation of support. As academic libraries move away from traditional roles and instead toward serving as facilitators and stewards of content creation, the Digital Makerspace (DMS) (digitalmakerspace.uncw.edu/) at the UNCW's William Madison Randall Library, in collaboration with the Technology Assistance Center (TAC), provides access to new and emerging technologies to all UNCW students and faculty. The DMS staff have integrated these services with classroom activities through development and implementation of programming and additional technologies for the purpose of:

1. assisting faculty with the design and development of learning experiences that leverage these technologies and
2. supporting faculty in their efforts to integrate these technologies in their courses and in their classrooms.

As an example of this classroom integration, Dr. Soon Goo Lee, an assistant professor in the Department of Chemistry and Biochemistry at UNCW, has incorporated his own research projects dealing with X-ray protein crystallography and protein 3D structures within chemistry courses to provide students with unique opportunities to conduct chemical research in laboratory classes and gain basic scientific knowledge through virtual reality at Randall Library. Since fall 2018, Dr. Lee, Jason Fleming (information technology librarian), and Peter Fritzler (sciences librarian) have led a successful VR workshop (see figure 28.1) for chemical education, Virtual Reality for Chemical Research. The main goal of our VR and 3D printing in chemistry education project is to introduce VR and 3D-printing technology as a tool for chemical education at higher education institutions.

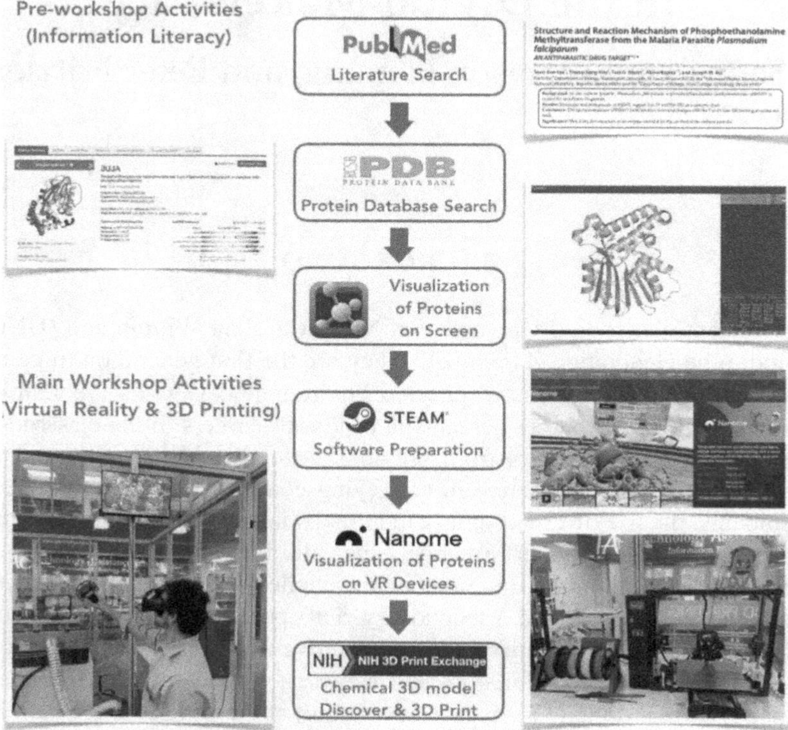

Figure 28.1. Schedule diagram of the "Virtual Reality for Chemical Research" at Randall Library. ***Soon Goo Lee***

SUPPLIES

VR

- Protein Data Bank (PDB) (www.rcsb.org/)
- HTC Vive or Oculus Rift
- Alienware Aurora R4
- Nanome (Nanome, Inc.)

3D Printing

- 3D printer lulzbot Taz 6
- Cura
- filament

INSTRUCTIONS

Pre-workshop Activities

The Introduction to Chemical Research course was originally designed to introduce information literacy and chemical research, including the use of chemical literature, experimental design, and proposal writing to undergraduates majoring in chemistry and biochemistry. As a pre-workshop activity for Virtual Reality for Chemical Research, undergraduates begin learning about the Framework for Information Literacy for Higher Education (i.e., Authority Is Constructed and Contextual, Information Creation as a Process, Information Has Value, Research as Inquiry, Searching as Strategic Exploration) and how to use scientific databases to find peer-reviewed journal articles on specific topics of interest in chemistry and biochemistry at the beginning of the semester (see figure 28.1).

Dr. Lee has expertise in X-ray protein crystallography, has solved more than fifty protein 3D structures, and has deposited forty-one structures (as of July 2019) in the Protein Data Bank (PDB) for public research and education (see tables 28.1 and 28.2). Two or three weeks before the Virtual Reality for Chemical Research workshop, students learn about protein X-ray crystallography and how to read and write research journal articles on protein 3D structure and function in the classroom. For example, students search a peer-reviewed research article "Structure and Reaction Mechanism of Phosphoethanolamine Methyltransferase from the Malaria Parasite *Plasmodium Falciparum*: An Antiparasitic Drug Target"[2] through PubMed, a free resource by the National Center for Biotechnology Information. Then, they access the PDB and download a deposited protein 3D structure, which is Phosphoethanolamine methyltransferase from *Plasmodium falciparum* in complex with phosphoethanolamine (PDB code: 3UJA) (www.rcsb.org/structure/3UJA). Using PyMOL, a free 3D-visualization software for education, students visualize their 3D protein structure coordinates and understand the overall structure and structure of the active site (see tables 28.1 and 28.2 and figure 28.1).

Main Workshop Activities

Activity 1: Introduction to VR devices and VR software (by TAC)

1. Before class starts: Open Nanome, log in, and create a VR room for students.
2. Demonstration: Open 3D model in Nanome and use controllers to move around.
3. Introduction: VR basic setup (e.g., VR BaseStation, VR controller, VR headset).

Activity 2: Overview class objectives and VR application (by librarians and academic instructors)

1. Discussion: What is VR? Show students Steam and what titles and software are available in the Digital Makerspace at Randall Library (see tables 28.1 and 28.2).

2. Discussion: Current use in academics and existing partnerships with academic departments (e.g., Chemistry, Anthropology, Environmental Sciences, Health Services at UNCW).
3. Introduction: VR contents developed for the humanities and sciences research in the Digital Makerspace.
4. Instructor Session: Short lectures with related materials (e.g., protein molecules).

Activity 3: Experience VR devices and 3D printing (by students)

1. Simultaneously with different groupings of the class (see figure 28.1)
   a. 3D Printing Tour: Demonstrate loading model in Cura and setting up print job and printing molecule from database.
   b. VR Experience (six students): Open chemical structure in VR protein visualization software and manipulate molecule looking for particular protein.

Table 28.1. Resources for the VR Workshop in Chemical Education and STEM Education

	Resources	*Websites*	*Description*
Database	PubMed	www.ncbi.nlm.nih.gov/pubmed/	Published by the U.S. National Library of Medicine, PubMed is the world's largest indexing database to biomedical literature.
	Web of Science	www.webofknowledge.com/	An indexing database to the leading journals within the sciences and social sciences.
	SciFinder	scifinder.cas.org/	A comprehensive indexing database to structures, reactions, and literature of chemistry.
	The Protein Data Bank (PDB)	www.rcsb.org/pdb/	A Protein Data Bank archive that holds 154,478 biological macromolecular structures (as of August 1, 2019).
	NIH 3D Print Exchange	3dprint.nih.gov/	NIH 3D Print Exchange allows for searching, browsing, downloading, and sharing biomedical 3D print files, modeling tutorials, and educational material.
Software	PyMOL	www.schrodinger.com/pymol	A user-sponsored molecular visualization system maintained and distributed by Schrödinger.
	Steam	store.steampowered.com/	A digital distribution platform for games and VR software developed and maintained by Valve Corporation.
	Nanome	nanome.ai/nanome/	A VR title for atomic, molecular, and protein visualization. Students are able to collaborate in real time at a VR space.

Table 28.2. Other Resources for Educational 3D Software

	Resources	*Websites*	*Description*
3D Design Software	Tinkercad	www.tinkercad.com	A free, easy-to-use web-based tool for creating objects that are ready to be printed in 3D. If you have never created a 3D design, this is a great place to start.
	Fusion 360	www.autodesk.com/products/fusion-360/overview#banner	A step up from Tinkercad, Fusion 360 lets you develop more complex models. Free three-year education licenses available.
	SketchUp	www.sketchup.com	A 3D modeling program for applications such as architectural design, interior design, civil and mechanical engineering, film, and video game design.
	Blender	www.blender.org	A free professional 3D computer graphics software product used for creating animated films, visual effects, art, 3D-printed models, interactive 3D applications, and video games.
	Maya	www.autodesk.com/products/maya/overview	Maya is a 3D animation, modeling, simulation, rendering, and compositing program.
	AutoCAD	www.autodesk.com/education/home	A professional-level tool for building and manipulating 2D and 3D models. Students are eligible for a free three-year license.
	OpenSCAD	www.openscad.org	A free software application for creating solid 3D CAD objects. It is not an interactive modeler but rather a 3D compiler. OpenSCAD reads from a script and renders a 3D model from it.
	Agisoft PhotoScan	www.agisoft.com	PhotoScan generates digital 3D models from an array of standard 2D photos of an object. A free thirty-day trial is available.
Find 3D Models	Thingiverse	www.thingiverse.com	A repository of 3D files from hundreds of users.
	MorphoSource	www.morphosource.org	MorphoSource allows researchers to store and organize, share, and distribute their own 3D data.
	NASA 3D Resources	nasa3d.arc.nasa.gov	A growing collection of 3D models, textures, and images from inside NASA.
	Smithsonian x 3D	3d.si.edu	A project to share 3D models developed from scans of their diverse collections.
3D Editing and Repair Software	MeshLab	www.meshlab.net	An open-source general-purpose system aimed at the processing of the typical not-so-small unstructured 3D models that arise in the 3D scanning pipeline.
	MeshMixer	www.meshmixer.com	A free experimental 3D modeling tool whose goal it is to make it easy to compose new 3D models from existing meshes.

Post-workshop Activities

1. Discussion: Future use in academics (after VR activity).
2. Since CHM350 is a writing-intensive course, students write proposals on the potential applications of VR for chemical and STEM education.

TIPS/SUGGESTIONS/CAUTIONS

1. Pre-workshop activities (e.g., information literacy session) are required. Through the prior workshop experiences, we have found that understanding scientific research articles helps students understanding VR contents (e.g., protein molecules) and makes them more interested.
2. Prior to the workshop, the academic instructors need to assign students specific protein and chemical molecules to download in Nanome.
3. Not all students want to try VR because of motion sickness. Program organizers should prepare alternative activities.

FEEDBACK/ REFLECTIONS

1. Instead of an instructor-led workshop, students need to create new 3D models for the purposes of printing them.
2. Due to space constraints, we need to find out how VR technology can be used in classrooms and laboratories.

NOTES

1. Adam Renfro, "Meet Generation Z," *Gettingsmart.com,* accessed October 12, 2019, gettingsmart.com/2012/12/meet-generation-z.

2. Soon Goo Lee, Youngchang Kim, Tara D. Alpert, Akina Nagata, and Joseph M. Jez, "Structure and Reaction Mechanism of Phosphoethanolamine Methyltransferase from the Malaria Parasite Plasmodium Falciparum: An Antiparasitic Drug Target," *J Biol Chem* 287, no. 2 (2012): 1426–34.

Chapter Twenty-Nine

Taking a Virtual Archaeological Site Tour

A Class Visit to the Baths of Caracalla

Jason Fleming, Eleanora Reber, and Stephanie Crowe

BACKGROUND

In March 2019, twenty students from the University of North Carolina Wilmington's Honors Archaeology class visited an archaeological site in Rome without leaving campus. Using Google Earth and HTC Vive virtual reality (VR) equipment in our library's new Digital Makerspace, the students traveled to the Baths of Caracalla, where they analyzed Roman history by investigating the site's features. Resource and time constraints would have made a physical trip to an archaeological site nearly impossible, so this virtual field trip allowed these students to gain an experiential understanding of what archaeological sites can tell us about the past and how to reconstruct political and economic structures via careful interpretation of architecture and artifacts.

This experience came about when the instructor for the class reached out via a form on the Digital Makerspace website.[1] At an initial meeting, the social sciences librarian, the information technology librarian, and the class instructor discussed some possible options for the experience. Since the instructor wanted her students to visit an actual archaeological site and not a virtual reproduction of what a location might have looked like, we had few options for the field trip. We finally settled on using Google Earth, where the VR equipment would allow the students to travel to any location. Trial and error led us to the Baths of Caracalla, which contained sufficient detail in its images for the students to take away something from their exploration of the site. The class instructor prepared a PowerPoint that showed additional relevant images and a worksheet for students to complete with questions about what the site's details might mean about Roman society at the time.

SUPPLIES

- HTC Vive (or other) virtual reality equipment—we have three VR stations
- monitors (for students not wearing headsets to see the site)—one for each VR headset

- computer with projector screen (if you also want to include a PowerPoint or similar presentation)
- worksheet: dl.uncw.edu/DMS/ VirtualRealityinArchaeologyExercise.pdf

INSTRUCTIONS

1. Prepare each VR headset with your location in Google Earth pulled up.
2. When the students arrive, introduce them to the space and the goals for the day.
3. Ideally, students should work in pairs, with one student on a VR headset and the other student providing direction and input. Depending on the number of students and the number of headsets you have available, you might need to divide them into groups and have other groups work on an assignment or work with the instructor.
4. Allow each pair approximately twenty minutes to explore the site (this can be adjusted as needed based on the amount of time you have available in the class period).
5. At the end of the class period, lead a discussion on what students learned from their field trip and the value of virtual reality for exploring archaeological sites.

TIPS/SUGGESTIONS/CAUTIONS

- If you have too many students for the number of available headsets, make sure you have an alternative activity set up for students who are not on the virtual reality equipment at any given time. For example, we conducted a tour of our 3D printing space.
- Leave yourself plenty of time to plan. It took more time than we expected to find a good site for the field trip.
- Provide cheat sheets or an FAQ sheet for students on how to navigate the VR environment.
- Additionally, make sure you have at least one person on hand who is well-versed in using VR equipment who can help students who need additional navigation assistance.

FEEDBACK/REFLECTIONS

During the session, students using the VR had a variety of reactions, ranging from slight motion sickness to extreme enthusiasm. We held a critical reflection session in the class period following the exercise. During the critical reflection session, students recommended some sort of orientation session on the use of the headset and navigation tools prior to the main exercise, possibly with a student using the equipment in front of everyone else, or a very detailed FAQ. Many students had navigation issues, in which they left the area of the Baths of Caracalla and found themselves elsewhere, or had difficulties with the VR controls and found themselves hovering in the sky above the Roman streets. A detailed navigation FAQ or an in-person orientation session would have helped with this problem and removed some of the demands on the staff assisting with the exercise.

Selection of site for smoothness of navigation was also more important than we originally expected. The Baths of Caracalla were chosen for the panoramic views within the baths, but several of these views were not linked to the Street View paths. They could only be accessed by clicking from above directly on the correct spot on the satellite map. These spots were marked on a desktop Google Earth window (figure 29.1) but not within the VR headsets. This led to some difficulty in accessing all the panoramic views within the virtual site.

Figure 29.1. Google Earth view of Baths of Caracalla. *Jason Fleming*

From a pedagogical standpoint, the students who had the PowerPoint station before the VR station tended to be more efficient and effective in answering the worksheet questions. In the future, this station should probably take place before the main field trip, either in class or as a homework assignment. Since students had a wide range of responses to the equipment, it was also important for the instructor to be flexible concerning how much VR time each student had.

NOTE

1. "Digital Makerspace," University of North Carolina Wilmington, accessed June 10, 2019, digitalmakerspace.uncw.edu/.

Chapter Thirty

Using Virtual Reality in Teaching Education Students

Lauren E. Burrow and Edward Iglesias

BACKGROUND

The Emerging Technology Laboratory opened in the summer of 2017 as a virtual reality–based makerspace. The early focus was on recruiting faculty who could use either VR or 3D printing as part of their pedagogy. An early recruit was Dr. Lauren Burrow, who during the course of two years brought her pre-service teachers enrolled in various pedagogy courses to the virtual reality–based makerspace at the Steen Library. The purpose of this exercise was to expose new teachers to the possibilities of VR in education in providing virtual field trips. For many, makerspaces allow individuals to make what was previously "impossible" or what was previously relegated only to imaginations into a reality. However, in rural settings, VR spaces allow teachers to take what is "real" and make it available to their students. One of the strengths of VR is the ability to take the user to locations that are simply inaccessible either because of cost (museums in Europe) or risk (outer space). Additionally, VR is useful as an "empathy engine" that can safely expose the user to situations to better understand at an emotional level the "realness" of a virtual experience; for example, witnessing the inequities of homelessness or following the perilous journey of a refugee. Essentially, VR creates an opportunity for students and teachers to become both consumers and creators of spaces that are otherwise inaccessible to rural communities. See figure 30.1.

This chapter will go into detail about the equipment used, the overall environment of the makerspace (including soundproof rooms), planning that went into programming, as well as efforts made to recruit faculty. Information will also be provided on how instructors can frame structured guidance to elicit transformative experiences with students, as evidenced by anecdotal feedback from Dr. Burrow's student-users, comparative data regarding pre-service teachers' confidence and commitment levels involving VR integration in classroom spaces, and notes on how this experience could be improved.

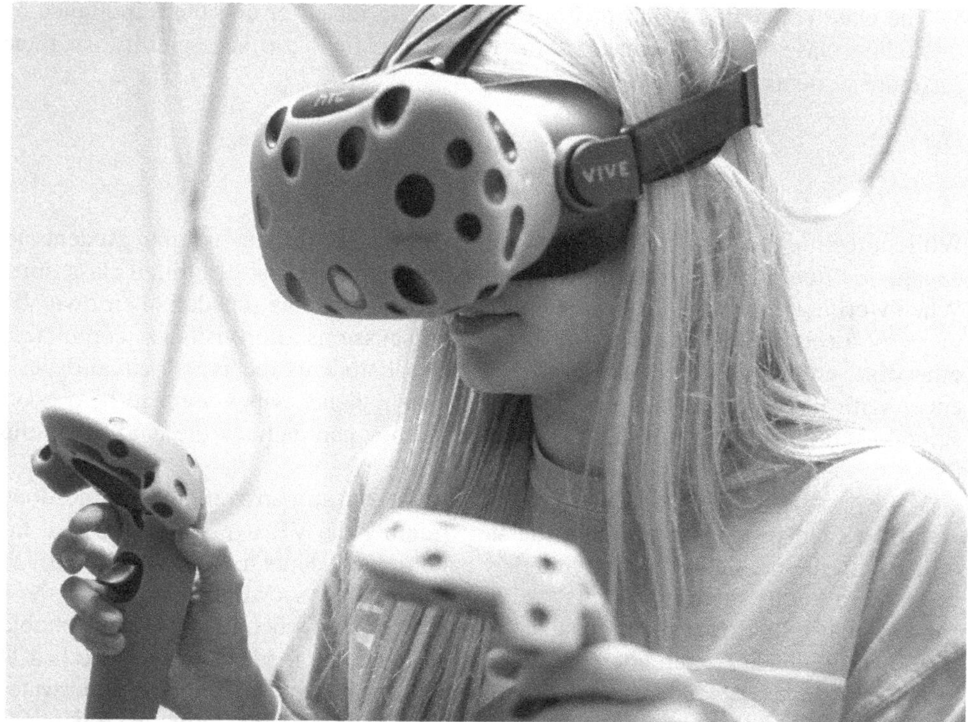

Figure 30.1. Student using VR equipment. *Lauren E. Burrow*

SUPPLIES

- four Oculus Rift VR workstations
- two HTC Vive VR workstations

INSTRUCTIONS

1. Prior to coming to the VR makerspace, students read a recent article about the destruction of about one quarter of the Great Barrier Reef due to coral bleaching and the need to turn attention toward protecting the remaining reefs for wildlife, weather, and tourist revenue purposes. The pre-service teachers completed a knowledge- and attitude-based reflection based on article content.
2. During the virtual field trip, students viewed theBlu experience (store.steampowered.com/app/451520/theBlu/) in the stand-up VR spaces. After their assigned field trip experience, students were able to explore VR scenes of their choosing at the sit-down stations.
3. After completing the VR field trip, students wrote up how the VR experience had impacted their knowledge about and attitudes toward this potentially endangered natural resource.

4. The class concluded with open discussion about ideas for and the importance of finding ways to use VR-based tools to increase field trip accessibility for their future students.

SUGGESTIONS/TIPS/CAUTIONS

While allowing students "free choice" can be fun, consider encouraging students to engage in "free play" during follow-up visits to make the most of limited class time. When working with large groups, we suggest having students schedule their own VR visits by a certain date and then hosting class discussions after visits are completed; otherwise, enforce "viewer time limits" so that all students receive an equal experience. With large groups, pay attention to ocular hygiene; wipes seem to be a good solution but must be administered with care as they can damage the coating on the lenses of the unit.

Make sure to preview the scene yourself so that you can answer student questions about the field trip, and make sure the staff running the VR experience are also familiar with the pre-chosen activity so they can guide students to scenes of interest or be ready to troubleshoot if students "get lost" during their viewing. Beware that some students may experience situations that are uncomfortable when using VR. If a phobia is known in advance, then alternate arrangements can be made; however, we had at least two instances of students who did not know they were afraid of being underwater until they were in that simulation. Finally, both HTC and Oculus now make wireless units, and these are preferable since the trailing cord tends to "shock" users out of the experience if they brush against it.

REFLECTIONS

From the instructor perspective, this VR experience provided an engaging, learning-based field trip to a "place" that most of the pre-service teachers had never experienced. The purposeful selection of the V-scene helped to build students' awareness about ecological damage that is currently occurring to coral reefs while also inspiring them to imagine the positive impacts of and innovative possibilities for VR field trips in K–12 classrooms.

For the student participants, seeing the coral reefs in a virtual setting helped build empathy toward scientists' calls to protect these natural wonders. One student reflected: "It's hard to care about something you don't know much about, but the VR trip brought the ocean 'to life for me' and made me curious to learn more about other parts of the world that might be endangered." Many students confirmed that the experience helped them reconsider and get more excited about the potential uses of VR field trips in their future classrooms: "Before this I couldn't really think of many places to take my students, but now I am so excited to take them all around the world." Another student, who had never been diving, shared: "It blew my mind. I couldn't believe how real it was or how immersed I felt. It was the most incredible feeling." But beyond the "wow!" factor, all the students agreed that there are so many possibilities for VR use in educational settings, with many sharing ideas beyond just field trips. One student stated, "This would be so cool to use for science labs. . . . I would much rather have my students dissect a virtual frog than a live one." And several students continued to return to the VR lab after the course ended so that they could "get away from the stress" of their studies or to "just explore" another new place.

Overall, the activity was a success: it helped build a productive partnership in which the professor was able to leverage existing university library services to enhance her course instruction, and it got pre-service teachers excited about innovative learning opportunities for their future students.

Index

About the Editors and Contributors

Jennifer Hicks is the circulation and reserves supervisor for Miami University Middletown campus. She holds an MLIS from Kent State University. Along with circulation, reserves, and student worker supervision, she also creates and runs programming in the library makerspace. Jennifer has presented at various state, national, and international conferences on the topics of student training, makerspaces, and fake news. She has held various board roles for the Ohio Library Support Staff Institute (OLSSI) and is a current cochair for the Distance Learning Interest Group for the Academic Library Association of Ohio (ALAO). Jennifer has a cowritten chapter about library gamification published through ACRL. This book is her editorial debut. Aside from libraries and makerspaces, her interests include animals, tattoos, and traveling.

Jessica Long is the outreach and instruction librarian and associate librarian at the Gardner-Harvey Library on the Middletown regional campus of Miami University (Ohio). She received an MLIS from Kent State University and a BA in anthropology from the University of New Mexico. As part of her outreach work, Jessica has spent time building connections between the library and other departments as cochair for the Center for Teaching and Learning for the Middletown campus and with the greater library community as cochair for the Distance Learning Interest Group for the Academic Library Association of Ohio. She regularly teaches how to structure arguments and complete effective research in a credit-bearing debate course for international students, as well as leading a variety of instruction sessions on topics ranging from course-specific research to how to combat misinformation. Jessica has presented talks on online learning courses and tools, gamification and game-based learning, fake news, and using makerspaces to help support community needs at various state, regional, and international conferences. In addition to her presentation work, Jessica has also authored and coauthored two book chapters that deal with gamification of the research process and interactive library orientations, respectively. This book marks her first time as an editor, and she is thrilled to learn so much about making and makerspaces from other librarians and library staff. When not in the library, Jessica can be found volunteering at her local animal shelter, traveling the globe, or buying new gnomes to add to her growing collection. She can be contacted via e-mail at longjh@miamioh.edu.

* * *

Camille Andrews is emerging literacies librarian at Mann Library at Cornell University, where she works on multimodal literacies and the mannUfactory makerspace. Since 2004, Camille has also been involved in outreach; instruction; information literacy initiatives; learning technologies; and assessment for learning outcomes, technologies, services and spaces. She is extremely interested in the intersection of library and information science, user experience, instructional design, twenty-first-century literacies, and new technologies. Camille graduated from the College of William and Mary with a BA in literary and cultural studies (focused on Francophone African and Caribbean literature) and from Simmons College with a master's in library and information science.

Cara Bolley is the emerging technologies librarian at the Defiance Public Library System's Main Library MakerSpace. She received an MLIS from Kent State University and a BS in digital media arts concentrating in animation at Huntington University. She provides classes at the main and branch locations and also provides one-on-one assistance in the MakerSpace. Her background in crafting and stop-motion animation helps fuel her creativity as she helps others in the local community make their own creations.

John J. Burke is the director of the Gardner-Harvey Library on the Middletown regional campus of Miami University (Ohio). John is a past president of the Academic Library Association of Ohio (ALAO). He holds an MS in library science from the University of Tennessee and a BA in history from Michigan State University. John regularly writes and presents on library instruction, makerspaces, and library technology topics and has just completed his sixth edition of the *Neal-Schuman Library Technology Companion: A Basic Guide for Library Staff* (ALA Publishing, 2020).

Lauren E. Burrow is an associate professor of elementary education at Stephen F. Austin State University. Her research agenda focuses on best practices in teacher education with scholarly and creative works typically exploring service learning as pedagogy, creative writing/the arts, and technology integration. As the mother of three young children, most of her most brilliant ideas come from listening to and learning from them.

Dianne Cmor has enjoyed an international career in academic libraries working in Canada, Qatar, Hong Kong, and Singapore. She is currently associate university librarian, teaching and learning, at Concordia University in Montreal where she is responsible for ensuring the high-quality and high-impact participation of the library across the teaching and learning endeavors of the university. She oversees various services, spaces, and cross-unit committees devoted to teaching and learning, user experience, and so on and plays well with other academic and student support units on campus. Dianne holds degrees from Trent University (BA Hons), McGill University (MLIS), and York University (MA).

Sarah Coleman is youth services/young adult librarian at the Bonita Springs Public Library, part of the Lee County Library System in Lee County, Florida. She received her MLIS and her BA in media, information, and technoculture from the University of Western Ontario. She has worked in public libraries since 2007 with children, teens, and adults. Sarah was active in the Colorado library community for ten years, presenting on topics such as STEM programming, social media for libraries, and programming for adults with disabilities, presenting at the Colorado Library Association Annual Conference and CLiC Spring Workshops. She also served as an instructor for the ILEAD USA Leadership Program in 2013.

Susan E. Cook is associate professor of English at Southern New Hampshire University, where she teaches nineteenth-century British literature, gender studies, and composition. Her research focuses on multi-media approaches to nineteenth-century literature, and her book, *Victorian Negatives: Literary Culture and the Dark Side of Photography in the Nineteenth Century*, examines the relationship between photography and nineteenth-century fiction. She and Liz Henley have cotaught a course on the industrial and digital revolutions and have coauthored articles in the journals *Pedagogy* and *Impact*.

Michelle Costello, education and community engagement librarian, is liaison to the School of Education and provides research help and library instruction to students, faculty, and community members. Michelle was co–project manager of a successfully developed and implemented learning community of pedagogical improvement for librarians (LILAC, Library Instruction Leadership Academy). Michelle earned her MLS from Syracuse University and a BA in psychology and elementary education from St. John Fisher College.

Amber R. Cox is a creative services senior librarian at the Pikes Peak Library District. She received an MS in library and information science from the University of Illinois at Urbana-Champaign and a BS in psychology from Southeast Missouri State University. She has eight years of experience in developing and implementing public library programming for teens and adults and has presented talks on maker-centered learning, the Repair Cafe initiative, and other makerspace-related topics at various regional and state conferences.

Stephanie Crowe is the coordinator of liaison librarian services at the University of North Carolina Wilmington. In this role, she provides oversight and vision for UNCW's liaison librarian program. She is also the liaison librarian to the departments of Anthropology, History, International Studies, Public and International Affairs, and Sociology and Criminology.

Stephanie Douglas is the adult services librarian at Golden Public Library in Golden, Colorado. She received an MLIS from Emporia State University and a BS in history from Southern Illinois University. She has worked for more than twelve years in both an academic and public library setting and is passionately dedicated to creating positive library experiences for adults.

Debby Emerson is the director of Wadsworth Library in Geneseo, New York. This public library serves the rural communities of Geneseo and Groveland, with a total "population served" of 11,252. Debby received her MLS from the State University of New York at Buffalo and her BA in American literature from DePauw University in Greencastle, Indiana. She was previously executive director of the Central New York Library Resources Council, assistant director at the Rochester Regional Library Council, and head of research and instruction services at Leroy V. Good Library at Monroe Community College. She has been an active member of the New York Library Association (NYLA) and served as the organization's president in 2016.

Gene A. Felice II is an assistant professor in digital art within the Department of Art and Art History at the University of North Carolina Wilmington where he is developing the Coaction Lab for interdisciplinary collaboration. His work has been featured nationally at the Yerba Buena Center for the Arts in San Francisco and internationally at Sussex University in the UK and at ISEA Hong Kong, and was most recently selected to be a 2018 American Arts Incubator/State Dept.–funded exchange artist based in Alexandria, Egypt.

Donna Femenella is the course reserves and makerspace coordinator at American University Library in Washington, D.C. In her role, she supports faculty with their courses and research. Her interest in staff development led to the creation of a program that allowed student assistants to enhance skills desired in their chosen future professions. She has presented at various conferences and colloquiums on promotion of services as well as building a community of makers in the library.

Jason Fleming is the information technology librarian at the University of North Carolina Wilmington Randall Library. His research interests include gamification, makerspaces, and information discovery. He received his master's in library and information science from the University of South Florida.

Peter Fritzler is the sciences librarian at the University of North Carolina Wilmington. His varied research interests include communication in science, undergraduate research, applied learning, public understanding of science, information literacy, blue spaces, and history of local surfing. He also serves as the faculty advisor to the UNCW Surf Club. He received his master's in information science from the University of Tennessee.

Tammie L. Gerke is an associate teaching professor in the Department of Geology and Environmental Earth Science and the Department of Mathematical and Physical Sciences at Miami University. She has taught geology and environmental sciences for approximately twenty years. Teaching interests include developing approaches on how to provide more positive and engaged learning experiences in the sciences at the college level. Dr. Gerke also has an active research program and provides undergraduate students opportunities to participate. She is the geology and environmental earth science advisor at Miami University Middletown (MUM) and faculty advisor for the

MUM Geology Club. In addition Dr. Gerke is active in outreach activities with the local community including monthly talks on the National Parks at the MUM library, an annual fossil hunting field trip, and overseeing service projects for MUM Geology Club with the U.S. Army Corp of Engineers and their participation in the education section of the annual GeoFair.

Elizabeth M. Henley is associate professor of computer information systems at Southern New Hampshire University. Her interdisciplinary research currently focuses on the connection between technology and the humanities and makerspaces. She teaches classes that utilize the SNHU Makerspace and has run workshops for other students to attend. She and Susan Cook have worked together on projects combining their disciplines, including assignments in Susan's classes and presenting at Dickens Symposium.

Adalia Hiltebeitel manages the Technology Assistance Center (TAC) at the University of North Carolina Wilmington, which includes seven full-time staff and about sixty student workers. The TAC supports approximately eighteen thousand clients via phone, in person, or online and ensures the TAC services are consistent with department and university policies and goals. She has a master's in computer science and information systems.

Edward Iglesias is a refugee from library technology now uncomfortably in administration. He is a serial creator of library makerspaces and is currently working on integrating VR and AR into the library environment. He has also published three books on library systems and technology and is now trying to learn about people.

Christine Keenan is the coordinator of the Innovation Lab and Makerspace at the Shapiro Library on the campus of Southern New Hampshire University. She enjoys engaging students, staff, and faculty to discover the joy of creating with emerging technology as well as sewing and painting. She has organized numerous collaborative quilting projects and has personally made more than fifty quilts. Her most recent creative interest is being a contributing artist for Art-O-Mat, and she loves hearing from patrons around the country that purchase her tiny treasures from upcycled cigarette machines.

Soon Goo Lee is a creative science educator and active researcher at the University of North Carolina Wilmington (UNCW). As a protein biochemist and X-ray protein crystallographer, he determined more than fifty protein three-dimensional (3D) structures and incorporated a diverse set of experimental approaches to solve unanswered questions about the biological roles of proteins in plants and microorganisms using biochemical research tools, especially X-ray crystallography. As an assistant professor of biotechnology in the Department of Chemistry and Biochemistry, he has been part of UNCW's STEAM (Science, Technology, Engineering, Art, Math) team and carried out a virtual reality (VR) and 3D protein structure project for chemical education with UNCW's undergraduates and librarians at the William Madison Randall Library. Currently, Dr. Lee is a member of the American Chemical Society (ACS) and the National Art Education Association (NAEA). He is interested in ways to use VR in interdisciplinary subjects and utilizes arts to improve undergraduate students' scientific knowledge and research.

Emily Lelandais is a circulation services specialist at American University Library in Washington, D.C. She helps manage the AU Library Makerspace and is responsible for maintaining the library's board game collection. In her role, she also serves as a liaison between the AU Library's Access Services unit and the Library's Strategic Communications unit and contributes to the creation of marketing material for library events and services. Emily has presented on the role of the Makerspace at the AU Library and spoken on panels about how to manage an academic library board game collection.

David Luftig is a science librarian at Washington State University's Owen Science and Engineering Library. He received his MSLIS from the University of Illinois. While there, he helped preserve the University of Illinois's historic Experimental Music Studio archives. Since getting into building electronic instruments in the late 1990s, David has organized numerous DIY electronics groups. He is enthusiastic about DIY electronic music as it provides a fantastic way to learn fun electronics skills while engaging with one's community.

Jessica Martinez is the science librarian at the University of Idaho Library in Moscow, Idaho. She received an MLIS from the University of Washington and her undergraduate degree from the University of Colorado. As a reference and instruction librarian, she enjoys working with the campus community in all areas of the library. This includes the library's makerspace, the Making Innovating and Learning Laboratory (MILL). She has presented on makerspaces, open educational resources, impostor syndrome in library instruction, and social media as a marketing tool. Jessica enjoys trying new things at her library like developing a board game collection and organizing library mini golf; she is always looking for ways to engage patrons from a variety of backgrounds and bring them into the library.

Thomas Mays started his first business shortly after finishing his undergraduate degree at Ohio University. His company provided marketing and communications services and consulting to a variety of for-profit and not-for-profit organizations. Much of this work involved helping businesses navigate the quickly changing technological landscape in the 1990s and 2000s as the Internet and then social media grew as mainstream marketing and communication channels. Dr. Mays completed a master's of business administration and a master's of science in social and applied economics at Wright State University and earned a PhD in educational leadership from the University of Dayton. Since 2012, Dr. Mays has been at Miami University, where he teaches courses in business analysis, small business innovation, and digital commerce. His research interests include social capital in higher education as well as academic integrity.

Laura Wiegand McBrayer is the associate director, Library Information Technology and Digital Strategies, at the University of North Carolina Wilmington, where she directs a team that supports, maintains, develops, and innovates all things related to libraries and technology, virtual and physical. In addition to technology and libraries, her areas of professional concentration include project management, leadership, organizational development, and effective teams. She holds a BA in philosophy from Loyola University Chicago and a master's in library and information science from the University of Wisconsin–Milwaukee.

James McKee is the makerspace operations manager at Mann Library at Cornell University, tasked with supervising day-to-day operations and coordinating logistics of the library's makerspace. Since 2015, he's been heavily engaged with patron-facing services and spaces, instruction, emerging technologies, and student management. He is especially interested in information policy and facilitating access to new technologies and is also a strong advocate for digital and user privacies. He graduated from Cornell University with a bachelor's of arts in history and completed his master's in library and information science at Syracuse University.

Eric Melbye has published short stories, poetry, a novel (*Tru*), and research in the fields of composition and creative writing. He is the editor of *Segue* online literary journal and the faculty advisor for the award-winning student literary journal *Illuminati*. Melbye currently teaches creative writing at Miami University Middletown.

Ethan Mills is an assistant professor of philosophy at the University of Tennessee at Chattanooga. He earned his PhD at the University of New Mexico, where he specialized in classical Indian philosophy, and he has since published several journal articles and a book, *Three Pillars of Skepticism in Classical India* (Lexington Books, 2018). He is also a lifelong fan of science fiction, fantasy, and horror (genres that occasionally find their way into his courses), and he blogs at *Examined Worlds: Philosophy and Science Fiction*. Starting in 2018, Ethan worked with Wes Smith to develop a filmmaking assignment in which students make their own short horror films with philosophical themes, all of which led, scarily enough, to Wes and Ethan writing an article for the very volume you are now reading. Ethan also loves cats, beer, whiskey, and rambling urban walks.

Bernadette Smith Mirro has been the digital initiatives librarian at Marymount University since February 2015 where she is the liaison to the fashion, interior design, and liberal studies departments. Prior to joining Marymount University, she was part of a team of reference and instruction librarians at Berkeley College in Manhattan. She holds a master's in library science from the City University of New York at Queens and a master's of arts and humanities from Marymount University. At Marymount University, she is responsible for developing unique online learning opportunities to ensure patrons can make the most of the library's digital resources. Her academic curiosities include exploring unique learning opportunities that include incorporating 3D printing into curriculums and addressing the information literacy needs of underserved student populations. Bernadette Mirro's research has focused on integrating library resources into Marymount's learning management system to ensure the library is at students' point of need.

James Mitchell is the systems librarian at the University of North Alabama and manager of the university library's makerspace, the Collier Experimental Learning Lab (CELL). He received his MLIS from the University of Alabama. Over the past four years, James has been responsible for makerspaces in both academic and public libraries. He has taught classes on video editing, computer programming, and 3D printing, among other things. His research interests include free and open source software in libraries, cloud infrastructure and libraries, and makerspaces and libraries.

Sarah Nagle spent three years as a librarian at Pikes Peak Library District in Colorado, where she worked to provide engaging programming for all ages and ability levels in the district's makerspaces. Sarah now serves as creation and innovation services librarian at Miami University in Ohio. She earned her MSLIS from the University of Illinois Urbana-Champaign in 2015. She supports transdisciplinary projects and curriculum relating to a wide range of experiential learning, maker, and innovation topics. Sarah's research interests include inclusivity in the maker movement and how maker-centered learning can enhance learning both in informal environments and higher education.

Courtney Pace is the manager of the Making, Innovating, and Learning Laboratory (MILL) at the University of Idaho Library, located in Moscow, Idaho. She received a BA in communication and society from Washington State University, with an emphasis in science communication. She manages the daily operations of the MILL, coordinates the workshop series, and serves as the main point of contact for makerspaces projects, visiting groups, and interdepartmental collaboration. She also serves on library committees dedicated to improving user experience; most recently, she served on a committee that developed a board games collection within the library. Courtney is dedicated to lowering the barrier for making and innovation; she focuses on free software and resources, as well as projects that accommodate lower-level learners.

Tracy Paradis is the archives and special collections librarian at SUNY Geneseo's Milne Library. She received an MLS from the University at Buffalo and a BM in vocal performance from California State University at Northridge. She was a research instruction librarian for fifteen years prior to her current position. She has presented on teacher-as-performer, social media, and library programming at various regional and state conferences. Tracy has also served as liaison to the Fine and Performing Arts.

Michael Price is the digital media and emerging technologies librarian at Carmichael Library at the University of Montevallo (UM) in Montevallo, Alabama. He received his MLIS from the University of Alabama and his BS in art (focus on digital media in art) from UM. He regularly works with faculty at UM to instruct students in the use of various digital tools, such as 3D printers, 3D scanners, virtual and augmented reality, laser cutters, and so forth. He has received several grants to support the addition of technology in Carmichael Library's Digital Media Lab.

Julia Ravindran joined Marymount University in 2015, having previously worked in NYC for a number of high-profile fashion designers. Some of her career highlights include developing both bridal and evening-wear collections annually showcased at NY Fashion Week, being a liaison to celebrities and high-end customers, and directly engaging with couture clients to produce custom-made gowns from concept to finish. She has extensive knowledge in pattern making, draping, embroidery design, and digital design using Adobe Photoshop and Illustrator. Her research areas consist of 3D printing in fashion design, fabric manipulation, surface design, and the transformation of technology and social media in fashion. At Marymount, she is the advisor to Pattern Makers Club and in 2017 introduced 3D printing into the fashion curriculum.

Eleanora Reber is an associate professor of anthropology at UNCW. Her teaching interests include archaeology, the archaeology of state formation, the archaeology of state collapse, the archaeology of the southeastern United States, and archaeological sciences. Her research focuses on absorbed pottery residue analysis and the archaeology of the African diaspora in the Cape Fear region.

Kathleen L. Schmand is the director of development and communications at Northern Arizona University's Cline Library. She is responsible for leading the library's efforts to provide excellence, organization, and innovation in fundraising, grant seeking, marketing, outreach, communication strategies, and operations. In partnership with librarians and staff across the organization, she designs messages and strategies to persuasively articulate programmatic concepts and initiatives. Since 1996, Kathleen has worked at Northern Arizona University in a variety of capacities including: head of Access Services; interim associate university librarian (twice); coordinator for community affairs, grants, and development; interim head of Library Technology Services; and interim head of User Services. Since 2016, she has been supporting and providing outreach for the Cline Library MakerLab.

Nancy Schuler is the e-resources, collection development, and instructional services librarian at Eckerd College, an undergraduate liberal arts institution located in St. Petersburg, Florida. She received an MLIS from the University of Washington and a BS in natural resources management and BS in geography from the University of Maryland. Her areas of interest include library spaces, unique collections, and information literacy instruction.

Andrew See is the head, User Services and Experience, an access and information services unit that, beyond maintaining a high-quality standard for user experience and research support, oversees all of the library's experiential learning spaces and technologies including the Cline Library MakerLab. He chairs two user experience groups, UX-Web and UX-Spaces, that collaborate with other library units to provide connected, clearly articulated, user-centered services. Andrew received his master's in library and information science at the University of Arizona and is a national presenter on innovation and making data-driven decisions.

Kelsey Sheaffer is the creative technologies librarian and director of the Adobe Digital Studio at Clemson University in Clemson, South Carolina. She received a master's of fine art in kinetic imaging from Virginia Commonwealth University. She has taught courses on animation and sound and collaborates with faculty to integrate digital media projects into the classroom. Her work in libraries is supported by an interdisciplinary creative practice, and she has exhibited regionally and nationally. Kelsey is also involved in scholarship on library space design, collaborative campus communities, and digital literacy pedagogy.

Wes Smith is a studio librarian at the University of Tennessee at Chattanooga. He earned his master's of arts in higher education and bachelor's of arts in sports administration from the University of Louisville. He has presented talks on emerging technology, nontraditional librarianship, and using online tools for media production at ALA, ACRL, and LITA. Prior to the start of his librarianship, Wes held various positions as a media content creator or video editor at various college and sports organizations.

Carli Spina is an associate professor and the head of Research and Instructional Services at the State University of New York's Fashion Institute of Technology. She holds a JD from the University of Chicago Law School, an MLIS from Simmons GSLIS, and an MEd from the Harvard Graduate School of Education. She has extensive experience working on projects related to accessibility, universal design, user experience, and technology as well as serving as a coordinator for services to patrons with disabilities. Her research, writing, and teaching interests extend to a number of topics, including universal design, accessibility, assessment, user experience, and inclusion. She is currently in the process of writing a book on Universal Design and its applications in libraries.

Jasia Stuart is coordinator of digital technology at Concordia University Libraries in Montreal, Canada, where she heads up the Webster Library's Technology Sandbox, a popular makerspace where staff and students from all faculties come together to play, build, and problem-solve using a variety of tools and methods ranging from knitting to augmented reality. Her professional interests include applications of machine learning in the visual arts and the training of artificial intelligence on library collections. Jasia holds a BS in computer science from the Université de Montréal and a BFA in drawing from the Alberta College of Art and Design.

Amanda Sweet is the technology innovation librarian at the Nebraska Library Commission in Lincoln, Nebraska. She received her MLIS from the University of Wisconsin–Milwaukee and a BA in English from Carleton College. She has trained librarians and volunteers in more than thirty communities to use makerspace equipment using a design thinking–based approach. She launched a statewide digital literacy effort in libraries across the state to help communities thrive in a digital world. To enhance this effort, she provides technology kits through the mail to introduce communities to the basics of artificial intelligence, the Internet of Things, mixed reality, drone technology, and web applications. She believes there is always something new to learn and that technology can change lives.

Antoaneta Tileva is a professorial lecturer at American University in Washington, D.C. She holds a PhD in cultural anthropology from American University. Her work is at the intersection of urban, gender, and development studies.

Stew Wilson is a research librarian in Palm Beach County, Florida. The project in this book was developed during his time as paralibrarian for network administration and technology at the Community Library of Dewitt and Jamesville in Syracuse, New York. Questions about this project can be e-mailed to stewartrwilson@gmail.com.

Bridget Rowan Wipf is the librarian for the College of Engineering, Informatics, and Applied Sciences at Northern Arizona University's (NAU) Cline Library as of October 2019. She spent the past three years working in Cline's User Services and Experience Department as the training coordinator and spent one year supervising student employees in the MakerLab. Bridget has her MLIS from San Jose State University and a BS in sociology from NAU. She has presented at conferences and webinars about empowering lower-level employees, gamification, and student employment. She is currently volunteering for the Library Collective while she learns the ins and outs of her new position.

Sara E. Wright is currently the librarian for space and service planning at Cornell University Library, where she works on space, service, and web design, incorporating accessibility and universal design principles into all three. Since 2012, she has been involved in managing and leading people and projects to assess user needs, develop and transform library spaces, and advocate for the value of user experience to inform planning and decision making. Her professional interests include library assessment, user experience, and creating engaging learning environments both physical and digital.

Mason Hongqiang Yang has been working as the electronic services librarian at Marymount University since February 2010. Before joining Marymount University, he worked as a reference librarian for the Loudoun County Public Library. After he graduated with a BS degree in mechanical engineering, Mason Yang worked as assistant mechanical engineer and later mechanical engineer in different manufacturing companies. Mason Yang's research interests include 3D printing, data visualization, augmented reality, mobile computing, and effective pedagogy in library instruction. During his academic career, Mason Yang presented his research findings of different subjects at several professional conferences and coauthored an article with his colleagues on using mobile devices in the college classrooms.

CPSIA information can be obtained
at www.ICGtesting.com
Printed in the USA
LVHW061607221021
701184LV00016B/903

9 781538 133323